FIELDS OF VISION

Essays on Literature,
Language, and
Television

D. J. Enright

Oxford   New York
OXFORD UNIVERSITY PRESS
1990

Oxford University Press, Walton Street, Oxford OX2 6DP

Oxford New York Toronto
Delhi Bombay Calcutta Madras Karachi
Petaling Jaya Singapore Hong Kong Tokyo
Nairobi Dar es Salaam Cape Town
Melbourne Auckland

and associated companies in
Berlin Ibadan

Oxford is a trade mark of Oxford University Press

First published 1988
First issued as an Oxford University Press paperback 1990

British Library Cataloguing in Publication Data
Enright, D. J. (Dennis Joseph), 1920–
Fields of vision : essays on literature,
language and television.
1. Television programmes related to literature
I. Title
791.45
ISBN 0–19–282698–0

Library of Congress Cataloging in Publication Data
Enright, D. J. (Dennis Joseph), 1920–
Fields of vision.
Includes index.
I. Title.
PR6009.N6F54   1988   824'.914   88–19513
ISBN 0–19–282698–0

Printed in Great Britain by
Richard Clay Ltd.
Bungay, Suffolk

To my mother
1890–1986

Author's Note

Acknowledgements are due to the editors of journals in which passages from the second and third sections appeared in a different form: *Encounter*, the *Listener*, *Meridian* (La Trobe University), the *New York Review of Books*, the *Observer*, *The Times Literary Supplement*.

Contents

TELEVISION

Books on the Box	3
Pity and Terror, and the Bottom Line	15
Mice in Cages	20
The Serious Stuff	35
Teaching and Talking	39
Stirring Things Up	43
Chambers of Commerce	48
Copulation Explosion	51
Mighty were the Auxiliars	55
Causes without Effects	62
The Masters	68
For the Children	72
Building Bridges	77

LITERATURE

Intermission	85
Perilous Sword-Dance	89
Evils be ye my Good	94
What Happened to the Devil?	98
The Third Place	114
Hell's Angels	117
A Doomsday Book	123
Master of Horror	130
The Executioner Himself	144
Is God an Endless Orgasm?	154
Signs and Wonders	161
More than Mere Biology	166

Contents

'A Bad Man, my Dears': Heine in English   172

'My Muse, Mnemosyne'   183

LANGUAGE

Vulgar Tongues   191

Words Deft and Daft   201

Truth, Beauty, and Bafflegab   210

The House of Joss   216

Death of a Thousand Typewriters   224

Broad Rumour   235

Index   245

TELEVISION

Books on the Box

Although in obvious ways indebted to books, or to people who write them, television is ill at ease with literature. Literature is something of an enemy, not a very potent one, but irritating in its assumption of superiority. It prides itself on appealing to a minute audience, few yet mysteriously fit; it also boasts about the blockbusters that it—or what is taken for it—comes up with: books whose world-wide readership makes even television ratings look almost modest.

The two activities start off in much the same manner, with pens, typewriters, word processors, and a human brain guiding them, but the end-products are very different. The trouble with words is, they are—wordy. No wonder, then, that strange things happen when television turns its attention to books. Its book programmes bear a resemblance to spy stories, perhaps because of the suggestion, unvoiced yet in the offing, that something discreditable is about to be uncovered, some shabby secret revealed. (That authors can be bald? Or tongue-tied? Or conceited? Or vapid? Just like the rest of us?) For television, books are foreign territory, intriguing, dangerous, seedy, out of Graham Greene—not places you would actually want to live in. Even the opening images are weird. What, you might wonder in the absence of the *Radio Times*, can they herald? A programme on skiing, the life-style of fashion models, the golden age of jazz? Something to do with computers, or acrobats, or well-educated criminals?

There follows an underground train in motion, presumably film from stock, but always effective in creating unease: will it crash, we wonder, will someone fall under it? Or the camera moves through a country landscape, or an urban scene, among walkers in a busy anonymous street, dwelling for a moment on a face, or a car, or a building. Or it swoops along hedgerows, through tall grass. Mutter, mutter, goes the sound-track. Is someone going to be raped, or a remarkable archaeological find about to be found, or is a conservationist complaining, or are we approaching a paddy-field in some disastrous south-east Asian country?

3

Mervyn Jones is of the opinion that book programmes are not meant to be about books so much as to provide opportunities for clever camera-work, which is why writers 'who are lured into the enterprise are always walking through beautiful scenery or playing football with their children'. The principal information conveyed about Colin Wilson in one such programme, Jones adds, was that while writing *The Outsider* Wilson slept under a tree on Hampstead Heath, and that 'he attracted the affections of a young woman whose father threatened to horsewhip him, so that the pair departed hastily for Cornwall'. Why bother with grey theories when you can film the golden tree of life? I recall another programme during which, at considerable length, a poet pushed his way worriedly through a street market so busy and crowded that he was lost from sight for minutes at a time. That may have been the intention.

But ah, the low voice is muttering extracts from a book, its tone and delivery, barely audible, insisting on a meaningfulness which might not be obvious could one hear the words; or, come to that, might be too obvious. It is much the same whether the programme concerns the author of an earnest documentary on abandoned coal-pits, a trendy feminist or gay ('brilliantly perverse'), a left-wing guru or a right-wing wit, an exotic Latin American or a home-grown scribbler. Television is the great homogenizer. Unless you are preternaturally alert you can easily miss the transition from one book or author to the next.

A similar confusion occurs when a programme suddenly begins to sparkle, and only later do you realize it is Independent Television you are watching, and a commercial has intervened. Television engages primarily with the eye, secondarily with the ear; the mind comes a long way behind, and the imagination, its power to make connections forestalled, may never catch up. The reader and the writer are always capable of error and misunderstanding, and of failing to co-operate, but books and the reading of them involve nothing like the distortion, concentrated irrelevance, and self-aggrandizement that television can generate.

For a lively literary interview you have to go to the chat shows. When, in mid-1987, Terry Wogan's guests were Jackie Collins and Barbara Cartland, Miss Cartland claimed to be concerned to save young people from the horrors of sexual incontinence, whereas Miss Collins professed herself as out to stimulate her followers, to improve performance and add to the world's enjoyment. After repeated prodding by Mr Wogan—ought she not, in view of we all know what, to modify the tenor of her novels?— Miss Collins, belatedly taking the hint, assumed a more earnest demeanour and made a vague promise to introduce condoms into her future action. There was no real confrontation between the ladies, only a tut-tut and an amused curl of the lip. Both were unshakeable in their self-assurance; both were assuredly at the top of their different ladders. We were left to suppose that virginity has been making a come-back while copulation continues to thrive.

Television does its duty by classical music: it gives pictures of the conductor, the orchestra, the choir, the soloists, and the audience. Plenty to look at—but you do get the music as well. Where books are concerned, the tuning up, so to speak, is of more consequence than the music; and so are the journey to the concert hall, the queuing outside, the finding of seats, the removing of hats and coats. For such things constitute visual movement. Television is adept at picking up the trivial detail and giving it the semblance of something else, for a moment. If as a rule it devalues serious writers, by focusing on what matters least of all about them, it can be good to third-raters. To those who have little to lose it gives generously. It is in its way a great equalizer. What Karl Kraus said of the press is equally, or more, true of television: its mission is 'to disseminate intellect and at the same time destroy receptivity to it'.

Perhaps we should cast around for another word than 'book', for some less unwelcoming expression. *Martin Chuzzlewit*—a leisure complex designed by Charles Dickens.

Television adaptations of Dickens, Trollope, Jane Austen, among others, have the effect of sending some viewers back to the novels, to renew acquaintance, to spot what has been left out, to clear up obscurities caused by truncation. The effect on other viewers may be to send them to the novels for the first time; pious hope would have it so. Such considerations are real, but of marginal import.

Film and television are arrogant without noticing it. During the scoring of *Fantasia* Walt Disney exclaimed: 'Gee, this'll make Beethoven!' (A sour little element of truth there.) Ken Russell remarked, of his film *Gothic*, that 'Shelley was the Elton John of his day'. (It must have been a very different day.) Brecht's *Baal*, starring David Bowie, was billed by the BBC as *Bowie in Baal*, thus—as an article in *Screen* had it—'giving a sense of their cultural and promotional priorities'. (But promotion *is* promotion, Bowie is, or was, Bowie, Brecht is—who? It was hard in this case to work up much indignation.) Alluding to his prime-time 'specials' in the United States and Canada, Billy Graham claimed that in a single telecast 'I preach to millions more than Christ did in his lifetime'. (It only remains for him to be crucified on camera and then rise from the dead during prime time.)

Debussy's *Prélude à l'après-midi d'un faune* isn't the same thing as Mallarmé's poem, or a prelude to it, nor is Mallarmé's poem Debussy's music. Tone-poems aren't poetry, 'sound poetry' isn't music. What we see as falseness to the original is found in every filmed or acted adaptation of a novel of any account; it is inevitable, however thoughtful or 'respectful' the adaptation. Though much is lost, something may be added. But in truth, to compare the two, while interesting, is a vain exercise, for they are essentially different experiences.

I have enjoyed some of the adaptations of 'classic' novels; *Bleak House* and *Oliver Twist*, for instance, though *David Copperfield* worked less well, its characters appearing as toddlers, spouses, and the dead and gone, on what seemed consecutive days, and there was a truly awful travesty of *Northanger Abbey*. Never mind that it was a travesty of the novel: it was awful in itself. Just as some of the others were good in themselves, on their own terms.

In his Alan Palmer Lecture, Kenneth Baker observed that the otherwise admirable series *The Jewel in the Crown*, based on four novels by Paul Scott more austerely gathered together as *The Raj Quartet*, left out 'the teeming presence of India' and 'the politics and turmoil of a nation moving painfully towards independence, within which the last of the British Raj were caught up and buffeted around'. Only a history book, a vastly comprehensive and quite unreadable one, could convey all that; and perhaps only a politician would want it all conveyed. I would have thought that we saw enough of the Raj, at any rate: *ex pede Herculem*. But the moral drawn from this deficiency is worthy of note: 'All television drama has a tendency to concentrate on intimate human relationships. Perhaps this is dictated by the medium itself.' It would certainly account for the high incidence of love-making in television drama; television demands movement, and the small screen, it seems, is exactly the size of a double bed.

Jonathan Miller is right to assert that 'there is no possibility whatsoever of synonymy between a text and a sequence of pictures'.* To sharpen what ought to be a truism, he quotes from the preface to *The Golden Bowl*, where James talks of illustrations to novels:

Anything that relieves responsible prose of the duty of being, while placed before us, good enough, interesting enough and, if the question be of picture, pictorial enough, above all *in itself*, does it the worst of services, and may well inspire in the lover of literature certain lively questions as to the future of that institution.

In his reference to a future that is our pictorial present, James spoke more prophetically than he could ever have guessed.

To begin with, if not to end with, the bulk of the 'responsible prose' of the novel is cast aside in filmed versions, words being the first casualty in this transmutation. Thus a dense sense of life has gone from *Bleak House*, with its intimate questioning of the cost to the spirit of 'shirking and sharking, in all their varieties', and not only (Kenneth Baker's favourite character) Mrs Jellyby. Every picture tells a story, it's true, but the story is generally short, simple, and segregated. Once again, imagination—which is no merely mental or sentimental phenomenon but encompasses the nerves and the flesh too—is starved, for the sake of an immediately striking and easily digested visual titbit. The dramatization of fiction does too much for us, and hence too little with us and to us. 'Piece out our imperfections with your thoughts,' pleads the Prologue to *Henry V*, nominally in excusing the 'wooden O' but more importantly as a reminder that the audience is to take an active part in the proceedings. Television is less modest than

* 'How to Kill Novels: A Talk by Jonathan Miller', *Strawberry Fare*, Autumn 1985, St Mary's College, Strawberry Hill, Twickenham.

Shakespeare; it is wholly 'perfect', leaving and allowing next to nothing for the imagination, that 'great instrument of moral good', to engage with.

Jonathan Miller remarks that no film-maker can provide a visual equivalent for Dickens's verbal visualization of John Wemmick Junior in *Great Expectations*: 'a dry man, rather short in stature . . . his mouth was such a post office of a mouth that he had a mechanical appearance of smiling.' Any attempt to reproduce that mouth would be a ludicrous disaster. When you read the words, Miller points out, you find yourself rehearsing what it means to have such a mouth, 'with your lip muscles undergoing the appropriate contortions to produce a satisfactory rictus': Dickens's metaphor, here as in the phrase 'shirking and sharking', is coercive. The mouth happens in your head and thence throughout the body: it isn't happening, even if it could so happen, out there on a screen located at a comfortable distance.

The best dramatizations are shadows of the novels they derive from—BBC's *Vanity Fair* was a very elegant shadow, a well-dressed skeleton—yet with the help of a skilful script-writer and producer, and of course first-rate actors, they succeed by their own lights, providing good, intelligent entertainment. For one thing, they do have a story, however stripped down, unlike those 'original' television dramas which are imperfect in another way, requiring (though rarely compelling) our thoughts not simply to piece them out but to make ordinary sense out of them.

By virtue of clever adaptation, a fine cast (from Wendy Hiller outwards), and splendid photography, Victoria Sackville-West's novel, *All Passion Spent*, afforded a charming piece of viewing. Given the mediocrity of the original text, this may demonstrate the unimportance of language in television, except as primitive pointers; the play would have succeeded had it been soundless and accompanied only by subtitles in Basic English. In *Television: The Medium and its Manners* Peter Conrad has said (actually of talk shows: 'What's showy about talk?'): 'On television, language is virtually a dirty word. . . . Television values an ad-libbing glibness with language, the capacity to run on inconsequentially and fill up dead air, but this is a different gift from articulacy.'*

---

* 'What's showy about talk?' Something Anne Robinson was quoted as saying, in *The Times* of 8 July 1987, provides an answer of sorts. 'I'm convinced that for

All the same, I cannot help feeling that the best dramatizations, notably of Dickens, owe much to the intellectual superiority, the seriousness and not just the humour, of the novels. Not only has something rubbed off on them, but some magic ingredient has inhibited the deadly knowingness and cheap topicality that infect original television drama. In the circumstances, Jonathan Miller's hostility—even if he is concerned to promote new writing for the medium—seems distinctly misplaced.

Take poetry . . . But that's unfair.

Long-term abuse leaves the self—which looms larger in poets than in other people, even other writers—distended, and spongy, and cold. Poets should be scattered, living far apart from one another, and from what they have in the way of a public. Put them together, and they form cliques, within which they form further cliques, eventually dwindling to one single member. Their characters deteriorate, even the nicest of them. If they live among ordinary people (as distinct from fellow poets and poetry-fanciers) then they may indeed—though one shudders at the expression—be themselves, what remains intact of their selves. Huddled together, they become something worse than themselves, akin to the grotesques in the old Humours plays. Minds of this class are like damp hay, one might suggest, drawing on Coleridge's analogies (albeit at the time he was speaking of people in whom the imaginative power is egregiously feeble): 'they heat and inflame by co-acervation; or like bees they become restless and irritable through the increased temperature of collected multitudes.'

Poets are customarily solemn and high-minded on the subject of their calling, reserving humour for their earnings, their ex-publishers, and the compilers of anthologies in which they do not

women what you're wearing on television matters much more than what you're saying. Some weeks we're inundated with letters about my clothes. Once I inadvertently wore a revealing black slinky top and snake-head necklace. Half the letters said how disgusting I looked and the other half just said "Cor".'

While the idea that there is anything inadvertent about what people wear on television is hard to swallow, the cheerful complacency—you lose one, you win one, the one you lost wasn't worth winning—rings true.

feature. Sometimes it is hard to know whether it is poetry, its nature and significance, they esteem so highly, or themselves, the two being virtually coincident.

Much of what ails them, no matter how it manifests itself, can be ascribed to the fact that they were once described as unacknowledged legislators. It is honourable, if less than wholly desirable, to be an unacknowledged genius, but for a legislator to go unacknowledged, and increasingly so, is mere ignominy. Consequently they find themselves dressed in robes that are both borrowed and invisible.

> Why do poets piss in the sink—
> Is it all that drink?
> Why is so much they write plain bad?
> And why do so many go mad?

These pathetic lines by Oliver Reynolds hint at a further calamity: in our permissive or liberal society their traditional bohemianism—potent shades of Shelley and Byron! And now Elton John!—cuts little ice. They can attract more attention by wearing sober suits, embracing temperance and monogamy, and working in banks or building societies; by becoming 'more like folks even than folks', as Malcolm Lowry's fictitious writer, Sigbjørn Wilderness, complained. (But look at his name.) Since so many poets are paranoid, perhaps they are at their best when genuinely persecuted. Persecution implies some degree of public *raison d'être*.

So of course does financial success. Now that money has become clean and virtuous, both the root and the flower of all good, prosperous writers prefer to describe their profession as a trade, while dropping in some modest allusion to its value as civilized entertainment: they do earn their living. It is left to writers who don't make money, including the majority of poets, to suppose that they do good, or hope to. Least pleasing, I dare say, are those who make lots of money and also let it be known that they intend to confer spiritual or moral or social benefits. Despite the rehabilitation of Mammon, some things still impress us as, not exactly wrong, but at least incongruous.

It is poetry that matters, not its practitioners. Johnson observed that people will be taken in if they imagine that an author is greater in private life than other men. 'Uncommon parts require uncommon opportunities for their exertion.' And poetry has at any rate retained a fair share of its reputation for beauty and truth. It is these latter qualities, and especially the first of them, that have suffered in their reputation. More than other art forms, poetry is still reckoned to concern itself with the nobler aspects of mankind, the higher if not necessarily the happier sides of life. This is the case whether or not one ever reads it; and notwithstanding its perfectly legitimate use for satirical purposes and—though some resistance is encountered here—its appearance in the shape of 'light verse'.

There does seem to be something in poetry that fends off the meanness and squalor commonly met elsewhere in the printed word. Efforts to shock by obscenity either crumble into bad, boring prose, or acquire too much tenderness or sadness to succeed whole-heartlessly. It is as though some rhythm of the language, not always determinable, meshes with a primordial, Edenic pulsing of the heart to carry us in a different direction. At all events, it cannot be solely preconceptions of poetry and what it is meant to be that account for this, for we are ready iconoclasts, keen to make a name by overturning received notions, in particular those that involve large claims. The phenomenon is more clear-cut in Eastern cultures, where the novel, a relatively late form, was considered good enough to embrace the gross antics of the Floating World, while poetry devoted itself to religious teaching and spiritual experience. (It must be admitted that the poetry was often rather tedious, and the fiction quite lively, and—in the hands of women, possibly by nature more nimble in passing between the facts of life and the feelings of the heart—elegant and subtle.) Secularized as we are, it is in our poetry that we come nearest to 'religious' apprehensions. I put the word between quotation marks because it isn't *juste* but I cannot find a better, a more precise one. Intimations of something, a kind of innate or atavistic 'respect' for life, or atavistic fear and awe, not too often provoked in the course of daily life? Dr Roget doesn't help.

That poetry is commonly used as a vehicle for 'self-expression', for self-pity and self-approbation, for the little whimsies which

11

(they are *our* whimsies) we so prize, is a sign of the respect in which we hold it, the unique if cloudy value we attach to it. We don't generally think of a writer unlocking his heart with a novel. (Though he perfectly well could; he could even unlock his heart with a book review.) Poetry almost redeems almost everything it touches, or that touches it. It can offer an unearned respectability, for while it is easy to be dull or inept in verse, it is hard to be downright cheap. If we misuse it, never mind, it's a tough plant; we only expose ourselves harmlessly, to the minimum of spectators. Poetry remains pure of heart. Even the writing of bad verse may do us good. I doubt the same can be said of bad prose.

I have left music out of these considerations because in an innocent way it cheats, or at least is unfairly unhandicapped, being the purest of all the arts, the most sheerly beautiful (yet what does *that* mean? It only drives us back to words): not intellectual, not forced into fidgety explanations and comparisons, or morals, or into the conspicuous absence of moralizing; occasionally erotic, or erotic after we have been told it is, but never pornographic. We don't know what music is, Adam Zagajewski says in a poem called 'Late Beethoven', or

> Why it is
> so obstinately silent.
> Why it circles and returns
> instead of giving a straight answer
> as the Gospel demands.

It preceded the Gospels, this first and most natural of the arts, truly of prelapsarian date, which is to say of divine origin. (That, although too good for us, it still means so much to us, is a happy omen.) And hence an art to whose condition, in a fallen world, no other art can aspire; or should try to.

For all that, we ought to reckon with the views of Thomas Mann's wearisome but well-meaning Settembrini, who is represented (*circa* 1913) as being sternly averse to music on political grounds. For it is 'the half-articulate art, the dubious, the irresponsible, the insensible': at best it kindles the emotions, whereas what is incumbent on us is 'to awaken the reason'.* It is the Word

---

* When working on *Doctor Faustus*, Mann said much the same himself: 'Music is both calculated order and chaos-breeding irrationality . . . the most unrealistic and yet the most impassioned of arts, mystical and abstract.'

that Settembrini, himself far from inarticulate or insensible, loves and reverences, 'the bearer of the spirit, the tool and gleaming ploughshare of progress'. Well put, dear organ-grinder! And yet, with their simple faith in reason and progress, and in words (not quite the same thing as the Word) as plough-shares, these sentiments, though by no means puerile, seem to come from an age and a world far removed from ours. What Settembrini says, shaking his head, serves as commendation of music rather than inculpation. For what this speechless art is unable or disinclined to tell us of is what we have heard so much about, and not very usefully, already.

Poetry is made of words; the tone of its voice is not always immediately clear; it carries its own pictures; it moves at the speed it deems fit; it turns silence to account; even at its most amenable it eschews ingratiation. That television is unhappy with it comes as no surprise; you can almost see the screen squirm-ing. How right-minded was the mother in Marshall McLuhan's joke, who, when a friend exclaimed, 'My, that's a fine child you have there!', replied: 'Oh, that's nothing. You should see his photograph.'*

The aptest way of conveying poetry on television would be to display the words on a roller. Short of that, and short of *An Evening with Pam Ayres* (rather different, but at home with the medium), the most authentic programmes I have seen allowed Dannie Abse and Tony Harrison to give virtually straight read-ings of their work. Admittedly, the roving camera fastened on what some of us with experience of these gatherings might think an unnaturally high proportion of attractive and ethnically varied young ladies. But it would be hypocritical to blame the camera for doing what we would do ourselves had we the chance. In general, however, no matter what television may seem to promise by way of a public reason for existing, in the event it confirms the absence of one.

* 'We're trying to turn boring old facts into visual symbolic images,' said Jocelyn Pride. 'We want to convey the inner meaning of the story, semiotically. You see, television is a very visual medium.'

'Ah,' said Sir Luke. 'And this explains why people sit in front of screens and watch it?' (Malcolm Bradbury, *Cuts*).

Television

Poetry resembles an obscurely holy mendicant or rumoured seer who, by some caprice of the great, has been hustled out of his cave and transported into an opulently appointed palace. All around stand potentates, viziers, warriors, pontiffs and mastiffs, flags and banners and strange devices, tables laden with rich foods and wines. On the fringe move odalisques and executioners, alchemists and fiddlers, jesters and eunuchs, magical engines on wheels. Although aware of a certain incongruity, the purported soothsayer is not necessarily daunted—he is happy to have what looks like an audience—but the rest of the company are suddenly ill at ease. It seemed a nice idea at the time—but what to do with the fellow now he's here?

Pity and Terror, and the
Bottom Line

In the Folio Debate held on 24 January 1985, on the motion 'That
Television is the Enemy of Literature', it was to be expected that
both the proposer, Michael Holroyd, and the opposer, Melvyn
Bragg, would pull their punches. Not so much because such an
occasion, staged in the Royal Festival Hall, is intended to be
gentlemanly or (in the manner of Barbara Cartland and Jackie
Collins) ladylike, or because nowadays we are slow to make or
imply great claims either for or against anything outside politics,
but because Holroyd watches a lot of television—'one of the neces-
sities of life' in our time—and Bragg writes a lot of literature.

Holroyd made the central point: that literature is a collabora-
tion between author and reader, the latter reading at his own pace,
'returning to previous pages at will to make specific connections
within the text, and controlling to some degree what is read'.*
Thus 'the words are provided by the author but most of the images
are evoked by the reader, and to some extent the sounds too',
whereas 'we are, in a sense, dictated to by television'.

Melvyn Bragg countered adroitly: the dramatic tradition is a
large part of our literature, and television contributes to literature by encouraging dramatists to write for it; not to mention
(which wasn't mentioned) presenting the classics of the past.
Still, our great dramatic literature is *readable*, and the greater
it is, the more amenable to being read. Personally—though to
say so is a confession of weakness, grouping oneself with that
big softie, Charles Lamb—I prefer to 'collaborate' with
Shakespeare, in the theatre of the mind, rather than be dictated
to by producers and actors.

---

* A truism that can do with repeating. Marina Tsvetayeva: 'Art is an under-
taking in common, performed by solitary people.' And Goethe: a literary work can
only really commend itself by compelling the reader to interpret it in his own way
(compelling rather than flaccidly allowing in the spirit of a free for all) and 'to complete it, so to speak, by creative re-enactment'.

15

Another shrewd if glancing blow was struck by Bragg when he submitted that, instead of replacing reading, television more usually replaces non-reading. A smart debating point, but a sad admission of defeat elsewhere. Bragg sought to put a brave face on things, though some might think it a doltish one, by arguing that in the past there have been splendid non-literary civilizations, and our own civilization, in its present phase, may be one of them. He included Shakespeare among those who lived in 'largely illiterate societies': the Elizabethan age illiterate, non-literary? What a stroke of luck that there was someone able to copy down the oralisms of Shakespeare, Marlowe, Jonson. Any state of illiteracy or non-literariness we are going to achieve will be the reverse of splendid.

His final, mollifying plea was that, instead of rejecting it, the literary world should take television for what it is. To my knowledge the literary world hasn't rejected television; it has envied it, grumbled about it, bowed the knee to it, and derived pleasure and instruction from it. But what *is* it that television is? 'A big, nervous, pimpled adolescent longing to have its friendship for literature recognized and returned.' (A true sitcom image, that.) Heaven help us when it stops being nervous and grows to its full strength! This is a case of television's admirers underestimating the object of their admiration.

After calling for a show of hands, the chairman, Frank Delaney, tactfully declared the result a draw. I would have come up with a clear winner, if only because of Michael Holroyd's description, when alluding to the humiliating way books rely financially on television, of a scene in a bookshop, a scene arousing both pity and terror but purging us of neither. There sat an actor who had portrayed Christ on television, signing copies of the Bible.

Yet, for all the thunderous assault on them, and their premature interment by people infatuated with the sheer idea of the new communications technology and never mind what is communicated, books, good and bad and indifferent, proliferate. People can be seen reading them on trains, and not hoary ancients alone. Kenneth Baker, Secretary of State for Education, announced in November 1986 that, according to their own accounts, two out of ten eleven-year-olds only read what they had to, and four out of ten didn't usually read at home, while among fifteen-year-olds one in four rarely read books at home, and then only if they wanted to find something out. By contrast, figures published in 1983 indicated that children aged between five and fourteen spent an average of twenty-three hours a week watching television. Nevertheless, if we return, in the confusion customarily engendered by figures, to the Education Secretary's 1986 calculations, we gather that nine out of ten among the eleven-year-olds did say that they liked reading stories. It cannot be that all the many children's books published these days are read by grown-ups alone.

New (and better stocked) bookshops have opened, and actors are not always in attendance. Public libraries are fairly full, particularly on Mondays when weekend reading is returned. There is even a Public Lending Right, payments from which grow smaller for the majority of authors, as more and more authors qualify for a share. Even those excited beyond measure by the electronic revolution don't positively malign books; they only pity them. When I used to spend my day with typescripts (mostly unpublishable), and with books in various stages of their hazardous development, I sought relief in television in the evenings, and found it. It took a job in publishing to make me realize that my appetite for the printed word was less than insatiable. But before sleep descended, I always returned to reading. Books do refresh—though the phrase itself shows the power of television—parts that other media cannot reach.

All the same, it must be saddening for a writer to perceive that a two minutes' appearance on the small screen, in whatever guise, 'means more'—attracts more attention, even leaves more trace —than a lifetime of writing. No doubt this is why writers can be lured away from their desks. In Kingsley Amis's *The Old Devils*, a wife muses on her husband: 'And that was a bit of a puzzle too, how he was always saying he wanted to be regarded as a writer first of all and then always going on television and being interviewed.'

More truly illuminating, in its murky way, than the Folio Debate was a BBC *Omnibus* programme called *Big Bang in the Book World* (19 June 1987), on the theme of recent take-overs and mergers in publishing, British and American, and the phenomenon of internationalization.

In general the taken-over publishers sounded pleased with what they had done, or what had been done to them, which indeed was the only course open to them short of admitting that their mistakes or misfortunes had led to them being taken over. Borne on the pasteboard wings of the spirit of the times, they imagined they were themselves that spirit. Moribund a decade ago, so the gleeful story went, a decade being the furthest bound of the past that most of them would countenance, British publishing was now becoming big business, dragged at last and late in the century into the twentieth century, out of the cottage and into—yes, into big business.

With a predictable exception or two, the few authors roped into the programme were less than whole-heartedly enthusiastic. (And plainly less bouncy than the publishers, as befitted their status.) Big business is geared to big sales, and it must have occurred to the authors, albeit now valuable properties, how improbable it was that publishers of this class of bigness would have given them their start in life. Big sellers, they ruefully and modestly observed, are commonly trash.

Small sellers—as which most authors begin, and as which many remain—need small publishers. (Not that 'small' in this context need mean diminutive.) 'Internationalization', a term that smacks of airport bookstalls and hotel lobbies, is irrelevant to them, their works, and their expectations.

Apart from a distinguished elderly British publisher and a distinguished middle-aged American one, either clear-eyed or green-eyed according to one's viewpoint, what the publishers here reminded me of was a vast American printing-plant set up some twenty years ago in Jurong, then a new industrial estate on the island of Singapore. This huge piece of machinery, its proud custodians explained, wouldn't dream of swinging into action for a printing of less than a quarter of a million copies: textbooks, naturally, for the Third World. Every office and corridor in the gleaming factory boasted a closed-circuit television camera, intended to discourage the native labour force from slacking off. I asked a Malay clerk what he thought of this; glancing nervously around, he murmured some pious words about the need to work hard. During the ceremonial opening, the best entertainment was to stand in front of the central viewing screens and watch the behaviour of the invited dignitaries as they perambulated: the canapés dropped, the drink spilt, the bottoms pinched. But that is another story.

The pictures in the *Omnibus* feature—however rich or flamboyant, people are never quite enough, and books never fully furnish a screen—showed playing-cards inscribed with the names of publishing houses and a hand, bearing presumably a trump card, hovering over them and moving, predaciously or perhaps beneficently, from one to another, pondering which to snap up, or salvage. It positively bristled with immediate images, as Henry James would have said. There was aptness in the symbolism; one of the most prosperous authors referred with becoming incredulity to the 'monopoly money' he had won.

With its excitement, its gung-ho talk of auctions and huge sums of money changing hands, of global markets, 'today's atmosphere' (big bang or else dead silence), publishing as the 'glamour industry', the intermittent hint of sinister consequences ('If someone pays millions of pounds to buy a house, he's going to move the furniture around'), its handsome greying (yet youthful) senior executives, its pretty girls (a gaggle of publicity managers toying with wineglasses in the Groucho Club and concurring that their increasingly arduous function was increasingly vital). . . With all this going for it, the show was a soap opera of the plushest kind. Produced by Mammon; directed by Mammon; script by Mammon; acted by Ego, Ego, and Ego.

It may be, after all, that the worst enemy of literature is—books.

Mice in Cages

The middlebrow is odious when contemptuous of the 'vulgar' or covetous (though incapable) of the 'elevated'. When television seeks to be highbrow, it is at best middlebrow. When it is content to be lowbrow, as in British soap operas, it can achieve middling heights.

The obvious secret of soap operas—I am leaving aside the scented bath-salts variety—is that, in however undistinguished a manner, they deal with basic and relatively homely situations. People die, people may be killed, but their heads are not discovered in hat-boxes, this being a sign of up-market, quasi-highbrow entertainment, as are also the more eccentric kinds of sexual activity. In soap opera, good intentions often flounder, bad intentions falter, and—less frequently—good intentions are effected and bad intentions are carried out. Justice is generally done but, as in life, only partially; the audience know that nothing is perfect, you are lucky to get half of the reward you merit, unlucky if you get more than half of the retribution you deserve. British soap opera doesn't run all the way to extremes; in a British fashion, it draws back.

This is why critics who pride themselves on adventurousness dismiss soap operas as 'nostalgic'. Elsewhere in the schedules the extremes display themselves so freely that extremity, we suppose, is what the people are supposed to want. Curious, then, that *Coronation Street* has lasted so very long, and that *EastEnders* has established itself so firmly. There must be a future in nostalgia, after all. But in fact, long ago, 'Ena Sharples' of *Coronation Street* declared: 'Don't talk to me about the old days! They're best forgotten!' What is curious is that if something is markedly violent or sexual, we hesitate to think of it as 'trash'. We might in an unguarded moment suspect it of being pornographic or otherwise pernicious in its effects; but then we pass over pornography with a smile, it seems, and we can't quite bring ourselves to believe in evil effects. Trash obviously isn't art; violence and pornography might be, you can never be sure.

A successful madam shoots to fame, partly through the ineptitude of the police, and appears on chat shows. Were she an actress working in a soap opera, the character she played would promptly be written out of the story, dispatched to the antipodes with an abruptly broken heart or, more sternly, mortally injured while crossing the street to the newsagent or the pub. Characters are disposed of thus because the actor wants to break free from the role before it takes him or her over irretrievably (when a woman wrote to Robert Robinson, apropos of one such 'death', complaining that an operation would surely have saved the character's life, his answer was: 'When an actor wants to leave a series, there's little that medical science can do'), or because the actor has taken to drink and the fact can't be covered up, or because he or she has fallen into public disgrace (one character met with a fatal accident soon after the actor concerned had been charged with indecency: that he was subsequently acquitted made no difference).

The story-line is subject to pressures other than those of the imagination, or of the ratings. When Pat Phoenix pulled out of *Coronation Street* after twenty-three years, the writer arranged for 'Elsie Tanner' to join an old flame who was running a bar in the Algarve. In *The Street Where I Live*, H. V. Kershaw relates that during an Equity strike in 1961 Miss Phoenix could continue working, since she was on a long-term contract, whereas Jack Watson, playing her boy-friend, a naval petty officer, could not. Kershaw supplied a scene in which Elsie Tanner told her invisible lover over the phone of an anonymous letter she had received intimating that their association could jeopardize her pending divorce, and so he had better keep out of the way 'until the trouble blows over'—or until the strike ended. Conversely, 'Ida Barlow' was due to be knocked down by a bus in Episode 78 and buried in Episode 79, but she was kept alive (though missing) for a week in revised scripts so that the cast of *Coronation Street* could decently switch on Blackpool Illuminations. It wouldn't do to have half the nation in mourning at that time.

On Bonfire Night fireworks are to be seen in Coronation Street. Christmas is Christmas for all soap operas. It was not the fault of the writers of *EastEnders* that snow fell in Albert Square when the rest of the country was enjoying a sudden summery day just after Easter in 1987. In 1986 'Ken Barlow' discovered that owing to a technical cock-up some thirty people had won the prize holiday offered by the local paper he edited; a few weeks later more than 3,000 readers of the *Daily Telegraph* were led by a misprint to believe they had won a holiday in the Seychelles in the paper's Passport Control Competition.

Whether inadvertent or not, this kind of realism is a pleasing bonus. But the term is an ambiguous one. I do my best to avoid what television offers as realism since it usually denotes some form of nastiness. What we need, rather desperately I would think, is something a little higher than the 'real'; and never mind if it resembles the escapism we once held in scorn. Isn't there more than enough realism around us? Newscasts alone are sufficient to do our dying for us. Observation suggests that the more analyses there are of the origins of crime, the more crime there is; the more commonly personal misery and discontent are aired, the more firmly these ills tighten their grip on us. When there was less talk about them, there was more resistance to them—dumb resistance, if you like. Television documentaries can be like dictionaries of symptoms: pick the fashionable disease you fancy. More directly emotive than printed words, and impatient of niceties, the medium is a great breaker-down of stoicism, by showing us people who are proud to be in distress, and insidious in weakening the will to responsibility and independence.

A brand of realism rears its head in television comedy. A young fellow has to rush home to go to the toilet (note the genteelism) because he couldn't find an unvandalized phone box to relieve himself in: roars of canned laughter. Vindicated by its realism, as phone boxes testify, the cult of loutishness coexists comfortably with the high ideals professed by the medium's managers, one ideal being that young people, like other people but even more so, have the right to get what they want, or are supposed to want, and plenty of it. (Another ideal has it that idealism is fuddy-duddy, obscurantist, or 'Fascist'.) It may be that these latter-day idealists are stuck in the past, when realism in the arts was execrated and outlawed, and they are still fighting the good fight against cosiness, prudery, and repression, a fight which is much safer nowadays and doesn't call for martyrs. Of course there is a less charitable explanation, for squalor is easily procured, it costs little and it makes a profit. Either way, as a society we are telling ourselves: Every day, in every way, we are getting worse and worse.

It is natural that American toy manufacturers should back children's cartoons, since these provide both inspiration and commercial springboard for their products. The more lurid cartoons—some of them have been shown on British television —can be enhanced, we gather, by toy guns that are fired at the television set, which then registers a hit or a miss. A peculiar realization of what two and a half centuries ago was called the 'delightful task': 'to teach the young idea how to shoot'. The next step in realism calls for the screen to exude a few drops of simulated blood in the case of a hit, preferably a substance that doesn't stain the carpet.

That much in *Coronation Street* and *EastEnders* is mildly boring is testimony to a more decent, less tendentious sort of realism. Viewers may not be highly educated, but they are not stupid; to borrow Kershaw's distinction, they can tell trivia—'the trivial round, the common task'—from trivialities. Soap opera can afford a measure of dullness, unlike news broadcasts. And also a sensible normality. 'Your father's self-employed,' a woman in *EastEnders* tells her young daughter. 'If he doesn't work, he doesn't earn. Then there's no nice clothes, no pocket-money, none of the things you like.' And when, with an allusion to past unhappiness which followers of *Coronation Street* will pick up, a character now in marital distress himself remarks of the editor of the local paper, 'Good at words, but just as mixed up as the next fellow', only middlebrows are going to complain of philistinism.

The trouble with soap opera is that once it is on to a good thing, it can't get off it. Den Watts, manager of the Queen Victoria in *EastEnders*, was forever ringing his lady friend just as his wife Angie came down the stairs. On the first occasion this may have touched a nerve; by the twentieth repetition we could only suppose that Den was egregiously stupid or else that Angie lived on the staircase. In *Coronation Street* Ken Barlow refused to give his daughter away because, with cause, he disapproved of the man she was marrying; he went on and on refusing, in episode after episode, so protractedly that in subjective time his daughter would have been an old woman before she ever wore a wedding-ring. In *EastEnders* Michelle's pregnancy, though it lasted for less than nine months of objective time, appeared to have gone on for several years. I doubt that the occasional slowing of pace and the repetitiousness are there for the sake of viewers who miss an episode or two, or that script writers are keen to avoid any imputation of artistic allusiveness. They seem to be inherent in the nature of the genre. Or in our nature.

At its inception *EastEnders* must have resolved to show itself different from *Coronation Street*: in its metropolitan setting and therefore its sharper-witted (or smart-alecky) characters and rackety behaviour; its introduction of Blacks and Asians; and most of all its high incidence of foul temper. Obviously it was to be less comfy or 'nostalgic' than its rival, and more 'realistic'. With the help of gifted and hitherto unknown actors, it has matured since then, though there is still an excess of nagging and wrangling, too much by the standards of any sort of realism, since little time is left for other activities. It might seem that why Arthur Fowler couldn't find a job was because demonstrating anxiety, shame, and self-pity kept him fully occupied. As the on-off marriage of Den and Angie grew tedious, so latterly has their on-off divorce. I don't share Mrs Mary Whitehouse's condemnation of the series for 'its homosexuals, its blackmailing pimp and prostitute, its lies and deceit and its bad language'—the prostitute and the homosexuals are far from stereotyped, and the lies, when not white, are shown to be shabby—but the sheer volume of what she calls 'verbal aggression' is preposterous and exhausting. Incidentally, it is a matter of interest that bad language is the language we always *do* take in. Four-letter words positively leap out of the set at us. Words can offend at least.

Far more than its relatively equable rival, *EastEnders* tends to bog down in obsessive cud-chewing or sink into stock squalor, and the prevalence of petty crime would send the residents of *Coronation Street* into deep shock. Yet its stronger or starker characterization has a credit side: one episode (2 July 1987) consisted entirely of a duologue between two ageing ladies—the neurotic Dot and the malapropic Ethel ('Are you accusing me of inconsequence?' she asked when Dr Legg recommended sheltered housing)—reminiscing and confiding, often at cross purposes. This rare cameo, funny and touching, made most 'serious' television drama look like the heavy-breathing, tiny-hearted stuff it is.

It's said that practically every pressure group in the country has been badgering Julia Smith, the producer, to bring their speciality into *EastEnders*. Shrewdly, when she featured a cancer scare, she had the tumour turn out to be non-malignant, by way of encouraging female viewers to go for breast screening. 'If we'd had malignant cancer they'd have all stayed at home worrying themselves to death thinking they'd got it too,' she said in an interview in the *Telegraph Sunday Magazine*. During the next fortnight, it appears, the clinics were inundated. The soaps are a staple source of copy for newspapers, who bring in psychologists to comment expertly on story developments. Does Bet Lynch, in *Coronation Street*, have sound enough reasons for marrying Alec Gilroy, despite not loving him? Yes, because in her mind love is associated with being horribly hurt.

The older homosexual receives a grim letter from the States about AIDS; the doctor pontificates on the penalties and rewards of old age; the wages of sin are about to catch up with a youthful criminal; a social worker runs round dishing out advice (at such a rate that we fear for her sanity) . . . *EastEnders* 'has seemed of late to be assembled, Lego-like, from pieces taken from a kit marked Social Ills of Britain Today', Brenda Maddox has complained, while admitting that the series has become 'a kind of group therapy for a group of 20 million'. We must hope that *Coronation Street* will sustain its gentler mood, and not feel obliged to tackle too many social problems; group therapy on that scale can damage the mental health. Kershaw notes that the programme never took advantage, 'if that is the phrase', of the growing permissiveness of the 1960s and '70s; not until Episode 190 was the word 'bloody' used, and then only in a moment of stress, and the speaker promptly made his apologies. We must rely on the sharp ears of its fans to keep the programme in order. And sharp those ears and eyes are: great indignation was voiced when, eight years after she had said she didn't like chocolate éclairs, Ena Sharples was seen eating one and asking for more.

The human spirit desires freedom, but not too much of it; it needs a goodly portion of routine as well: a mixture of the every-day and the extraordinary. Soap operas contrive to provide the exciting feeling that things are about to ensue, along with the assurance that nothing untowardly radical is likely to occur. Following them, even irregularly, can impart a sense of immortality, or at least of timelessness. And also of fearful boredom, when more than ever seems it rich to cease upon the midnight. During a year when I watched *Dallas* on and off, the only thing that happened was that Bobby Ewing died. Twelve months later it turned out that he hadn't. British shows, though they might tactfully delay a death or prudently arrange one, wouldn't venture into such outright inexplicability.

The stories told within the *Coronation Street* serial, Kershaw says, were real enough: 'what was unreal was the sheer amount of dramatic event on that one street.' The happenings of a hundred streets, as he puts it, had been encapsulated into one. In *East-Enders*, in rapid succession, a woman gives birth unexpectedly late in life, her schoolgirl daughter has a baby by an unknown father, her husband suffers a nervous breakdown and goes into hospital, and then into prison for making free with the Albert Square Christmas Club money. Some encapsulation! Yet, such is the diversity of clocks we carry inside us, all this helter-skelter seemed reasonably unhurried. Although there may be but a minute of fictional time between the end of one episode and the beginning of the next, the few days of our own living which intervene—either two or five in the present scheduling—serve to space out the thronging events. Reality and unreality, speed and leisureliness, a proliferation of incident and a sense of nothing much going on—these coexist in soap opera, and probably that coexistence accounts for the ability of the genre, at its best, to hold us without bruising us, to engross us, and then (with luck, before the experience cloys) to let us go.

An interviewee cited by Laurie Taylor and Bob Mullan in *Uninvited Guests: The Intimate Secrets of Television and Radio* comments that while the personnel of *Dallas* and *Dynasty* are allowed to stab and shoot and rape, they are never permitted to swear. True, they grow impassioned over what really matters—not bad language, not even rape or mayhem—and what really matters is oil wells. Humour occurs sparingly in British soap opera, but the American species is virtually devoid of it. (Hence the great send-up, *Soap*, is continuously and frantically comic.) And probably for the same reason that humour is unwelcome in pornography: it would destroy our illusions and delusions. Smiles in American soap opera are sour, or sinister, or once in a while tender, but a belly-laugh would be most unseemly, ruder than a rape. The only instances of humour I have noticed in *Dallas* both occurred in the same episode. J. R. had been roaming the family house at night, checking on security; over breakfast the next morning his wife, Sue Ellen, remarked that she had observed him entering her bedroom: 'I was so excited I fell asleep.' Later, for some reason, there was a parade of models wearing bathing-costumes, and a bystander, not overly taken with the fashions, granted that at least the models had pretty faces. In fact the models were in the foreground of the picture, cut off above the waist, and all that viewers had seen of them was their pretty *fesses*.

In 1986 a writer in the *Daily Telegraph*, nominally discussing *EastEnders*, said: 'Watching the English soap operas is like viewing the tiny lives of mice in a cage. Watching the American series is like watching expensive leopards prowling round a luxurious cage. Either way it's not the jungle of life, just a zoo.' So be it, we are mice, the Americans are leopards, expensive ones at that. (The animal metaphor doesn't fit too well, but you can hardly talk of expensive jackals or vultures.) As regards the British programmes, the 'zoo' looks to me close enough to the jungle of life; though perhaps remote from the famous jungle that used to be Fleet Street. At least the mice are distinct and diversified, and quite nimble, whereas the leopards do little but slink.

When an imposter arrived in Southfork claiming to be the patriarch, Jock, returned from the dead, Miss Ellie, the matriarch, hitherto the programme's most sensible person, took him for the genuine article. In all likelihood the sons would have followed suit but for the paranoid fear that the fellow was after their oil wells. A letter in the *Radio Times*, defending Dennis Potter's play *The Singing Detective*, or specifically its 'notorious wood scene', invoked the greater incidence of adultery in *Dallas* and *Dynasty*. But the lay figures in those 'glossy soaps' cannot truly be said to commit adultery, because they cannot truly be said to *commit* anything. Any adulteries that manage, even so, to take place can be forgiven on the grounds that all the women look much alike and all the men sound the same.

According to Taylor and Mullan, some of the people interviewed said that what they welcome about the American series is that they are 'so unreal', whereas the British programmes are 'like watching yourself'. Unlike its unreality, so skilfully reinforced by abysmal acting, the alleged sophistication of *Dynasty* is gainsaid somewhat by the Denver hotel called '*La* Mirage': a strange name, at best, for a hotel, possibly born out of a confused association with oases. Although our soap operas have been judged too parochial for the USA, *Dallas* and *Dynasty* are sufficiently catchpenny for the UK.

These remarks do not imply a wholesale condemnation of American television, American culture or lack of culture, the sensationalism, vulgarity, and other qualities or lack of them that Europeans are swift to detect and curl the lip at. No one but the Americans, and perhaps Jaroslav Hašek, could have created *M*A*S*H* ('I always think people volunteer better if they're forced'; 'Do they always fly that low?' 'The ground's very high round here'). No one but the Americans could have made *Taxi*, *Hill Street Blues*, *Cheers*, or *Soap*, all of which need to be *listened to*, not merely looked at. I am inclined to add the much-despised *Star Trek* to the list, for the sake of its stolidly preserved—albeit simplistic—morality and the ensuing ethical dilemmas, and its crude but likeable dabbling in old myths; Apollo was once discovered on an obscure planet, dragging out his immortality in sorrowful neglect. Terrible things happen in deep space, where, through the agency of the good ship *Enterprise*, America engages in a respectful and benevolent form of colonialism, including replays of the Third Reich, the Wild West, Chicago-style gangsterism, and the Roman arena, but at least mankind survives with honour, and niceness too, which *is* something. Adept in sophisticated comedy, the Americans are equally good at the near-sentimental, sweetness held just this side of the twee, as in *Perfect Strangers* and *The Cosby Show*. In *Television Today and Tomorrow* Christopher Dunkley comments that in the 1980s the Americans were sending us programmes such as

Rhoda and some of those mentioned above, while Britain was sending them *Benny Hill*. 'Which way does that suggest the rubbish was travelling?'

No doubt the leer, visually symbolic of the innuendo, is universal in its appeal. I wonder how many of our best situation comedies, the anguish-free counterpart of soap opera's social and psychological ministrations, have travelled across the Atlantic. Can it be that the Americans are really too parochial to enjoy *The Good Life, No Place Like Home, Last of the Summer Wine, Me and My Girl, Steptoe and Son, To the Manor Born, Only Fools and Horses . . ., Fresh Fields, Open All Hours, Ever Decreasing Circles, Sorry!, Yes, Minister, Rumpole of the Bailey, Fawlty Towers?**

Brian and Gail Tilsley in *Coronation Street*, and Hilda Ogden; the sorely tried Pauline Fowler, deserving of Mrs Whitehouse's (and Mrs Thatcher's) unreserved admiration, in *EastEnders*, and wayward young Michelle and clumsy, worried, good-natured Lofty ('You can't speak to him,' Michelle is currently complaining, 'all you can do is hurt him': what misery lies ahead?) . . . There have been passages in both series to touch the heart, simple but not mawkish, free from the self-conscious sensitiveness of many a well-regarded novelist. Language doesn't play a great part, fine language no part at all. Television is at its most natural and authentic where true inarticulateness is concerned, where words honestly can't be found but facial expression and physical gesture can be. So much is owed to a happy combination of tactful script-writers and proficient actors, who slip so dexterously into their roles that we cannot imagine anyone else playing them or (a professional embarrassment to them) the actors playing any other roles. Quite probably the art in which contemporary Britain is richest is that of acting: the large body

---

* It appears that *Fawlty Towers*, at least, has achieved 'a small cult following' in the States. And in January 1988 we heard that a New York station was to launch *EastEnders*, 'the steamiest and most successful soap opera ever' (advertisement), preceded by a two-hour lesson on the characters and—words assume a special importance when you can't understand them—their language: exotic usages like 'sweet F. A.', 'give me a bell at the nick', and 'I gave him a kick up the orchestras' (fortunately glossed by Eric Partridge: 'orchestra stalls', rhyming slang). Thus coached, the Americans should find the dialogue easier to follow than most Britishers do.

we are blessed with, not merely of celebrities and elderly knights or dames, but of diversely talented, ever-ready performers of all ages.

There have been shrewd moments, too. 'I wouldn't wrap my chips in the sort of filth you write,' Sue Osman tells a reporter who is trying to ferret out a story about the dead hero Andy. (Sue is another of those admirable, unglamorized women in which both programmes abound: the males are posturing shadows by comparison.) Later in the same episode of *EastEnders*, when the reporter, now in the pub, alludes complacently to his 'profession', Den says: 'Oh, writing for the *TLS* now, are you?' I haven't noticed any reference in *Dallas* or *Dynasty* to the *New York Review of Books*.

That, despite the narcissism of the medium, characters in soap operas are rarely seen to watch television may be simply because watching television is a relatively solitary occupation, and a more or less placid one. The proper place for a TV set is the pub, where gossiping, unbosoming, and quarrelling drown it out. Significantly, as if television, though it gave birth to soap opera, is the enemy of soap-operatic life, the first and gravest sign of poor Arthur's decline was that he took to squatting in front of the set, staring glumly into it, instead of occupying himself with his family's affairs.

The pub is the pivot of both *Coronation Street* and *EastEnders*, no doubt because it is public, and even among such assiduous busybodies as feature here you can't have everybody forever gathering in somebody's house. (On the rare occasions when neighbours or friends are invited in, generally for tea, you can be sure that something is up, a secret is in the air.) The Rovers Return and the Queen Vic are characters in their own right, with their varying fortunes: staffing problems (a pretty barmaid, or a competent one?), favour or disfavour found with the grub, management ambitions, keeping peace between the customers (for whom licensed premises are a natural battlefield) . . . When in mid-1987 the Rovers Return was taken over by the shifty Alec Gilroy, the regulars wondered whether they would ever get used to him, and a shopkeeping woman replied that well, she'd got used to VAT and breakfast television. That *EastEnders* has sprouted a second boozer—a classier place, run by an alleged yuppie who is far too ingenuous, and eager to fit in, to rise very high—is an indication of its proneness to split into warring factions and vehement though short-lived cabals. In *Coronation Street* a drinking-club deputized while the gutted Rovers Return was being restored and thereafter was discarded, in accord with the programme's centripetal disposition.

In *EastEnders* alternative foci are a modest café and—probably no allusion intended to the genre's first sponsors—a launderette. Incidentally, Peter Conrad describes a commercial in which a dishwasher volunteers to relieve viewers of their chores: 'Sit, America—we'll do the washing up.' He adds, 'But what do we do while we're not washing up? Television's answer is smugly self-referring: we watch television, and on it we see the dishwasher uncomplainingly toiling on our behalf.'

That even the poorest members of the dramatis personae have money to spend on beer is a convention we accept; often someone better off pays for it, and no embarrassment is called for. (Of late non-alcoholic drinks have made great advances.) At times we may wish we had a local like the Rovers Return or the Queen Vic, where we could drop in and chat with friends when there was nothing worth watching on the telly. More soberly, we may reckon those places a form of hell, loud with an interference more insistent than Muzak, and not a chance of being left in peace to read the *TLS*.

Soap opera instils a sense of continuity, of life going on, which older people in particular are grateful for. We all need to be hooked on something. The world can't end while *Coronation Street* still stands. To let it go would amount to *lèse-majesté*. (The working title at the outset was *Florizel Street*—delusions of glamour? A sad tale's best for winter?—and it narrowly missed being called *Jubilee Street* before its inspired title, linking it with the first great television occasion, the crowning of Elizabeth II in 1953, was arrived at.) The only time when the world seemed, for a short while, to be ending was when the Rovers Return burned down in June 1986.

The sense of permanence and continuity is bolstered by the echoing of events in the outside world. In late August it's time for anxiety over O-level results. During the run-up to the general election of 1987, in *EastEnders* Ethel's unappetizing dog, Willie, was petted more than during the rest of its life. (Given the hyped excitement on all the media, it was not unwelcome that the residents of Coronation Street paid no attention, being devoted to eternal verities rather than temporal matters.) On National No Smoking Day the moralistic shop assistant Mavis Riley (whom no one takes very seriously) refused to serve a customer, Jack Duckworth (whom everyone would love to refuse), with a packet of fags. Were there a National Euthanasia Day no doubt someone in the Street would be found to do his or her public-spirited bit, and with some semblance of reason. (Pure coincidence that the grocer bears the same names, Christian and family, as Mrs Thatcher's father.)

And traces of 'public service' are dutifully woven in, as when it was pointed out to a victim of theft that you should ask for identification when men come to the door wanting to inspect your gas pipes. In harmony with the spirit of the times, *EastEnders* introduced a couple of amiable, troubled homosexuals; when the AIDS campaign was in full flood, Dot was seen waxing hysterical over touching articles they had used, and spraying Flit in the air. Since Dot had long been known as unbalanced, a religious crackpot, the point was easily taken. As usual, rather too much was made of it during the following instalments, and even the splendid actress taking the part couldn't deliver her shrieks of horror with much conviction. The subject was dropped: Dot has a short memory, she can always find something new to expend herself on. And the programme had made its contribution to the cause, quite a civilized one at that.

An odder variety of relevance or timeliness emerged elsewhere, in the days preceding the wedding of Prince Andrew and Miss Sarah Ferguson, when a rash of discussion programmes, virtually indistinguishable, broke out on all channels, the theme being the perils of marriage and the high incidence of divorce. Let joy be confined was the message of the medium. A little later, joy was to rage unconfined as television turned away from Disturbing Realities to Fairy-tale Romance. Like justice, the media are even-handed; they give with one hand and take away with the other.

Mice in Cages

It has often been said that the British Royal Family constitute the biggest and longest-running of all soap operas; and one, it seems, immune to the charge of parochiality. (Notwithstanding the verdict of one journalist: '. . . the life of genteel, suburban Britain writ large, but with a reverential element of mystique'.) In respect of pageantry and glamour, the plushest American series fall far short, with mere oil wells to offer, and ranches, boardrooms, boring frocks and females. And indeed some members of the Family display palpable if subdued acting powers. (In one case, unsubdued.) Naturally television makes the most of this inexpensive, ready-made, and sure-fire entertainment. In August 1986 the media told us in grim tones that the Queen had gone to the National Heart Hospital for a check-up—without consulting them first—and they listed reasons why she could or perhaps should be feeling the strain: her age (not very gallant, that, and not very convincing if you think of her mother), the recent wedding of Prince Andrew (although his not getting married might have entailed a greater strain), the touted disagreement with the Prime Minister over South Africa and the feelings of the Commonwealth (a source of distress, if that was what it was, for which the media were partly responsible) . . .

A few days later, the interval between two instalments of soap opera, television brought us equally sensational news—the Queen had been observed to climb 125 stairs to the top of a lighthouse in Scotland, and without puffing! There was no hint of an apology or recantation in respect of the earlier story about a putatively wonky heart. It was as if that canard, now happily refuted by our doughty fourth estate, had been the dirty work of a gang of malicious subversives.

The very next week, as if to keep the ball rolling or, in her graciousness, to keep the media in countenance, the Queen Mother was rushed into hospital by helicopter with a sinister ailment of the throat. And then rushed out again. Two stories for the price of one. *

* It has been said that the Queen Mother was once thought suitable for *Crossroads*, as a background figure lending genteel tone to the foreground (not to mention 'a reverential element' etc.). One wonders how Equity would have responded.

Television

Outside hospitals, helicopters, horses, and inheritances, and as distinct from their character parts, we don't know much about the truly private lives of the Royal Family, despite the efforts of the press, those stout foes of mystique. This is how it ought to be. An inevitable weakness of soap opera, springing from the bi-weekly need for fresh material, fresh trivia, is that everybody knows everybody else's business. There is no mystery, not for longer than thirty minutes at a time. In view of the sort of mysteries television regales us with, this is rather endearing.

The Serious Stuff

In *Amusing Ourselves to Death* Neil Postman has declared that 'The best things on television *are* its junk, and no one and nothing is seriously threatened by it.' I wouldn't myself describe the British soap operas as junk, but I often think they are the best things on television.

Postman's thesis is that 'television is at its most trivial and, therefore, most dangerous when its aspirations are high, when it presents itself as a carrier of important cultural conversations', and hence we should all be better off if television got worse rather than better. It is to be hoped that the paradox—foul being fair, and fair foul—will not obscure the message.

Peculiarly bad (in no ironic sense) are the 'superior' dramas, the up-market thrillers, that television is proud to screen, such as *Dead Head* and *King of the Ghetto*. Items in this class avoid the various kinds of conventional ending by failing to end, a dodge which (though the argument may be that *life* is like that) fails to persuade us of anything except that the writer, having enjoyed all sorts of generally unfunny fun on the way, doesn't *know* how to end. We are let down, and that's all. Much cleverer, and logically satisfying, were the old Charlie Chan movies, but then, they lacked factitious 'relevance' and pseudo-Dostoevskyan overtones.

There are other tricks. Still rejecting the 'escapism' which itself escapes most of us, intellectuals incline to assume that a feeling of unease is an indicator of serious art. It can indicate merely that the 'artist' is wobbling desperately between genres, either lacking conviction or else keen to conceal his convictions as shameful little weaknesses. Unease is only too easily procured on film; all you require is a repeated shot of a celluloid doll, perhaps bashed in, or a happy laughing child, or a pram, or a kitchen knife, or somebody chopping wood. These appurtenances can be quietly dropped in the event, whatever the event may be. (The more vulgar thrillers, like *The Sweeney* or *The Professionals*, usually follow up such hints, if indeed they have time to drop them in the first place.) Or you can switch back and forth between colour and

35

black and white or sepia; or you can interpolate silences, since where noise is the rule silence is bound to seem menacing.

Unease is a delightful substitute for making sense, sense being harder to arrive at. Now and then we hear that something is 'suffused with irony'—the word 'irony' here signifying vague praise—when in fact it is simply muddled. Worst of all are the aesthetic gestures, violence in the guise of ballet. Thus, in a serial called *Brond* (classy name, sort of like Ibsen), the repulsive artiness of a man pushing a sword-stick right through another man in slow, swirling motion: a gimmick employed also in representing sexual passages, a modern mutation, perhaps, of the old rule that nudes on stage had to stand still. *Brond* was another of those unsavoury and befuddled thrillers which—in the assurance that, unlike the novel, acted fiction doesn't need to tell a story—set out, through episodes of tarted-up violence, cryptic emotionality, and portentous stillnesses (and, in this case, with the conscripted support of a plangent ballad), to bully the viewer into supposing that they mean more, much more, than they say or do. Swift noted that something may pass as wondrous deep for no better reason than that it is wondrous dark.

The thrill of violence, of the thing in itself . . . While 'copy-cat' crimes are a current feature of the scene, no one can *prove* a connection between this sort of entertainment and the comparable happenings in our streets. (Though one of the bored teenagers who set fire to a school with Molotov cocktails claimed that he got the idea from watching the Tottenham riots on television.*) Yet I find Christopher Dunkley's rebuttal startlingly frivolous, a ripe example of the intellectual's shallow perception of human nature and, in this instance, of nonchalance towards the subject he has chosen to examine: '. . . it was not an addiction to *Starsky and Hutch* which sent Genghis Khan on his wicked way . . . Torquemada did not need video nasties to give him his nasty ideas . . . the whole of recorded history shows that the

---

* In January 1988 it was reported that in a scheme sponsored by the Independent Broadcasting Authority children in selected primary and secondary schools were being taught how to watch television: that is, how to distinguish between fantasy and fact and thereby avoid 'desensitization' by screen violence and the consequent temptation to mimic it. The only wonder is that the tuition, also described as 're-sensitization', isn't to be conducted by television itself.

absence of sadistic television does not by one iota reduce the incidence of sadistic crime.' Nobody has suggested that evil came into the world with the first television transmission or the first film. We can do nothing about Genghis Khan, Torquemada, and the rest of 'recorded history'—one might wonder, by the way, how Mr Dunkley managed to calculate the non-effects of a non-existent agency—but, since some of us still incline to believe that good art does us good in one way or another, we ought to be prepared for the possibility that bad art does us bad in some way. Television is a comparatively new phenomenon, and there are comparatively new crimes in evidence, such as vandalism, motiveless mugging, and the beating, rape, and murder of elderly people. As I write, it is reported that a woman of seventy-nine has been robbed and raped, and sentence has been passed on two men who set fire to a tramp's shack and burned him to death, while yesterday a girl of five was raped. How can Mr Dunkley, and the many who cling to similar libertarian views, be so *sure*?

Possibly it will be argued that why we have more crime today is because we are more civilized; Genghis Khan was unacquainted with the concept of 'crime', and for Torquemada it belonged inside a specific and specialized frame of reference. Dunkley's researches will tell him what, in part, produced the two of them and their behaviour. Certainly television and video nasties (what a roguish locution!) will not produce their like out of a top hat, so to speak. The germ of sadism has to be there already, and in all of us excepting saints it is there already; abetted by what seems its domesticated or tamed condition, television can foster sadistic behaviour by a slow erosion of the more decent, humane qualities. Evil grows ordinary, it flickers away in your living-room as if it were a Christmas tree; you too can be a Genghis Khan. We *are* influenceable creatures, even the most sturdily independent of us, and 'recorded history' records no vehicle of influence to approach television in respect of potency, relentlessness and ubiquitousness. Nothing, I believe, has *no* effect. And if what I say betrays my own need of protection, then so be it; I doubt I am unique.

When a letter in *TV Times* took exception to the 'gruesome violence' occurring in an episode of the crime serial *Taggart* —a man was killed by a bolt from a crossbow fired at close range, and the camera lingered on the 'horrible wound', returning to it several times in close-up—the Controller of Drama of the company who made the serial replied thus: 'The tone of the programme was that crossbows are dangerous and should be respected.' (The killer had the utmost respect for his crossbow!) This is akin to the standard apologia proffered by the more literate among the pornographers of yester-year. As witness John Cleland's *Memoirs of a Woman of Pleasure* (1749) and the moral tailpiece he contrived for Fanny Hill: 'If I have painted vice all in its gayest colours, if I have deck'd it with flowers, it has been solely in order to make the worthier, the solemner sacrifice of it, to virtue.' A virtuous man. So are they all, all virtuous men.

Teaching and Talking

Films about nature and animals are television's greatest and least ambiguous successes in the documentary line. Animals don't talk about their joys, sorrows, grudges, and secret ambitions; they preen themselves unselfconsciously, or lament without the need for speech. Even the camera can't stop them being natural.* Documentaries concerned with human nature and the human animal are liable to be less irreproachable. In reflecting that wildlife programmes have increased public interest in and understanding of animals, Messrs Taylor and Mullan feel obliged to add that television apparently hasn't made viewers more interested in politics.

Nevertheless we are better informed today than ever before, on scientific and medical matters. There is no excuse for thinking we shall live for ever; no excuse for not knowing where babies come from—nor when, for it is generally at mealtime, an hour when we are also treated to intimate details of the Life Story of the Maggot. Of course, as they are always telling us, we can switch off; or change the times of our meals. (Don't leave supper till too late, or you'll eat to the sight of a charred corpse, and a young policeman throwing up at his first sight of a charred corpse.) Quentin Crisp wasn't altogether flippant in alleging that television is to blame 'for contributing to the madness of young people by bombarding their consciences with the lurid spectacle of world-wide injustice'. One disaster, injustice, scandal, succeeds another at such a pace that not the young alone are thrown into a state of incoherent, undirected anguish; not one thing is wrong,

* Some weight—I don't know how much—should be given to the qualms intimated in J. G. Ballard's novel, *The Day of Creation*, where makers of television documentaries are characterized as 'the conmen and carpet-baggers of the late twentieth century', purveying raw nature homogenized into palatable and reassuring packages. The fictitious Professor Sanger contends that, far from lying, television makes up new truths: his contrived wild-life films—'soap documentaries', the stern narrator terms them—remould nature into forms that reflect people's real needs. 'Sooner or later, everything turns into television.'

I suspect we should make allowance for science fiction's distrust of facile technology, its minatory tenor and partiality for doom.

but practically everything. But what—short, of course, of switching off—is the alternative to this protracted miasma of universal misery, except to treat pictures of starving, disease-ridden people as a lowering sort of soap opera with little variety and not much plot? Horrors are numberless—they run together in our heads—and hence ephemeral, but (we know) only in the sense that those who suffer them are ephemeral.

Apart from the purely archaeological, subjects relating to the past are especially tricky to handle. Film wasn't invented then. In *The Celts* (1987) the sad message that the Celts were 'all out' was illustrated by the presenter, Frank Delaney, appearing in white flannels and getting bowled out in a village cricket match. (A metaphor which the printed word would never get away with.) Whatever the medium's aspirations, history on television tends towards the condition of *1066 and All That*. Pictures speak louder than words, but they are rarely as precise or capable of nuance; even the picture of a scalpel making its mysterious way through anonymous flesh shocks more than it instructs. Television threatens to correct this imbalance by reducing the precision of words, by confusing them one with another, and transforming their meanings. But that process began elsewhere, in print, alas; television only accelerates it. Jacques Barzun has observed that without the written word, seconded by the art of printing, 'a widespread language would slide about and, by uncontrolled change, scatter its resources in so many directions that it would fail of its single purpose', that purpose being the readiest possible communication among the largest possible number of fellow speakers.

'Many large-breasted women find themselves the objects of unwanted sexual attention from men and resentment from women. Donahue talks with women whose breast size have [*sic*] affected their lives' (*TV Times*, 12–18 September 1987). On chat shows in general, the less said the better. It is they who will finally kill off the so-called art of conversation, itself a sickly survivor from earlier and less egalitarian times, and not simply by doing it for us. It is evident now that to hold a conversation you require someone like Terry Wogan as master of ceremonies, and then a form of theatre or tame arena, a set of stairs by which to make an entry, tasteful seating arrangements, and special lighting effects. It's easier just to switch on the set, and relax. You can always hope that urbanity will fail, blows be exchanged, the lights fuse. This rarely happens, but you can hope. You could have a better conversation with your milkman—ours has nine children, five of his own, two stepchildren, and two adopted—except that he's not famous, and nor are you.

In preparation for a talk show of his own, Robert Kilroy-Silk, a former MP, visited America. There, he reported in the *Listener* of 23 October 1986, they tackle issues in a fashion unheard-of in Britain. In the *Oprah Winfrey Show* three convicted rapists were brought face to face with an almost exclusively female audience, some of whom had themselves been sexually assaulted. 'What did you do, Keith?' asked the presenter, microphone in hand. 'Um, well,' Keith answered shyly, 'I was a child molester.' 'What ages were they?' 'Oh, any age from five to thirty-five.' (Disapproving noises from the audience.) 'Well, it was mainly oral sex . . .' Keith may have been shy, but words didn't fail him.

Another show in the States featured two male guests and their sex therapist, who described how Maureen, the therapist, had dealt with their problems, including premature ejaculation. 'It was riveting,' said Mr Kilroy-Silk. 'There was, of course, an element of voyeurism present. Who could deny it? Like the story told by the three rapists, it was a fascinating subject, however distasteful the former might also be.' (Come now, in this sphere 'fascinating' and 'distasteful' are practically synonymous!) He went on to praise the 'good television' these shows constitute, their vitality and freshness, and 'the consummate skill and sensitivity' with which the presenters handle the issues. In television discourse 'sensitivity' frequently means dispassion carried to the point of insensibility.

In Britain, Kilroy-Silk added, television treats its guests shabbily, 'unless they're VIPs', leaving them to wait in dismal reception areas, whereas in America those concerned treat their guests 'in the same way as they would friends entering their own home'.

One imagines the scene. Do come in, Keith. Don't be shy. Would you care for a sherry, or would you prefer oral sex with one of our kiddies?

Mr Kilroy-Silk claims to admire such shows for discussing 'topical and controversial issues'. But what is *controversial* about the issues he mentions? Only the propriety of airing them on television. There are those who will do a lot for a chance of getting on television; and there are more who draw their norm of human behaviour from what they observe on the screen. Ignoring something may not make it go away, but talking about it can encourage it to come closer. That at least one of Kilroy-Silk's issues is *topical* cannot be gainsaid. The great discovery of 1986 was that ten per cent or more of adults had been sexually abused during their childhood, many of them by members of the family circle, and that cases currently reported were doubling in number every year. We thought we were a nation of shopkeepers; we find we are a nation of child-rapists.

The other major discovery of the year was that AIDS was all set to wipe us out. The first discovery at least served to moderate the sense of grievance engendered by the second.

Stirring Things Up

Twenty years later, even ten, a satirical programme celebrated in its time is virtually incomprehensible; only the giggles and gasps from its original audience reveal that it must once have had some pertinence. We can read the *Epistle to Doctor Arbuthnot* and much of the *Dunciad* as if, changing a few names or simply ignoring the names, they had been written yesterday. Ours is an age not of satire, but of joshing at one pole and libel at the other, with little in between. While libel is as socially acceptable as joshing, it may cost more, and on the whole shadow-boxing is the order of the day. After his dismissal from Radio 4's *Start the Week*, Kenneth Robinson was quoted in the press as saying, 'I am told people want me to stir things up—but not too much.'

Small chance, then, of our seeing some bug with gilded wings getting flapped, but a much greater chance of watching television poking fun at television, the commonest targets being its best-known items: the commercials. These are such old friends that in BBC 2's *Naked Video* the studio audience began to laugh well in advance of the pointed barb, which was thus rendered supererogatory. No matter, since the witticism that fails to detonate is comparable to the fashionable thriller that fails to make sense: it must be clever. Wildlife occasionally gets its satirical revenge, as when a fly, a real wild one, settles on the screen, pat on the nose of a self-satisfied wiseacre or an obnoxious game-show presenter.

The comedy series *Yes, Minister* and *Yes, Prime Minister* are very witty, sometimes prescient, and rightly admired by Mrs Thatcher: an instance of satire pitched just a little too high, or too cultivated, to be hurtful to anybody. *Spitting Image*, however, has been deemed daring, controversial, remorselessly savage in its treatment of top people. All the same, you have to be a celebrity to figure as a victim—though a different satirical show accommodated Henri de Toulouse-Lautrec, a not tremendously familiar brothel-patronizing French painter—and figuring as such confirms your status. Politicians seem happy to be victims, or, more likely, are unhappy to be ignored. People don't mind being roughed up in televisual public: it looks much like being caressed.

Now and again *Spitting Image* has let fly a shaft of true satire, as in its modest proposal that Libyan babies were killed during the American bombing of Tripoli because 'according to reliable information' they would have grown up to be adult Libyans. If more such gems have blushed unheard, this is due to the unintelligible sound-track. My inadvertent confusion of the senses might suggest that either the latex figures by themselves or the printed script by itself would have a stronger impact. But not much stronger, for there are no positive values in sight, or in earshot, whereby the antics are to be judged; it isn't sufficient simply to give the Queen, say, an ugly phizog or some silly lines to squawk. As it is, pandering to voyeuristic *schadenfreude*—a shabby transaction for which we lack native terms—the show has merely added to what we already have too much of: vulgarity.

And yet, talking of impact . . . Though I haven't followed *Spitting Image* at all assiduously, its faces have more than begun to edge out the real ones. Mrs Thatcher appears regularly on the screen *in propria persona*, but it is her 'spitting image'—high marks, I suppose, for that low title—that more often comes to my mind's eye. I have met the Queen once, and thought her a handsome woman, yet it is the latex caricature that now usurps the real features, or at least competes with them on equal terms. I must be shamefully impressionable.

Maybe Heine was in the right when he remarked that we were all of us sick enough in this great lazaretto, and polemic and satire (in which he certainly wasn't behindhand) reminded him of a revolting scene he had witnessed in a Cracow hospital, where the patients were mocking one another with their various infirmities, the consumptive jeering at the dropsical, the dropsical at the cankerous, the cankerous at the lockjawed.

Not long after I had jotted down these wretched reflections, I happened to be looking distractedly, in the last stages of lunch, at what I took to be a medley of highlights (that televisual term!) from *Spitting Image*. Eventually it dawned on me: this was the final programme of *Pebble Mill at One*, a nippy cavalcade of the celebrities who had appeared on the show over the years. The single state of one man, at any rate, had been sadly shaken. How can one not be disturbed by the insidious force of the televisual image, which owes nothing to our imagination, and asks nothing of it except compliance? Insidious not despite the unmeaning or inaudible words that accompany it, but seemingly with the help of them.

'Sin of self-love possesseth all mine eye.' All the arts show narcissistic or self-referring tendencies. We are all connection-makers. Paintings feature bits of other paintings, variations are composed on somebody else's musical themes, and writers commonly allude openly or covertly to other writers' writings.

This is natural and commonplace, a tribute to (and turning to account of) our awareness, despite so much evidence to the contrary, of community and continuity. But narcissism in television is something else—blatant and habitual, an unremarked matter of course. Television refers to television in the calm assurance that nothing of significance exists outside television. Its relationship with itself is comparable to that which a writer, say, hopes more diffidently to establish with life, with other people. For television practically the only outside life is other television; and even the word 'other' implies a distinction, an otherness, a something out there, which doesn't certainly exist. Television, you might poetically say, is a great imperialistic power, its colonies constituting most of the known world. No nonsense about free cities, or principalities, or autonomous republics, or self-sufficient islands. This is what you let yourself in for once you invite receiving equipment, the Mephistopheles or Dracula of our day, into your home.

A power so inbred in its operations threatens to breed out diversity and singularity. Parody and what is parodied become indistinguishable; if laughter precedes the joke that should elicit it, never mind, it all comes out in the wash. When they are not impersonating one another, comedians hard up for jokes joke blandly about other comedians. Situation comedies make knowing allusions to other situation comedies, currently showing or recently screened, unconscious of any 'unreality' that might ensue. (How could it? This *is* reality.) A budgerigar in a sitcom is reported to greet visitors with the words 'Dirty Den', the nickname of the licensee of the Queen Vic. The presenter of a cartoon show for children, whose staple discourse is baby-talk, quotes a catch-phrase, itself ponderously ironic, from Kenny Everett's 'adult' show: 'all in the best possible taste'.

Newscasters take part in quiz shows (will this impair their authority? Not in the least), or perform dances on comedy shows (to prove that they do have legs). People who have appeared in news items reappear on panel games, and may turn out to be experts on unexpected subjects. Adverts feed off programmes, programmes feed off adverts. The process at work is not one of deliberately making or happily discovering connections: it is as spontaneous and uncalculated, as 'natural', as breathing—no matter how stale the air. In a similar *esprit de corps*, participants in game shows can win a TV set, a video-recorder (a device for compressing a multiplicity of channels into one ever-running programme, so that nothing is wasted), a freezer containing three months' supply of TV suppers . . . But never a book token, a subscription to the London Library, or a set of The World's Classics. For here we have what is very nearly a closed system, set to last for ever, so long as licence fees and advertising budgets keep pace with inflation and wage-claims.

It may be objected that all the phenomena listed above are merely the forgettable clutching at the forgotten as they both go down into oblivion. It is true that empires depend on change and novelty, within limits, since the empire that rigidifies is dying; if the sun is never to set on it, there must always be a seemingly new day, and the abridging of memory this entails. (We are told that within television's empire its satraps are competing with one another, yet the benefits of their rivalry are hard to discern.) Christopher Dunkley allows that not many programmes really seem to need watching at all, once the video-cassettes have been lying on the shelf for a few days. But that television is largely forgettable—and conceivably we have developed a rudimentary defence system: a refractory memory—is no guarantee of its innocuousness. It is not only that it has swallowed up some of our finite time, but it encourages us to forget, as well, what we ought to remember.

Moreover, while I don't imagine that a rapist's life, along with all those pornographic mags and blue movies, flashes before his eyes as he jumps on his victim, I suspect that—in no specialized Freudian sense—it is quite possible to forget and still be marked. 'Slowly the poison' (which may be no worse, no more immediate, than a clogging sediment) 'the whole bloodstream fills.' We don't, as the saying goes, know what hit us.

Chambers of Commerce

'Zapping', jumping from channel to channel by the grace of remote control, is an undemanding way of avoiding the commercials. (The caretakers of the French language have honoured the practice with a formal indigenous term: *saute-chaîne*.) Nevertheless I have noticed in myself and in others a tendency to come alert just as the ads begin, and to sink back into a semi-doze when they end.

We know of old ladies who regard the ads as more consistently agreeable than the rest of television, but that this is not necessarily a mark of advancing years is suggested by a story of Marshall McLuhan's. When, during the Second World War, the United Service Organization sent the armed forces special issues of the principal American magazines with the advertisements omitted, the men insisted on having them restored. 'Naturally the ads are by far the best part of any magazine or newspaper,' McLuhan comments. 'More pain and thought, more wit and art, go into the making of an ad than into any prose feature of press or magazine.' Ads are *news*. 'What is wrong with them is that they are always *good* news. . . . Real news is *bad* news.' We may feel, and not only in time of war, that good news, even if we know it is chiefly good for those who announce it, at least makes a pleasant change.

The ads for Hamlet cigars have as much entertainment value as anything else on television: a recent variation on the consolatory theme has Dracula finding he has left his false teeth in a glass at home. And the winsome puppy unwinding a toilet roll in the garden is a brilliant piece of euphemizing, and puts the condom campaign to shame. Some of the lager commercials are clever, too, though it's hard to remember brand names which are Germanic or consist in an uncertain number of alphabetic symbols. (I had to give up IPA because of repeatedly asking for IPC or ICA and getting a queer look.) Curiously often, the cryptic is mistaken for the clever and striking; obliquity or inconsequence, exploiting technical gimmicks, may catch the eye, but collages or hodgepodges of noisy images that have nothing to do with the product do nothing for the product. Equally, a message expressed too economically can be obscure; 'X Kills Germs Longer' makes one wonder whether other disinfectants only knock them out fleetingly. Some genius conceived the idea of calling a brand of soap powder 'Biological', even (as I recall) 'Biological (pat. pend.)', though I don't see how you can patent the word: we are all of us biological. Before long all soap powders became 'biological', and copy-writers had to come up with a 'New Biological' label, something more efficient, as it were more biological, than 'ordinary biological powders'.

In the matter of 'taste' considerable care is taken with television commercials. In the near past, no matter what else might be seen on the screen, an anaphrodisiac sanitary towel wouldn't be. In 1987, in the wake of the shootings in Hungerford, a Pilkington Glass ad showing a gunman firing at someone behind a sheet of glass, the glass shattering but resisting the bullet, was withdrawn on the instructions of the Independent Broadcasting Authority. Saatchi & Saatchi, who produced the ad, were later reported as asking whether a ruling made because of a specific incident, like the Hungerford shootings, should be a ruling for ever. Exception was also taken to a Procter & Gamble ad for Fairy Snow showing a young girl donning a night-dress, presumably on account of the current concern over child abuse. It was Procter & Gamble, by the way, who back in the 1920s sponsored a show called *The Goldbergs*, and thus inspired, if not the genre, the designation 'soap opera'.

Some ads are so abject, so sheerly irritating, that one cannot comprehend how they ever reached the screen: planted there, it might be thought, by Machiavellian rivals. In some quarters the original meaning of 'commercial' seems to have been forgotten. (The BBC has referred to an AIDS warning against the use of infected needles by drug addicts, shown on ITV, as 'a commercial'. If paid for by the makers of hypodermics, then so it was.) Lengthy ads are invariably tedious and self-defeating. One such consists of hectic, disjointed shots from an old cult thriller, *The Prisoner*: a brutal interrogator shouting 'We want information!', the browbeaten prisoner piteously insisting he is not a number but a free man, and at long last the advertiser's name, bound to have acquired a sinister ring by now —'LBC, The Information Station'.

In an ad for Vauxhall cars, a prospective customer, taking a car on a trial spin, drives an elegant young lady to the beach; returns to the dealer, takes out another model, and wins a rally; returns again, drives a third model to Switzerland, where he has a whirl with a local maiden and tootles on an Alpine horn; goes back to the dealer, murmurs 'Most stimulating, thank you', and walks away without making a purchase. A novelist *manqué* at work there, we suspect. The best ads are the haiku of television.

Viewers grumble about the timing of commercial breaks, and maladroit or abrupt cutting does seem to betray contempt either for the programme the sponsor has subsidized or for the sponsor's potential customers. And more serious aesthetic objections are brought: for instance, that when John Hurt was playing the Fool in a 'prestige' ITV production of *King Lear*, his voice was heard unmistakably during a commercial screened in the course of the play. Confusing to be sure, as well as galling, but he who pays the piper . . . and if you cannot smile as the wind sits, you will soon catch cold. How much worse it would be if the State called the tune. 'It should be understood that when Lear spoke of scurvy politicians he was referring to people who defraud the Inland Revenue, claim welfare benefits without entitlement, or enjoy the pleasures of television without paying a licence fee . . .' Or even, 'This government intends to carry out what King Lear could only dream of, and show itself more just than the opposition parties by shaking the superflux to houseless heads and unfed sides . . .'

For all their eccentricities, advertisers are hardly to be numbered among those who believe that television's influence on the viewer is inconsiderable. (Nor are the charities engaged in famine relief.) Yet the impression remains that to some degree they are altruistic, and more dependable than the State. Were it not for them, we should have virtually no sport, a limited choice of entertainment, and less in the way of high (i.e. expensive) art. Literature would stumble along, as ever, irrespective.

Copulation Explosion

It can't simply be one's age that causes love-making (an expression sensibly replaced by the menu-like 'having sex'), as represented on television, in films and plays, in books, to seem so peculiar. On a Sunday not very long ago—the better the day . . . —copulation was in full swing on two television channels simultaneously, unmistakable although stylized. Interesting, how grunt and groan, reminiscent of the previous day's televised wrestling, combines with the arty effects connived at by camera and lighting and indeterminate bodily parts. It seems more indecent than similar activities described in print, perhaps because more directly voyeuristic, while written accounts manage to be more disgusting, perhaps because more disgusted.

The sexual act has been around for a long time; it is no stranger to most of us. Why, then, this modern preoccupation with it? Because, however ancient, it hasn't for obvious and deplorable reasons been fully explored in the past? It can only be explored, fully or otherwise, in the doing, not in the viewing. Paradoxically, it remains a dirty little secret long after it has ceased to be secret. It is easy to do—in words, that is, or in images—much easier than furthering a story, or creating character, or simply writing well. (Anything is easier than writing well.) It will attract attention, even the attention of those who consider its representations peculiar or indecent or all too easy. Lawrence spoke of men despising sex and living for it. It 'sells books', it fills (or half-fills) the cinemas. It is the primal act, unquestionably important. And as we watch, we hope, yet again, that something extraordinary will happen; not what most commonly and comically can go wrong in real life, but—say—a famished vampire bursting in on the lovers, the sex-havers, or the bed collapsing, or carried off by a tornado.

I remember when the floodgates were opened, and novels abounding in sex arrived at publishers' offices by every post. There was one thing their authors could write about, and how

51

long, how yearningly, they must have been waiting for the green light! Their offerings fell into two categories: the clinical or unrecognizably 'realistic', and the unimaginatively grotesque. Often the authors would mention—modestly, as if to avert any supposition that they thought themselves engaged in high art— that sex, they gathered, was currently a big seller. With rather less reason, writers of poetry sometimes make the same claim for their speciality: they 'understand' or 'have been told' that this is the case. Who told them? What led them to understand? This remains a mystery.

That the ever-interesting topic should have become the only interesting topic is readily comprehensible in a society rich in leisure time, or unemployment, and religiously egged on in its natural curiosity by the media. But no topic is inexhaustible or infinitely interesting, except in the hands of genius. In John Updike's novel, *Roger's Version*, the attempts of one of the characters to establish the existence of God with the aid of computers were absurd, no doubt, doomed to failure, since a being notoriously reluctant to reveal himself, and scornful of the appetite for signs and wonders, is unlikely to be trapped by the most sophisticated of electronic appliances. Yet this side of the novel was brilliantly original, as well as gently captivating, in comparison with the successful attempts of practically all the characters to establish the existence of sex. That computers can prove more interesting than couplings ought to serve as a warning.

What is interesting about the sexual act, from our present point of view, is the impossibility of representing it. (This may have momentous implications.) The more operatic the style, as in Updike's writing, the greater the failure. Those who have come nearest to succeeding are those who have abstained from attempting to depict; the act is more honoured in the breach than in the observation. Now those old printed dot-dot-dots have come to seem pregnant with significance: they invited us to press the imagination into service, or even fall back on experience.

The hoary fear evinces itself—that in some distressing way life will come to imitate what one is loath to call art. While we have to resist such melodramatic notions as that life will collapse into the black hole of the television screen, like a sequence out of a

Disney cartoon, there is in humanity a strong urge to self-corruption—what we used to reify as the Devil seeking whom he might devour—as well as goodness and kindliness. At least I feel a little less absurd when recalling how Wordsworth worried over his feeble endeavours to counteract the 'degrading thirst after outrageous stimulation' catered for by 'frantic novels, sickly and stupid German Tragedies, and deluges of idle and extravagant stories in verse', paltry villains (stories in verse! German tragedies!) though these must appear to us. What saved him from melancholy was his belief in 'certain inherent and indestructible qualities of the human mind'. While today we may retain some faith in the survival of those unspecified qualities, if less perhaps than Wordsworth, we ought to know better than to subject them to further strain. How desolating to see the artist, once thought to constitute the growing point of the race's consciousness, now wielding the flame-thrower, the defoliant, the bovver boots.

As we have heard, television is as yet but a pimply adolescent, nowhere near the maturity reached long ago by literature. It is literature, or books rather, that must stand the gravamen of the charge of doing dirt on life. *Corruptio optimi pessima*. When a puff for a new woman poet alludes to her 'direct language and unorthodox subject-matter: that of contemporary sexuality'— unorthodox?—we detect little more than the desperation of blurb-writer and publicist. More germane is a generalization thrown out by D. J. Taylor while reviewing a batch of recent fictions in *Encounter* for June 1986: 'So painstakingly are human defects conveyed, so sharp are the physical sensations engendered, that you end up hating large parts of the dramatis personae: a characteristic, possibly, of all the best-regulated fiction.' To which we should add, as an acknowledgement that the phenomenon is by no means new, Karl Kraus's aphorism: 'Today's literature: prescriptions written by patients.'

That our self-disgust antedates the Holocaust and other contemporary or subsequent horrors, though these must surely have intensified it, is evident. It was over sixty years ago that Edwin Muir wrote, in contrasting Joyce, Huxley, and Lawrence with Scott and Jane Austen: 'The historian writing fifty years hence of the literature of today will find in it a certain note of inhumanity. He will speak of our hostility to mankind . . . A thorough dislike of their creations characterizes, indeed, the majority of modern novelists.' The sinister, the barely admissible question is: To what extent *post hoc*, to what extent *propter hoc*?*

In one of the Sunday night sessions mentioned above, the faces of the participants, under the pitching and rolling camera, were distorted and bathed in a ghastly mixture of chalk-white and mauve lights. Was it seasickness? The onset of heart failure? Or had they suddenly remembered AIDS? On the following day anxiety was expressed on television as to whether the general public would stomach plain speaking on the subject of AIDS and how exactly it is contracted. Which brings us by ineluctable process to the next chapter.

---

* Writers have customarily reposed trust in a posterity, superior in perceptiveness to the present, which will appreciate them at their true value. It could be that as standards decline from generation to generation posterity is simply less fastidious.

Mighty were the Auxiliars

The screen doesn't much like to preach; it has seen so many preachers come to grief over the years. And viewers don't fancy being preached at in their own living-rooms. The campaign against drugs has surely had some effect: it made 'good television'. And perhaps, if less so, that against smoking. Neither of these impinged on the bedevilled business of sex, except that in its feeblest moment the anti-smoking campaign thought to scare off young fellows by insisting that those whose breath was tainted wouldn't pull as many birds as would their clean-living coevals.

Sex has never been an easy subject to talk earnestly about. It was all very well for Boswell, after his one and only tête-à-tête with Johnson on 'the sensual intercourse between the sexes', to declare that this subject 'when philosophically treated, may surely employ the mind in as curious discussion, and as innocently, as anatomy; provided that those who do treat it keep clear of inflammatory incentives'.

In the case of AIDS, it seemed at the outset a question of introducing uninflammatory disincentives. Though eager to play its part, British television failed to find a middle way between the mealy mouth and the dirty mind. Nobody wanted to throw the first moral. ('We are advocating chastity not because we are moralizing, but for practical prevention': the Bishop of Birmingham.) The initial government warnings were a trifle quaint, and possibly misleading, in that one of them, featuring a worker chipping away at what eventually turned into a gravestone, might be construed as touching on the dangers of silicosis, and a second, involving icebergs, bore some resemblance to a nature film. It was decided that people couldn't understand these warnings, and hence something plainer was needed.

Something plainer was provided in ITV's *First AIDS*, a show of ninety minutes' duration including rock stars, comedians, pop music, and sketches, all those things that appeal to (or induce trust in) the low-IQs who spend their time copulating instead of doing their schoolwork. Even so, the studio audience, 'a cross-section of Britain's young people', were largely responsible for what brightness and good humour the programme afforded. Much of the material was of a vulgarity, visual and verbal, so grotesque as to be barely believable. Stand-up and lie-down comics inflated condoms, stuck them on their tongues or their heads (a variant of the Direct Method in teaching: you kids are pretty dumb, but you can't be as stupid as this), or flicked one another with them (demonstrating the fascinating properties of rubber). At last they could work off those smutty jokes so long banned from the air! A speaker on another programme was said in a letter printed in the *Radio Times* to have had condoms 'on the brain', but this was a figure of speech.

Sensitive young people, one might fear, would be permanently put off ——. Naturally 'having sex' was the expression favoured in the programme, a locution nicely stripped of lust as well as of love. (What could these striplings know of either?) One or two of the studio audience opined that condoms would have much the same effect, such was their naïve attachment to spontaneity. They were rebuked sternly. For these ninety minutes composed the apotheosis of what in a mean racist way, and in a more furtive age, was called the French letter—a saviour rising out of the mists of oblivion, the sordid past forgiven.* Casanova used condoms, so they must be fun!

Youngsters who may well have had no sexual ambitions whatsoever were exhorted to carry condoms in their back pockets or handbags whenever they went out—an exceptionally low-life and perhaps hand-picked Casanova in the audience boasted of carrying a dozen or so—and the clear feeling of the panel was that they would be at it as soon as they left the building.

So one turned to BBC 2 for the really highbrow stuff—like a take-off, in a series entitled *Now—Something Else—Again*, of the Piat d'Or commercials: 'The French. They'll let you screw their daughters for a bottle of wine.' And thence to Channel 4, where it was being demonstrated how easily a bawd (sorry, a hostess) can become a national heroine.

* Rumour has it that long ago, when the academic journal *German Life and Letters* proved successful, plans were afoot to found a companion journal in the French discipline with a matching title; in the nick of time this was changed to *French Studies*. In 1980 a juggernaut was spotted, carrying the inscription: 'If the French won't buy our lamb we won't use their letters.'

What was on BBC 1 that evening? Among other things, a short item called *AIDS—The Facts*, which assured us that you could at any rate *give* blood without risk, and that it was reasonably safe to kiss. Knowing what a kiss can lead to, the presenter then showed, with the aid of a plaster of Paris erection, exactly how to don a condom. There would be no excuse now for sticking it on your tongue and hoping for the best.

I spoke too soon. The press has since reported that of a party of eight young men who recently went to Thailand, 'six had disasters with a reputable brand which is made to the highest specifications'. *The Times* added that many disasters are caused by sharp finger-nails, rings on the fingers, and trapped air bubbles. How disastrous the disasters were was not divulged.

On 12 March 1987 *The Times* reported that the Duke of Edinburgh had astonished MPs and peers at the Commons the previous night by praising condoms. During a meeting of the all-party conservation committee, the Duke suggested that manufacturers should produce variously coloured models calculated to appeal to different ethnic groups and religions. (Those designed for Roman Catholics, one fancies, would burst into flames a few seconds after placement.) Thailand, the Duke was said to have said, is the most imaginative country by reason of producing multicoloured condoms, certain colours being considered lucky at certain times of the year. (This might explain the young men's disasters: temporary blindness—'mine eyes dazzle' —brought on by bright pigments.) 'They choose yellow if they are happy,' the Duke continued, 'and black if they are in mourning.'

The association of black condoms with widows is a hoary joke; and the Duke may have had at the back of his mind the diversely flavoured sheaths that were on the market well before the advent of AIDS. Still, the ethnic cause is always a good one, so why not Pakipistles, Chinese scrolls, Caribbillets, India rubbers . . .? And perhaps heartening accompaniments from a micro-music box: 'Eternal condom, strong to save', 'O shield us lest we die', 'I need thy presence every passing hour', 'Let me hide myself in thee', and other old favourites.

It is probable that the Duke was speaking ironically, and alluding obliquely to the fact that the first element in the old maxim, 'Be good, or if you can't, be careful', had dropped utterly out of sight. Irony is always prone to misconstruction, and is never expected of royal personages.

A leaflet put out by one concerned agency was headlined 'LOVE CAREFULLY . . . Use a condom', and carried the advice, 'So *love carefully* and know the one you're with.' Biblical language? No, nothing so grand: just, you ought to find out the other person's name. Far defter was the TV condom commercial sponsored (no irony, please) by the Virgin Group: 'You make love; they make sense.'

The most effective blow against some of the misunderstandings surrounding AIDS was delivered at the end of March in the course of *EastEnders*, where, as noted, the subject was brought up plausibly, by way of long-standing characters, and even humorously. Later in the year the Independent Broadcasting Authority stated in its annual report that more fictional characters were to die of the disease on television, and promiscuous characters would be answerable to new restrictions. 'Not every young lover in television drama has ended up in bed. But the conventional presumption is that couples do couple. That presumption is now challenged.' Whose presumption would that be? We can't tell from the phraseology how the responsibility or the blame—not that much of either is implied—is to be shared between television and the public. The moguls have such a winning manner of yielding; when they are persuaded to mend their ways, it turns out to be our ways they are mending.

And so the condom madness swept across the land. In my own neighbourhood a band called Johnny Pinko fell foul of the Wandsworth Community Health Council, not for being sponsored by a manufacturer of condoms—the Council thought well of the general idea—but for being sponsored by a brand which had failed a safety test prescribed by the British Standards Institute. Posters advertising a concert to be given in Putney displayed members of the band dressed in giant-size Jiffies. The manager of the band claimed that it was only one specific batch of Jiffies that was unsafe: the articles had come via a German company who had acquired them in good faith from the Far East. (One wonders what colour they were.) When last heard of, the Johnny Pinko band was proposing to play in an AIDS benefit concert.

By this time no eyebrows were raised when a magazine called *Sky*, subtitled 'A New Magazine for a New Generation', announced an article on 'Safe Sex', describing it thus: 'Once the subject of seedy sniggers, condoms are now a mixture of practical protection and style accessory. *Sky* presents an international guide to the condom.' Some sharp entrepreneur designed an 'accessory' for incorporation in Filofax—lest we forget—but the Filofax people considered it *de trop*.

One theory has it that contraceptive sheaths were invented in the mid-eighteenth century by a Londoner named Condom, and made from the blind guts of lambs.* Mr Condom's was the unhappy fate of many a benefactor of humanity, and he was obliged to change his name. Incidentally, a rather wittier sketch in the satirical programme *Now—Something Else—Again* had a young woman in a chemist's shop asking for Durex, to the smiling approval of the other customers; she then asked for a packet of Tampax, and the bystanders froze in horror and disgust.

Nevertheless some doubt remained as to whether the young, indeed the middle-aged too, innocent of history and accustomed to better things, would actually utilize these precious articles. A BBC 2 programme, ostensibly on the merits of massage, spread the message that there was another sort of sex besides the genital, namely 'touch'—touch, which we all require, including the aged, who make do with stroking their pet cats—and that this has the inestimable advantage of being safe. To celebrate the practice, there followed an idiotic scene in which two loquacious wrestlers, one heterosexual, the other homosexual, discussed the

* But Fritz Spiegl has pointed out that there is a town in France called Condom, and therefore, if a connection could be established, the offensiveness of 'French letter' would be (more or less) expunged. Condom, he notes, is a few miles away from a place known as Sore.

A late item of news is that Australian health advisers have found Aborigines unenthusiastic about condoms because the word sounds like *quandong*, a fruit tree also known as 'native peach'. 'We've changed the term to frenchies,' an adviser says.

pleasures of massage while going about their professional business in the ring. Having begun with various parts of the body, including the feet and the neck, the programme moved on by a natural transition to recommend what used to be called 'heavy petting'. Once upon a time we were told this was bad for our health. Not any longer. *Au contraire.* The word 'masturbation' was not uttered once.

Some three months later *Porterhouse Blue* was screened, an adaptation by one of our leading contemporary novelists of a novel by another leading contemporary. A protracted sequence in it, illustrating the difficulty of getting rid of unwanted, unused condoms, involved the blowing-up routine on a grand scale. It is unlikely that this low slapstick was intended to play any part in the AIDS campaign. Mighty were the auxiliars which stood upon our side, us who were strong in love!—as Wordsworth observed of a different revolution—the meek and the lofty both found helpers to their hearts' desire, and stuff at hand, plastic as they could wish. But by now the excitement was fading fast, though not before making condoms a fit theme for popular entertainment. Dedication doesn't last long in these circles, and pre-crisis humour soon reasserted itself; in a comedy show starting just at 9 p.m. a joke moved from designer condoms to designer diaphragms and 'cervix with a smile'. It was about this time that the IBA gave clearance for the advertising of condoms, on the understanding that the ads should be 'in good taste, restrained, and not show unwrapped products'. Commercials are ruled by a sterner code than the rest of broadcasting, and much of their distinction stems from the fact. Amid fear and trembling the first showing took place at 9.15 p.m. on Saturday 1 August, in the form of an enigmatic little story of boy and girl separated by wire netting, but finally brought together by courtesy of Durex. One TV critic admitted to thinking it was the white saloon in the background that was being advertised. The IBA reported having received only two calls after the screening, one in favour and one against.

Should all these efforts fail, one course still remains open. Namely, the vigorous promotion of personalized foam-rubber manikins and inflatable mates. The assorted fruits of human ingenuity *à la* Frankenstein are prefigured in Stanislaw Lem's book, *A Perfect Vacuum*: among them, sexercisers, copul cots, incubunks, porn cones, push-button clitters, phallophones, sodomy sofas, and flagellashes, besides plastic androids created in the image of Greek gods and goddesses for those with a taste for history. As Lem saw it, the outcome of this technological revolution was that 'the old methods of home fornication' were at last laid to rest 'alongside the flints and clubs of the Neanderthals'.

Causes without Effects

To assess with any certainty the effect of a television programme on even a single viewer is impossible. How to separate it from other effects? What about the subject's prior state of moral health? So much is incalculable. And we tremble at the lengths to which censorship, whether well-meaning or self-serving, can go. There was a case in Malaysia some years ago of a young boy who died by throwing himself out of a window in an attempt to emulate Superman's feats, and talk ensued of banning the Superman films, which in fact incorporate copy-book maxims about Good and Bad. Should a party claim that reading the divine Marquis led them to commit ferocious torture and murder, they may well be hoping to shift the blame: 'a pander was the book, and he who wrote it'; if their reading had been the *Boys' Own Paper* their behaviour might have been the same. Or so it will be argued.

Sociologists both professional and amateur have agreed implicitly with Ruskin's saying, 'Tell me what you like and I'll tell you what you are'—what teenagers like, we hear, are films such as *Conan the Barbarian* and the *Rocky* series —but the vast majority of them decline to explore the possibility of a relationship between 'what you watch' and 'what you do'. All the same, it is hard to believe, if I may repeat myself, that what we see and hear has no effect on us, and it is certain that much of what we see and hear can't have a good effect. We have noted the contention of clever people that there was violence, murder, and rape long before television was born; and some (though probably not the same) people will point to the even longer existence and greater ubiquity of original sin. But there still seems something odd when a retired headmaster writes to the *Radio Times*, mocking parents for their 'over-protectiveness' by disclosing that 'the language in an average eleven-year-olds' playground could never be broadcast'. What sort of a school was he headmaster of? These days, I fear, it would be difficult for parents to be over-protective. The defenders of television freedom are forever selling the medium short.

As witness Michael Grade, then BBC Television's director of programmes, when he rushed to acquit Dennis Potter's play, *The Singing Detective*, of charges of offensiveness brought against it, specifically against an episode of explicit love-making in a wood. Mr Grade had vetted the scenes and decided they should not be cut: 'There are very few people in television drama you are prepared to trust with scenes like this. Dennis Potter is one of them.' Mr Grade has failed to perceive the odiousness of the scene in question, and the truth that *no one* could be trusted with it. The viewer was by invitation—yes, we know, invitations can be declined*—a voyeur, perched on his or her chair, watching the small boy, perched in a tree, watching his mother copulating below.

The episode was preceded by a strong warning to viewers about its sexual content (the fact that I missed this was no fault of the BBC), and a spokesman was cited later as saying, 'Interestingly, a number of complaints were received after the warning about the explicit scene, but before the sequence was actually shown.' What was meant by 'interestingly'? In all likelihood complainants registered their objections in advance because they had a shrewd notion of what was to come, and there was little point in protesting after the deed was done. The spokesman's implication was that they were all cranks or prudes, zealous not to let ignorance stand in the way of self-righteous condemnation.

To take the present line, some will say, is to commit an act of self-exposure more disgusting than anything we shall ever witness on our screens. A *reactionary* bleeding heart! I recall how a

* The 'you can always switch off' argument—comparable to that other knockdown remonstration: 'If you don't like it here then go somewhere else'—was recently extended, in a letter in *TV Times*, to embrace programmes screened before 9 p.m. (toddlers' bedtime) in which parents might conceivably anticipate an unsuitable ingredient, such as a joke involving Fokker planes. (The word was printed 'Focke'. One tiny side-benefit of reading is that, with luck, it helps us to spell correctly; not on this occasion, however.) Parents were advised to scrutinize the guest lists of chat shows; if possible unsuitability should be deduced—this would require an extensive and intimate knowledge of celebrity-type guests, the sort of 'interest' television companies hanker after—then: videotape the programme. Thus the strategy proposed. One could of course send the children out for a healthy walk in the streets, or (which is more prudent) lock them in the coal-hole.

Alternatives to switching off include putting one's eyes out, in the manner of some moral weakling of classical antiquity, or driving a spike through one's ears. In a society committed to freedom of choice, the onus of choosing lies on you.

publishing house I once worked for took on a novel about a man whose custom it was to creep up on couples in parked cars, shoot them both dead, then lift the female off the male and remove her to a cool cave, in the hills of Tennessee, where he kept an inanimate and docile harem. My colleagues, eminently respectable people, considered the book perfectly acceptable and likely to sell well, though they turned out to be mistaken about the sales. When I confessed to find it merely and sheerly disgusting, and perfectly rejectable, it was suggested that I harboured suppressed urges to necrophilia. Proving that you are not a necrophile is no easier than proving you were never a spy. My boss expressed surprise that I felt no compassion for the book's hero. 'It's the only way he is able to communicate.' I was the villain of the piece, patently pitiless and probably perverted.

It may be the saddest part of Freud's legacy that no one can be allowed an honest, impersonal opinion on anything relating, however indirectly, to sex. Useless to say you love your mother because—well, because she is lovable. Even in—or especially in—sophisticated circles, morality, or indeed 'taste', is construed as a means of justifying our prejudices or needs, or—as in this case of necrophilia—covering them up.

A rather less ghastly ingenuity, in another novel published around that time, comprised a woman making love to (having sex with) a mushroom. There may have been a distinguished precedent skulking around, though I fancy it went unnoticed, in the genus *Impudicus* mentioned by Doctor Krokowski, the poetical psychologist of *The Magic Mountain*: suggestive in its form of *l'amour*, and among the ignorant still passing for an aphrodisiac, and in its odour, when the spore-bearing fluid drips from its bell-shaped top, suggestive of *la mort*.

The Singing Detective captured an audience of some ten million, approaching the ratings for *Dallas*, and drew panegyrics from the most grudging of television reviewers. Radio 3's *Critics' Forum* judged it 'an extraordinary work of art'. True, Dennis Potter is genuinely clever and—what's rarer—driven by some obscure daemon. The play had flashes of power and of wit, and (again) the advantage of first-rate actors; it was a thoroughly 'professional' piece of work, whatever that adjective means, and, which was quite brilliant, it contrived to arrive at a happy, or at least agreeably sentimental, ending. But once you took away the strong (or uninventive) language—'Fuck. Dirt. Death'—and shouting matches, the repetition of significant moments (you can't have too much of a bad thing), and the amiably nostalgic songs, there wasn't so very much left, hardly enough to make an extraordinary work of art. The relating as cause and effect of what the boy saw—and what therefore, the argument goes, *we* must see—to the Nessus-shirted adult lying in bed is simple-minded and banal psychology. At least the hero summed up in blunter terms: 'Sex and lies, that's what it's all about. Sex and lies.'

It must be owing to his talent, and the strength of his feelings, that Dennis Potter inspires so much double-think. When another play of his, *Brimstone and Treacle*, was televised, eleven years after it was banned, a television critic cited the author's own inserted warning:

> If you are a nervous type out there
> Switch off or over for some calmer air
> But you have to be very smug or frail
> To believe that no man has a horn or tail.

Good strong stuff, almost Jonsonian. The critic amplified: 'Or, in other words: certain scenes may be offensive to those of a bigoted disposition.' He had summarized one scene, clearly a 'certain' scene, thus: 'A student with cloven feet rapes a brain-damaged girl and, in so doing, cures her.' Ergo a bigoted disposition is one that doesn't find the rape of a brain-damaged girl conducive to good entertainment or art. Replying to protests printed in the *Radio Times*, Michael Grade insisted that great care had been taken in pre-publicity 'to ensure that there was little risk of unsuspecting viewers stumbling across the transmission of the play', which, 'like all of Potter's works, is highly moral'. No reference to suspecting viewers here, and certainly no solace for one of the protesters, mother of a handicapped girl, who feared an invitation to the taking of sexual advantage.

Brimstone and Treacle was very nearly a forceful, updated variation on an old comic and serious theme, that of the Devil, who must do something, willy-nilly doing good in a world where further incitement to evil is otiose. Here the point was amply and aptly pressed home by the cloven-footed student's proposal to shove Blacks and other undesirables into concentration camps and let them starve, or else shoot them, and by its effect on the National Front supporter he is addressing. 'That—that's going too far,' the man says, as might the auditors of Swift's *Modest Proposal*, and he decides not to renew his subscription to the organization.

What went wrong, possibly because the whole concept of conventions is reckoned out of date, is that the dramatist, represented by the critic as 'a hell-fire moralist', ignored the conventions which all forms of art lay down for themselves, within which alone they are potent, and so subverted his own intentions. No matter how 'tastefully' mounted, as in this production, rape cannot be enrolled in the service of satire, nor moral or religious aims achieved through its supposed therapeutic effect, least of all on a brain-damaged girl—not unless, as Swift contrived to do (and the serving up of babies at table is a manifestly more horrific postulate), the ground has been very skilfully prepared, a particular atmosphere established, and our complicity partially secured. What today is called 'black comedy' is most often a throwing together of raw incongruities, productive of gratuitous shock, not shaking us out of our complacency but freezing us in moral paralysis.

I do not mean to pick on Dennis Potter, or only to the extent that he is worth picking on.* Programmes of this class are the ceremonial flagships of our day, while the real enemy, guerrilla-like, is less definable and more malignant. I mean the brittle smartness, the generalized jumble of sneering and sniggering which runs through the arts, and is more distressing in television than elsewhere because television carries a semblance of 'normality' not present during the act of reading a book or going out to a theatre

* *Brimstone and Treacle* was originally banned after £70,000 of licence money had been spent on it, Dennis Potter says in his introduction to the printed version, published in 1978. The play was first produced on the stage in 1977. The seriousness of its intent—the mocking of the smug and sanctimonious—is made plain in this introduction: 'There is, in the end, no such thing as a *simple* faith, and we cannot even begin to define "good" and "evil" without being aware of the interaction between the two.'

or cinema or art gallery: a presumption of typicality, centrality, even 'homeliness' (television happens in the home), which insinuates a specious authority.

Purveyors of popular entertainment have taken over that ageing principle of high art noted earlier: that the authentic view of human nature is a decidedly low one. If we could believe that this arises out of those huge disgraces well within living memory, we should necessarily feel some respect for it. But we know that the media are not punishing us, but pandering to us, to our mean destructiveness and the pleasure we feel in seeing others brought low, even though we ourselves sink in the process. It is almost laughable to hear the top men, who have (as no doubt they must have) an eye to the main chance, wailing about 'witch-hunts' when exception is taken to their products. Or to see, in *TV Times*, the producer of *Emmerdale Farm* piously trotting out the old argument that 'a programme which portrays people's lives dramatically quite properly deals with the fact that life has a sexual dimension'.

We cannot suppose that our masters are acting for our own good—'Therefore that he may raise, the Lord throws down'—and so we must assume they are giving us what, with some wretched reason, they reckon we like. Far from breaking new ground, they are following the fashion, settling for the soft option. However inconsiderable its manifestations are, singly and in themselves, that fashion, because of the deadening silt it leaves behind, is much like the 'negation' which in the past was identified with evil.

The Masters

On 15 July 1987, at the Royal Society of Arts, the Richard Dimbleby Lecture was given by Sir Denis Forman, Deputy Chairman of the Granada TV Group, under the title 'British Television—Who Are The Masters Now?' To begin with, the masters were declared to be 'the people': 'the viewer is king', which is to say, the majority of viewers will get what they want, although at the same time the minorities are to be catered for. It is *de rigueur* on such occasions to stress the latter assurance, since the invited audience, like those who listen to the lecture on television or read it later in print, are likely to belong to one minority or another.

All the same, Sir Denis came out with some strange remarks in passing. One of the three threats to television, we heard, is a noisy minority who agitate over obscenity. Whether this minority was to be catered for was left unclear. It is, we are to suppose, a very small minority, since Sir Denis, presumably basing his calculations on the minority who had made themselves heard, stated that whereas a minority saw obscenity as a threat, a majority ('far more') saw censorship as a threat. Given modern psephological techniques, it surely ought to be possible to provide figures less nebulous for this majority and that minority, and even to indicate how many (if any) saw obscenity and censorship as both of them threats. And, understandably, no attempt was made to define either of them, the assumption being that everyone knows what they are. Under certain regimes, incidentally, the liberty of the press, in the shape of uncensored circulation of pornography, has actually served—by distracting the attention—as an indirect auxiliary in the censorship of political material. *

---

* Eager to eschew any hint of censorship or (which is seen as personally more shameful) self-censorship, the managers of BBC TV and ITV invoke 'taste' when, for example, a 'disaster film' involving aircraft is withdrawn pro tem after a particularly dreadful accident. A letter in *The Times* of 5 September 1987 asked whether programmes featuring gun-play, withdrawn because of the Hungerford shootings, were truly considered 'well-made, acceptable viewing, ready to beam into family living-rooms', and if not, then why were they scheduled in the first

Together, Sir Denis stated, the minorities to be catered for—
yet how do you bring minorities together?—are 'just as numerous
as the *Dallas* audience'. A little later, however, in a projected
future of maddened market forces, the central theme of the lecture, the viewer was reduced to a mere constitutional monarch
with no real power: we shall have to take what 'our masters' think
fit to give us. And so the problem of minorities and majorities will
have vanished.

Apart from an amused and dismissive allusion to the idea of a
jury having to consider, apropos of *The Singing Detective*, 'how
many inches of bare behind could legally be exposed during an
act of *al fresco* copulation', on the subject of specific obscenities or
alleged obscenities Sir Denis confined himself to a mention of
how now and then we meet a truly shocking sight in the street—
'dog and bitch going at it hammer and tongs'—and yet this
spectacle would never be allowed on British television. What this
aside betokened I am not sure; judging by the blank expressions,
the invited audience were equally baffled. That all shock-
ingnesses are relative? That television is pretty decent, con-
sidering, and even (though with no suspicion of self-censorship)
self-denying, and we don't know when we're well off? Or simply
that we expect better things of the brute creation than we do of
ourselves? The thought comes to mind that the sight of coupling
dogs is decidedly anaphrodisiac. (Though in this matter too there is
a dissenting minority, Molly Bloom among them.) British television doesn't show us people defecating in the street, either.

Casting the squint eye on history that we have noticed elsewhere, Sir Denis observed that in the past there were more prostitutes per head in Britain than there are now—there was more
chastity too, in those unenlightened days of black and white
—and that, moreover, rape was common in the past, so common
that it wasn't thought of as a crime. (As in the days of Genghis
Khan? Perhaps it was out of considerations of taste that no reference was made to child abuse.) The implication was that, while
we may not be getting visibly better, the difference now is that

place. Anticipating Saatchi & Saatchi, though not in the same spirit, the writer
wondered when the programmes would become acceptable again. 'Ten days?
Two weeks? Or is it all right now that the funerals are over?'

But there lies the charm of 'taste': two weeks is about its maximum life
expectancy.

things are out in the open, the open consisting largely of our television screens. That glorious 'open', *al fresco*, with its aura of spaciousness, healthy breezes, benign sunshine, and gentle cleansing rain!

Though jokes are always welcome in lectures, detached from anything that could be deemed felt convictions they attest to nothing. It would shock us as we walked along the street to see a baby stoned to death, yet in her book *On Iniquity* (1967), written directly after the Moors murder trial, Pamela Hansford Johnson quoted what the then Director of the Royal Court Theatre said, in the *Spectator* in 1965, regarding Edward Bond's play, *Saved*: 'Have you ever seen a baby stoned to death on the stage before? Or a flabby old bag rousing sexual excitement in a young man? I think it is a triumph to have these things put on the stage.' One can only echo Miss Johnson: What on earth can William Gaskill have meant by 'triumph'? Only a paranoid terror of censorship, an insane, gloating exultation over its defeat, could induce us to see this statement as other than simultaneously heartless, perverse, and ludicrous.

Miss Johnson, who had attended the Moors trial, was suffering from shock (a shock that in some others one would call salutary), and she was conscious, almost too acutely so, of that fact. Regarding Ian Brady's select little library, she did no more than imply, though I think clearly enough, that if there is the faintest chance of a causal connection existing between such books—the Marquis de Sade, Brady's 'major hero'; histories of torture; down-market titles such as *Kiss of the Whip*—and the killing of a child, then the libertarian principle of free availability must be relinquished. Reason tells us that there can be this causal connection, and here the evidence shows that there was. Miss Johnson did not ask for *Justine* or Krafft-Ebing's *Psychopathia Sexualis* to be burned wholesale, removed from the face of the earth. But she knew what an unpardonable offence she was committing. For some considerable time it has been considered élitist, hypocritical, or patronizing to hold that some people—those who, as George Steiner expressed it at the time of the trial, 'do not have countercurrents of wit, intellectual detachment, literary recognition'— are more vulnerable than others to sadistic erotica. If they were merely *vulnerable*, and there an end to it, the freedom to damage oneself if one chooses could be upheld; and the debate reduced to how much public money can rightly be spent on repairing the damage. Instead, when they emerge as child-torturers and murderers, we hear, not of wickedness or evil, terms proper only to the Bible, but of 'sickness', as if such phenomena belonged to the same category as bilious attacks or hay fever.

Appalled as she was, and yet cool and scrupulous in what she uttered (she must have taken great pains in choosing her title), Pamela Hansford Johnson's thinking contrasts sharply with the shallowness and insouciance of those passages of the Dimbleby Lecture I have cited, the which amount to a mock trial where judge and jury and nominally accused are one and the same person. Her book, soon dismissed from mind, I imagine, as uncomfortable inquiries often are, has recently acquired an unhappy timeliness.* As I write, a police inspector has said, in connection with paedophiliac pornography, that 'Today's looker is tomorrow's doer.' It may be that Brady encountered some slight difficulty in assembling his little library, perhaps more than he would today. (Though there are signs that the climate is changing.) Miss Johnson spoke of how we were then 'seeing the most fantastic growth of a semi-literate reading public'; the public for video films, as for television, doesn't need to be literate at all.

In the light or darkness of the misgivings that some of us—a minority? a majority?—are now experiencing, *On Iniquity* must strike us as brilliantly original. And what we may find most original about it, and (let's hope) thought-provoking, lies in the dedication, something the author's daughter said to her: 'Don't ask what does people harm. Ask what does them good.'

---

* A 'highly prejudiced and emotional book' was how John Calder described it in 1970, sounding rather like Malcolm urging the bereaved Macduff to pull himself together and 'dispute it like a man'.

For the Children

I ought much earlier to have stated my qualifications for writing about television. Probably what deterred me was the thought that no qualifications were required. But I now recall that in the early 1970s I wrote a piece on a children's programme for the *Listener*, in which I laid claim to one qualification, though an ambiguous one: television was new to me. After many years abroad, living in countries where either there wasn't any television or else it had just been introduced as a prime tool in the processes of 'human engineering' and therefore wasn't taken very seriously, I had returned to this country—England—where television was both firmly established and basically free.

Now that I have learned to look on television not as in the hour of thoughtless middle age, would I enjoy *The Basil Brush Show* as much as I did then, when the set seemed apparelled in celestial light and its buttons and knobs were still a mystery to me? I think so, albeit the show might register as quite outlandish—both artless and intellectually demanding—at a time when children are offered in the same breath a simplified version of Beatrix Potter and a choice of sexual life-styles. At all events I reproduce the old text, largely unchanged, as a historical document.

The pun is the essence of poetry, or its microcosm. The scorn frequently professed for punning is merely a sign of the higher illiteracy, in all likelihood linked with the taste for ponderous formulations and the concomitant suspicion that punning is a sort of cheating. Punning is at or very near the heart of a television programme in which the visual is combined with the verbal in a partnership of equality, something rarely come across—a children's programme, nominally, and truly.

The Basil Brush Show is a team effort, and credit is due to the producer, Robin Nash, to the writer (of course), George Martin, and to the cameramen. It is also due to Derek Fowlds, most graceful of feed-men, who really seems to enjoy the proceedings and behaves as if Basil's interventions were unexpected (perhaps some of them are), thus providing a sense of spontaneity to counteract the obviously drilled and sometimes less than gripping insets or side-shows. The feeling conveyed of a continuing relationship between Basil and Mr Derek, an intimacy still open to new discoveries, must have done much towards the show's sustained popularity. But the lion's share of thanks must go to Ivan Owen, the prime mover, or (as Basil puts it when he has let his brush down) 'my man, who speaks for me and generally lends a hand'. Though outwardly simple and uncomplicated, Basil is an expressive creature, intelligent, nervous, and cunning. Just as *onnagata*, the Japanese actors specializing in female roles in the Kabuki theatre, contrive to be more like women than women are, so Basil is more like—no, not exactly a fox—more like a living being than many living beings are.

A coward made bold by curiosity; affectionate and yet unsentimental ('Oooo! You're not like this when we're playing hospitals together!'); vain, for his brush means a lot to him, and he has a soft spot for his snout; with strong likes (for peanuts and jelly babies: 'it ain't what you chew, it's the way that you chew it') and dislikes (for 'eerie-wigs' and his Auntie Florrie's lap-dog, who bit him every time he sat on its lap); inclined to brief bouts of sanctimonious indignation ('Ali Baba and the Forty Thieves—98 per cent of the leading characters are dishonest!'), to sudden freezes and equally wholesale meltings; given to self-admiration ('Boom, boom!'); quick on the uptake (found ignorant of the fact that Rugby Union players don't get paid for their pains, he recovers himself nimbly: 'They do it for kicks'); richly vulgar—earthy, rather—yet quite the little gent when he wants to be (he apologizes to Lady Luvaduck for addressing her as 'Your Ladyboat': it was a 'fox par'); a cuddly innocent and a hard-boiled sophisticate; a fantasist who can suddenly turn cool and rational ('Between you and me, Basil, marriage is marvellous!' 'Between you and me it would be ridiculous!') . . . Basil Brush belongs to the small band of anthropomorphized animals, headed by Toad of Toad Hall, who function successfully in both worlds.

The show follows its own conventions closely. The two principal characters are discovered in the act of welcoming a duly appreciative audience of children. Then comes a passage of chit-chat, perhaps making play with one of Basil's many relatives (naturally there is a Herr Brush in Hamburg), or Basil scores a point or two off his colleague: Mr Derek is getting to be almost as well known as his jokes. Now and then Basil falls into a pensive mood, and from the gravity of his demeanour one would suppose him musing on the wickedness of blood sports or the transient nature of jelly babies. On one such occasion he had simply misheard a reference to Khartoum, and confided to the audience how fond he was of cartoons, Yogi Bear in especial.

A guest appearance follows, a marionette theatre (a nice touch) or a magician, the Little Angels of Korea, a school choir or a pop group. This yields to the main course: a playlet, often topical in flavour, minimal in plot and with guest help as applicable. Basil and Mr Derek set about buying a house; they get into trouble at the Customs; they rehearse *Romeo and Juliet* ('It's a bit of a drag!' complains Basil, dressed up as Juliet); or they find themselves on holiday at the North Pole instead of Nostra Palma, that sunny little spot on the Med. The Christmas edition featured a party given by Mr Charles Dickens for some of his more congenial characters. Music intervenes again, mercifully brief, and the show concludes with the serial reading by Mr Derek of a book, latterly *The Adventures of Basil the Buccaneer*. The story is skeletal and the style unembellished, but Mr Derek is helped out or hindered fruitfully by Basil, who by turns is absorbed in the tale, at cross purposes with the text, and engaged elsewhere, perhaps with his pet mouse or a bag of peanuts.

'I say! I say! I say!' At times the manner is close to that of the traditional music-hall. 'How do you make antifreeze?' 'I don't know. How do you make antifreeze?' 'Hide her dressing-gown!' A joke much enjoyed by the children—it doesn't matter if they don't get the antifreeze, the idea of hiding auntie's dressing-gown is enough—as was Basil's explanation when Mr Derek wondered how he ever got into television: 'Through the holes in the back.' And likewise his Groucho-like comment that 'Quack medicines can come in very handy sometimes . . . if you've got a sick duck.' On a slightly more elevated plane is the punning that surrounds Pierre from the South End (Southend Pierre), the bank robber who eludes the police by disguising himself as a children's nurse: 'I hope you searched every crook and nanny,' Basil remarks.

Lavatorial humour of a traditional and innocuous kind (even Freudianly relieving, maybe) crops up regularly. Mr Derek assures Basil that babies' high chairs always have a hole in them: 'that's the whole idea.' 'I think it's a potty idea,' says Basil. And after some talk of Nell Gwyn, when Basil hears that Charles II spent twenty-five years on the throne, he comments, 'All those oranges, I suppose.' The subject of underwear attracts repeated variations: 'Don't get your knickers in a twist/combs in a commotion/undies in an uproar/tights in a tangle.' The audience identify with Basil, he is one of them, just a bit bolder and more privileged, and delight to see him putting down an adult, even one so amiable as Mr Derek. For all the excursions into Frankie Howerd country, Basil is unfailingly shocked if he thinks Mr Derek has used a naughty word—'Unmentionables must not be mentioned'—and his extreme delicacy obliges him to spell out the title of a children's book, 'Winnie the . . . P.O.O.H.', 'Mrs Light-house' being one of his bugbears. A riskier joke occurred when he wished he could act in the theatre and Mr Derek told him, 'You're no Thespian'; he replied, 'You don't have to be like that to be an actor, do you?' The children laughed like mad, presumably at the expression of shock and concern written all over his body. Like other good artists, Basil Brush can give pleasure at various levels simultaneously.

This being a serious occasion, we should attend to the pro-founder aspects of Brush's art and thought. I am not thinking so much of his dealings with Sir Gerald Nabarro, Lord Longford, Mr Edward Heath, traffic wardens, or the Trade Description Act ('Half a pound of *tuppenny* rice!'), nor of his alertness to pressing problems like gazumping and traffic congestion ('Oxford Street, yes. That's where you sit in your car and watch the pedestrians whizzing past'). But disciples of Zen could meditate profitably on Basil's *koan* in a letter to his cousin Cyril: 'I am writing this letter slowly, because I know you can't read very fast.' The piece of advice about not mentioning the unmentionable should be pondered by writers, and also Basil's answer when asked what style he paints in, traditional, primitive, surrealistic, or impressionistic. 'Mine is more the . . . contemptuous style.'

On the subject of mental health, tribute is paid to the value of psychiatry: Basil's brother was in the habit of drawing everything in black—black grass, black sky, black sun—but a clever psychiatrist found out what the trouble was. 'Some sort of complex?' ventures earnest Mr Derek. 'No, he'd lost all his crayons except the black one.' When Lord Luvaduck maintains that there's nothing wrong with living in the past, Basil is pleased to agree: 'For one thing, it's a darn sight cheaper!' He once confided that he would like to be 'an executive . . . running a factory, or something . . . about fifty quid a week'. It was pointed out that he had had no experience and therefore couldn't expect a highly paid position. The pundits might care to study his rejoinder. 'And why not? The job's a lot harder to do if you don't know anything about it!'

'Boom, boom!' (*bangs head against Derek*) (*laugh*) . . .

Building Bridges

Will television bring the races and religions together, and shape a united Britain? It looks set to do both that and the opposite, in roughly equal proportions. Rather than the somewhat exclusive and sore-rubbing 'ethnic' programmes—more likely, I fear, to exacerbate and perpetuate division—its happiest contributions lie in those series, such as *EastEnders*, which include West Indian and Asian characters: people who, without being egregiously admirable, are understandable, who are part of the scene, the mixed, human scene, without forfeiting their racial characteristics. Naima, say, affects us as no more exotic than Angie; in both of them, as the narrative unfolds, individual peculiarities preponderate over the obvious racial ones. Ultimately we are all ethnic, we are each of us a minority. As long as it hasn't a too palpable design on us, the representation of what is desired—living both together and separately, as best we can—does far more than any amount of hortatory talk.

And after a united Britain a united world? To comprehend all is to pardon all: the saying is as problematical as it is noble. Possibly there are still things that can only be done, in as far as they can be done, by individuals in person, in the living, unprotected flesh.

But the impulse to moralize can grow overbearing, and we need to escape for a while into stories. The artist in us, to quote the world-famously spiritual Tagore, 'man of a hundred good intentions', must be allowed to be 'naughty and natural' once in a while. Though perhaps not exactly as television understands those adjectives.

The faces of the officials of the Writers' Association were either stern, or expressionless, or battered. The English visitor thought he preferred the battered ones. Among them was—let's call him Chen. Chen was best known, it appeared, for his translation of *Quo Vadis?*, in three volumes, made from an English version of the Polish original. A set had been given to each of the British delegates.

Like apparently everyone else, Chen had suffered in the customary way during the Cultural Revolution; he had been assigned to clean latrines. The Englishman had seen some public lavatories, and knew that cleaning them was a grimmer punishment and a deeper humiliation than might be supposed. He suspected that worse things had happened to Chen than mucking out latrines. There could barely have been enough of them to go round. Chen was less guarded than the others, readier to show his feelings, or perhaps more jittery.

For the Chinese, as for the Japanese, translating texts from foreign languages is a simple matter because foreign languages are simple matters compared with theirs. Getting the tongue round the barbaric sounds is more arduous and less agreeable. During recent times Russian had pushed out English, though the latter was now making a come-back; there were even English lessons on television, and the presenter had become almost a national heroine. Chen spoke very little of the language, most of that little consisting of a line of Shelley's: 'If Winter comes, can Spring be far behind?' When one of the delegates asked him, rather daringly, how he felt when he met those who had ill-treated him in former days, he replied after a pause, 'If Winter comes . . .' (Indeed, the Cultural Revolution was generally adverted to as if it had been a purely natural disaster, like a bad harvest, or else an unprovoked and irresistible assault from outer space.) Whether the talk was of the past or present or future, 'If Winter comes . . .' always fitted, and served to change the subject. The Englishman began to wonder if the phrase hadn't been cleared at the highest levels as a felicitous all-purpose response. But no, for Chen it really did have a meaning.

The two of them managed to converse, for the most part through gestures, exaggerated smiles of approval or deploring frowns. It struck the visitor as bizarre: here were professional writers demonstrating the superfluousness of words. 'Great Britain!' cried Chen, with a large, bruised, angelic smile. 'Not so very great now,' the Englishman replied modestly, thinking of the Opium Wars. Chen made no attempt to deny this palpable though sorry truth. Never mind, he indicated, patting the other's arm consolingly: 'If Winter comes . . .'

'Honourable Elder Brother' was how Chen came to address his

new friend. The Englishman felt this unsuitable, for Chen looked older by a good ten years. Tactful questioning proved 'Elder' to be correct, and thereafter he addressed Chen as 'Honourable Younger Brother'. The others found this quietly gratifying, a true and impeccable cultural interchange.

The people in the streets and markets, or strolling round parks and historical sites, looked cheerful enough. Far less so the writers. Exhorted to forget the regrettable past and to express themselves without fear or favour, as writers should, they remembered only the regrettable past. Spring had been announced, but they weren't confident that it would last. The Association's ageing chiefs presented their guests with little printed books written by themselves and turned into jaded English, containing essays on topics such as 'Musing in the People's Park', 'Sweet Water from the Fields', and 'On the Slopes of the Mountain'. Not so long ago it was production targets and dedicated truck-drivers. There must have been other writers somewhere out there, some of them young and with other things to write about, or other ways of writing. Maybe they weren't members of the Writers' Association. Or maybe they were busy writing.

At official dinners the chairman or vice-chairman of the local branch made speeches welcoming 'the famous writers from Britain'—though on one occasion, when even the seasoned interpreter looked faintly disconcerted, it was 'who, I am informed, are famous'—and alluding to the bridges that by their mere presence they were helping to build between the two nations. Of course clichés are indispensable to social life, most certainly to official life, but when voiced by writers they take on a sinister tone. Chen obviously wasn't trusted to make speeches, and he and the Englishman spent the time toasting each other and exchanging cigarettes. Chinese writers hadn't heard of the cancer revolution.

Once the two of them disappeared clandestinely into a humble drinking-shop—the party was on its way to a Chinese opera—and smartly downed four large bottles of beer. It was the Englishman's idea; he was determined to do something spontaneous, something that wasn't on the programme. Later in the evening the words 'If Winter comes . . .' were heard loud and fairly clear: Chen was doing his best to explain the opera's enigmatic plot.

Another time, in the hotel, the visitor had persuaded Chen to try some of his duty-free Scotch, which surely couldn't be stronger than the *maotai* served at banquets. Poor Chen had to go and lie down, while his colleagues stood guard outside the room.

Afterwards the Englishman would ask himself whether their hosts hadn't perhaps found them disappointingly docile. Free people might be expected to conduct themselves freely and easily. But the sightseeing was pretty exhausting; akin, you might think, to the sedatives popularly thought to be mixed with the tea dished out to the brutal soldiery. But no, it was a mistake, and self-flattery, to see plots everywhere.

Another thought that came to his mind later was that the speakers and writers he had met might well have digested a passage of Lu Xun's.

It seems to me that the spoken and written word are signs of failure. Whoever is truly measuring himself against fate has no time for such things. As to those who are strong and winning, most of the time they keep silent. Consider, for instance, the eagle when it swoops upon a rabbit: it is the rabbit that squeals, not the eagle. Similarly, when a cat catches a mouse, the mouse squeaks, but not the cat. Or again, remember the Tyrant of Chu: in his golden days, as he was leading his victorious armies from one end of the country to the other, he did not say much. When he began to play the poet and to sing lyric laments, his troops were beaten and he knew that his own end was near.*

Do only losers turn to words? For once the renowned humanist had permitted himself to over-indulge in the detestable mode of irony, the letter of his discourse being the contrary of its spirit. But the spirit, they would know, could kill, and the letter was safer.

There was an untoward incident just as the delegates were making their farewells. His cases full to bursting, the Englishman had abandoned the three volumes of *Quo Vadis?* on the bedside table in his room. The amiable maid—plainly you couldn't offer her a cash tip—might appreciate the novel. But she came running out to the group gathered round the cars, waving the books and shouting gaily. Ah, such honesty! (A woman delegate had been pursued by a hotel maid brandishing a toothless comb she had

* Translated by Simon Leys in *The Burning Forest.*

thrown into the waste-paper basket.) And such a sweeping loss of face! The officials made understanding noises, fought back their smiles, and confiscated the books so firmly as to suggest that they were out of bounds to the proletariat. Chen showed no sign of injured feelings. He embraced his friend vigorously, and the bystanders smiled benignly. The expression of emotion was perfectly admissible on parting. 'If Winter comes,' Chen murmured. 'Take care, Honourable Younger Brother' was all the other could say, sounding as elderly as possible and returning the hug. Almost certainly they would never meet again; they couldn't even exchange letters.

So many little bridges built, and all in the course of a fortnight. They could hardly be other than frail. Would anyone, anything, ever pass over them? You never can tell. Writers are forever making do with imponderables.

LITERATURE

Intermission

Television has its irreproachable uses. It offers handy and pleasurable relaxation after a long day of reading or writing, or of office- or party-going. Sitcoms administer concealed therapy by representing humorously some small failing or eccentricity, or mild misfortune or problem: lack of competence or confidence, the trials of retirement, shared accommodation, a change of job, grown-up children who decline to leave home. The sports coverage is generally admirable, not solely in bringing home to us the savagery of football fans (inevitably and inaccurately described as behaving 'like animals') and the burning down of stands and spectators. It is somehow reassuring to hear that a five-year-old girl doesn't like watching football 'because they hurt their knees'. Besides introducing us to the boredom of American football and (unless a calamitous storm blows up) yacht racing, with the aid of colour it has redeemed such once coarse games as snooker and darts, and brought out the allure of bowls, previously deemed an inactivity suited to old age. In this sphere the human expertise and technical gimmicks elsewhere deployed in tarting up inferior material and transforming the vapid into the senseless are put to an honest and worthy purpose.

Larger claims have been made for television, and graver fears of it expressed. Passages in Don DeLillo's novel, *White Noise* (1985), reflect both the fears and the claims in the lightly distorting mirror of urbane satire.

That night, a Friday, we ordered Chinese food and watched television together, the six of us. Babette had made it a rule. She seemed to think that if kids watched television one night a week with parents or step-parents, the effect would be to deglamorize the medium in their eyes, make it wholesome domestic sport. Its narcotic undertow and eerie diseased brain-sucking power would be gradually reduced.

Concerned parents of a certain educational level do adopt similar procedures—if you can't beat the set, join it, and look bored —and not American parents alone. We note with initial misgivings that the narrator, the father, is chairman of a university department of Hitler Studies, but then we acknowledge that enterprising universities need departments, just as their enterprising staff need distinctive fields of inquiry.

However, one of the father's colleagues, a visiting lecturer in living icons (which include the late Elvis Presley), takes a more solemn and impassioned view of the matter. For him, television is a primal force in the American home, 'sealed-off, timeless, self-contained, self-referring'. We can agree with him there, though we may diverge in our feelings about it. He goes further, much further. 'It's like a myth, being born right there in our living-room, like something we know in a dreamlike and preconscious way.' He isn't thinking of how we sometimes nod off. Oh no, for television offers unbelievable quantities of psychic data. 'It opens ancient memories of world birth', it 'practically overflows with sacred formulas if we can remember how to respond innocently and get past our irritation, weariness and disgust'.

It is true that myth fills a human need, and all the news items, the scandals, the tales of heroism, the personalities, the prize-winners, the record-breaking athletes, even the soap operas, have failed to satisfy the need. Here, we take it, the teacher's task, as the lecturer in living icons sees it, is to help his pupils recover an innocence of response which will strike through the irritation and weariness induced by a literal interpretation of the 'little buzzing dots' that make up the overt picture, and enable them, through cracking the codes and deciphering the messages, to reach into the growing myth beneath. Inevitably, little—or nothing— specific can be said about the myth, since it is still growing.

But the professor's students disagree with him. Television, they contend, is 'worse than junk mail' and 'the death throes of human consciousness'. In the traditional manner of youth, and requiring no encouragement from solicitous parents, they reject outright what the present offers them. They would much rather talk about movies, the debilitated myth-makers of times past.

No doubt all this tells us something about the mythopoeia characteristic of academic life, and most commonly observed among teachers of arts subjects, who live in terror of finding themselves listed in the courses handbook under some such lowering rubric as UNDERSTANDING or APPRECIATION.

Even so, there is a limit to what can be said about television; and much of what can be said will be tautologous. Formulas are arrived at, programmes are programmed; however many channels we are eventually blessed with, there will be nothing remotely comparable to the book published in a short print run for a small audience. To bring to bear the critical scrutiny appropriate to the novels of Dickens or the poems of Donne would be the depth of absurdity. Television needs attention, but attention of another and, alas, more uncertain and hazardous nature. Of what kind or kinds, and of what degree of potency, can or may its effects be?—assuming, as is prudent, that not the whole of what rains down on us will evaporate like water off a duck's back, that it is not utterly a neutral, affectless agency for filling empty time with pure emptiness.

Neither in that inquiry nor (with trifling exceptions) in criticism of the arts are there dependable objective tests or trusty guide-lines. Subjective judgements are admitted in the latter, sometimes grudgingly, but in the former they will be sent packing. We shall be expected to furnish incontestable objective evidence that the rapist or the killer was actually watching some sex/violence passage on the screen—or, in the case of the more literate, reading *Justine* or *Kiss of the Whip*—immediately before the act. Shakespeare and Donne, Dickens and George Eliot— what a simple task of assessment, after all! There is this to be said for the academic—it is at any rate academic.

The gentle viewer is at all times free to switch his or her set off. It is the ungentle, or the immature, developing personality, less likely to press the off-button, whom we must fear for, or fear. To tell ourselves that our fears are merely subjective is not to dispel them.

In the remainder of this book I turn, though in no incontestably academic spirit, to literature, in particular specimens of writing which are remote from television in their means and their ends, and unamenable to televisual usages, and then to questions of language, which itself (I have suggested) is commonly a minor adjunct to television, harmless necessary chat, the grease that keeps the pictures moving.

The gentle reader is, of course, always free to switch off. The ungentle one will never have switched on. Printed words are susceptible to a catch-22 of their own, and Tonio Kröger observed, in more wounding terms than I would care to employ and not without traces of hyperbole, that writers never capture the audience they really long for.

Perilous Sword-Dance

That terrible mania for sentences! An amateur graphologist told Felice Bauer that her friend Franz Kafka must surely have artistic interests. Kafka protested that what he had wasn't exactly a 'bent for literature' or a 'way with words'. Rather, 'I have no literary interests, but am made of literature, I am nothing else, and cannot be anything else.' Flaubert, as Henry James observed, was born a novelist, grew up, lived, and died a novelist; to be literary was for him an 'overwhelming situation'. 'His case was a doom because he felt of his vocation almost nothing but the difficulty.' Even so, the fascination of what's difficult . . .

The relationship between literature and life has been discussed often enough and at length. For the writer—who, far from having a bent for literature, consists of literature bent into something resembling human shape—there is no clear distinction between the two. In that sense, all serious writers are aesthetes: except that the term is irretrievably tainted by its assignation to literary playboys, and disqualified by its dictionary definition, too: 'professed admirer of the beautiful'. The only time you will find a writer professing admiration for the beautiful is when, in holiday spirit, he is gazing at a famous work of art or listening to great music—something, he thinks, that is enviably and yet also enfeeblingly distant from his own trade with its tricky, malevolent, and cherished tools. (Whose tool, rather, he will know himself to be, most of the time; and the rest of the time merely an accomplice.)

But yes, the writer also 'lives'; he cannot leave living to his servants to do for him. He may vote in elections, he may have a family. Perhaps he backs horses or collects stamps. If he is guilty of the baseness which (in Kafka's words) can be traced to 'that core which you can call literature, or anything you like', then other people are guilty of basenesses traceable to other sources. He may (no bad thing) even have a secular job of work to do, because he certainly eats and drinks. All this points to an uneasy balancing trick between two sorts of existence, yet it is, or can be, a rich imbalance. Thinking about it makes it seem less an over-whelming situation than a totally untenable one; left unthought about, it works. Writing is already strange enough, there is no call to make a mystique of it.

Many dedicated writers, those 'made of literature', have led as full a secular life as most people. They have guarded themselves against encroachments—Kafka more consciously and agoniz-ingly than most—but we do not get the impression that they spent all their time in an ivory tower. Even Flaubert, most extreme of 'aesthetes', even Rilke with his string of towers: we do not feel obliged to pity them for what they putatively missed. What *did* they miss?

Tonio Kröger, in Mann's tale, talks at length about his envy of ordinary healthy people, those fine and not excessively fastidious lads and lasses with blue eyes and dancing legs, who live in har-mony with all the world. (The kind of good souls who, to borrow Flaubert's expression, were *dans le vrai*: but who would take that for granted nowadays?) Alas, those favoured people are alienated by the sign they detect on his brow. (The mark of ink-stains.) All he ever dances is 'the cruel and perilous sword-dance of art'. Literature, he tells us, in much the same strain as Kafka, is not a calling, 'it is a curse!' Worthy folk reckon humbly that artistic talent is a 'gift'; they never dream that the gift in question is 'a very dubious affair and rests upon extremely sinister founda-tions'. The mania for sentences, as Flaubert's mother saw, dries up the heart; or, more accurately, dislocates or displaces it. Worth noting in this context—whether or not they know best, mothers deserve to have their say—is what Kipling's told her young son when he grew angry with her for criticizing his poems: 'There's no Mother in Poetry, my dear.'

Kröger places life on one side, and on the other (in a phrase that dates him) the 'sickly aristocracy of letters'. He is in the same boat as Doktor F. Kafka, when the latter asked Herr Carl Bauer how someone like Bauer's daughter, gay, healthy, and self-confident, could possibly marry anyone like Kafka, morose, hypochondriac, and selfish, all in the name of some mysterious higher necessity. But Kröger is not lamenting what he has missed, the forfeitures he has suffered (must one die *entirely* to life to be entirely a creator?), so much as priding himself on his superior gains. And he contrives by sleight of hand to accredit himself with the best of both worlds: what can make a littérateur like him into a poet, he claims, is his 'bourgeois love of the human, the living and usual'. On a visit to his native town—the family house, he finds, has been turned into a public library!*—he is taken briefly into custody as a suspected swindler. We are not sorry in the least. The irony is lenient; other times, other places, and he wouldn't have got off so lightly.

There *is* a form of symbiosis between 'the life' and 'the work', but it persists in remaining unanalysable. Not only do circumstances vary, but there are factors of which the outsider is totally ignorant, and the insider barely conscious. The writer deploys his consciousness in other fields; he knows better than to pull up flowers to see how their roots are progressing: let the unsleeping worms go about their business undisturbed.

The notorious wildness of writers, or what used to be notorious when wildness was less commonplace—sex, alcohol, drugs (now impossibly vulgarized), brawling, lust and rage plaguing every age—can be ascribed to the flatness of ordinary life as compared with the extreme condition of writing, the commitment there of every fibre of the being. This isn't necessarily an existence on the peaks, and can just as well be an existence in the depths: that love of the work which Flaubert described as frantic and perverted, like the love an ascetic has for the hair shirt that scratches his belly. Yet to relinquish the work, perhaps because those 'tools' of yours don't feel like using you at the moment, evinces itself as a descent, a switching into neutral gear, a mere coasting, briefly a relief, then a disappointment. And hence the resorting to whatever other extremes are available, the attempted escape from 'the common dream' into 'dissipation and despair', as characterized by another of those energetic aesthetes who did considerably more than articulate sweet sounds together.

* Truth can be harsher than fiction. In 1945 Thomas Mann's son, Klaus, returned to the former family home, then in ruins, and found that the Nazis had converted it into a *Lebensborn*, a place where the right kind of young men teamed up with the right kind of young women in propagating the Nordic race.

Dissipation because it promises a venture into the unknown, another exploration (in which, often, little is discovered); despair because of the fear of never writing again, of never getting back into that equivocal paradise, that factory without clocks. The accomplished Egyptian courtesan, Kuchuk Hanem, couldn't have competed with the 'perpetual orgy' of literature; when Flaubert didn't have a book on the stocks he could, he said, howl with boredom. Drinking, the self-consumption of one's woes, is by no means confined to manifest failures; indeed it can happen that failure sobers one up. Statistics affirm that out of eight American winners of the Nobel Prize for Literature three were alcoholics and another three were heavy drinkers. The so-called Protestant work-ethic alternates with an unholy and obdurate profligacy: those nights when no man can work. If it were possible to write continuously, allowing of course for moderate eating and sleeping, writers would be the most placid and biddable of creatures, the best behaved (if they could be said to behave at all), until they ran mad or died of something analogous to sexual excess.

Poets, it appears, are peculiarly vulnerable in this respect, more violent in dissipation, in their despair turning to suicide, *âmes damnées* of art, and not invariably its best friends, conceivably on account of the known fickleness of their muse— who either hangs around the premises continuously, feeding false promises, or else, if she stays away too long, forgets your address altogether—or because of the more arrantly uncooperative behaviour of their tools. Prose tends to perpetuate itself; novelists do their stint of 10,000 or a hundred words every day.

We desire and require that there should be something larger than ourselves, and outside ourselves; art is that, and it has the further advantage that at the same time we are very much inside it. ('And tho' I call them Mine,' Blake said of his designs, 'I know that they are not mine.') The total—it seems rather more than total—involvement of the writer in the act of writing, as much prisoner as pioneer, strenuous searcher and also beneficiary of unanticipated and unearned gifts, won't be found too commonly in those who write for television. Such a *modus operandi*, such a harsh blend of addiction and obsession, would kill their products stone dead. A line of verse, said Yeats, may take hours to get right, but it must look like the thought of a moment. On television, unless a line of prose is seen not to have taken even a moment of thought, no Christian ear will endure to hear it.

Evils be ye my Good

Allied to dissipation, and sometimes a result of it, is suffering. Not only does art make you suffer, but suffering makes you an artist. Lots of people suffer in one way or another without writing a word—or composing a bar of music, or painting a stroke—but it is true that affliction can transform potential writers into actual ones by impelling them to seek a mode of escape, or alleviation, or a coming to terms. Bring your drugs, asked one of Cavafy's Byzantines: they relieve the pain, at least for a time. And out of our great sorrows we make our little songs, and on occasion our great ones. Charles Tomlinson puts it less portentously:

> Art grows from hurt, you say. And I must own
> Adam in Eden would have need of none.

It was once remarked of a Poet Laureate fallen into critical disfavour that he had been seen in the street talking to himself, so there was still some hope for him. I knew a writer who courted distress on principle, in that the absence of it was a sign of commonplace bourgeois smugness, itself a cause of creative sterility. (This was a time when 'bourgeois' was an unquestioned and ever-ready contumely.) His courtship proved successful; even those nearest to him felt obliged to comply with his desire, and to a degree surely not anticipated by him. Dreadful experiences, Nietzsche said, raise the question whether he who experiences them is not himself something dreadful too. At best, if you gaze for long into an abyss, the abyss will gaze into you. The man's hunger for suffering may have done less to improve his work than to shorten his life.

The appropriation of suffering as an artistic appurtenance or distinction is both absurd and repulsive. Yet there is something, one feels, to George Gissing's temperate theorizing in *The Private Papers of Henry Ryecroft*. Writing, he observes, has come to be recognized as a profession, much like the Church or the law, and

94

a young person may enter it with parental approval and support. 'I heard not long ago of an eminent lawyer, who had paid a couple of hundred per annum for his son's instruction in the art of fiction—yea, the art of fiction—by a not very brilliant professor of that art.' An astonishing fact, when you came to think about it, 'a fact vastly significant'.

Gissing, who knew about going hungry, adds that, while starvation doesn't guarantee the production of fine literature, one does feel uneasy about 'these carpet-authors'. One evening, having no money to buy supper with, the narrator of the *Private Papers* loitered on Battersea Bridge, was beguiled by the scene, rushed home to write a description of it, and sent it to a newspaper. The paper promptly published it, paying him a couple of guineas with which he bought the next day's supper. To the few who possess 'a measure of conscience and vision'—Gissing continues—he could wish, as the best thing for them, some calamity that would throw them, friendless, on to the streets. (Calamities do not need to be excruciating; Anthony Powell's tutor at Balliol held that it was impossible to exaggerate the advantages of having a drunken father in forcing a man to think for himself.) They might perish, 'but set that possibility against the all but certainty of their present prospect—fatty degeneration of the soul—and is it not acceptable?'*

Gissing wrote at the beginning of the century, and his is an unpopular view nowadays, when for some time past people have expected to receive writing grants well in advance of showing any aptitude for the activity. More often than not, the sponsor is to be the State, an institution quite likely to feature as the villain of whatever pieces they may thereafter compose. No one will carp at mere, cheerful chutzpah, but you need agility like Brecht's to bring this off, and ability like Brecht's to make it worth bringing off.

A dozen or so years ago, asked by the *Observer* to supply a piece

---

* Christopher Dunkley extends the pathos of the starving artist to embrace, more pathetically, workers in television. 'The genius in a garret who paints a picture can reach his public by hanging his work on the Hyde Park railings but his brother who makes a television programme needs a transmitter network or a communications satellite before he can reach an audience.' As Johnson remarked, uncommon parts require uncommon opportunities.

on the subsidizing of writers,* I proposed what could be styled the negative-grant or, on the analogy of the subvention, the subduction. This might take the form of seducing the applicant's wife or husband or otherwise loved one; infecting him or her with a painful disease; blacking his mail; breaking his spectacles; imposing a heavy tax on typewriter ribbons (or word processors now); calling in his mortgage; interviewing him about his work on television . . . The underlying principle could be formulated as Make It Hard And It May Be Good. I left aside Rimbaud's more demanding recipes: you make yourself a poet by degrading yourself, you make yourself a seer by a massive, tenacious, and reasoned derangement of all the senses, you go through unspeakable torture to become sick and criminal and accursed on the grand scale, and thus and only thus do you attain to knowledge of the unknown. 'Knowledge of good bought dear by knowing ill' is how Milton summarized it in a larger connection. That sort of thing is rather too Continental for us. Instead I quoted the words of Shelley, a poet who was tormented at Eton and later banished from Oxford for disseminating an atheistical pamphlet, words chiming with Gissing's, albeit nobler in tone:

> Most wretched men
> Are cradled into poetry by wrong,
> They learn in suffering what they teach in song.

No learning, then no teaching; no suffering, then no song. Surely any author worthy the name would be prepared to be wretched as a man if it saved him from being a wretched writer.

I concluded this ill-natured piece by cautioning against the over-enthusiasm shown in certain countries, where governmental intervention or subduction had resulted in the maiming and even the killing of artists.

Irony, we know, is a wayward servant, especially unreliable when employed not simply in saying the opposite of what you

* What are called 'creative writers', that is. Scholarly writers are generally supported by university salaries and substantial holidays and sabbaticals, as also by grants from foundations and research funds. But the end-product tends to be larger in size than the odd poem or story, and is deemed a contribution to knowledge. Since size is an assessable quality and contribution to knowledge is by definition meritorious there can be no equivalence between scholarship and creative writing in respect of subsidy.

mean but in heightening an opinion which you believe to contain a measure of truth. It wasn't surprising that the sole response I had should take the form of a virulent though not wholly apposite postcard, on which the writer inveighed in storm-trooperly language against those—chiefly, it seemed, contributors to the 'Sunday Jewspapers'—who by undefined ruses were preventing him from publishing his own unspecified works of literature.

Well, to suffer from nothing worse than anonymous postcards is a beginning.

What Happened to the Devil?

In *Lucifer: The Devil in the Middle Ages* Jeffrey Burton Russell considers it strange that, 'at a time when evil threatens to engulf us totally, when evil has already claimed more victims in this century than in all previous centuries combined', one should hear less and less on the subject from theologians. 'Why is there a tendency to reject belief in the Devil today?' When reviewing his book, I offered the facetious answer that while churchmen appear on television, the Devil doesn't; and then needed to add that the Devil did so appear, in light disguise. When the Witch addressed Goethe's Mephistopheles as the *Junker Satan*, he ticked her off:

> The name has been a myth too long.
> Not that man's any better off—the Evil One
> They're rid of, evil is still going strong.*

If churchmen seem barely to believe in God (a sometimes bearded, patriarchal Being, otherwise a dispersed Presence unamenable to visualization) we cannot expect them to believe in the Devil (a goat-like figure, with dirty habits and a nastier sort of beard, and horns and talons). Like most of us, they still believe in Good, but rarely in Evil, a word which even sounds like Devil. Evil—a term which indeed most people would go far to avoid using†—is simply the absence of Good, and often accounted for by the absence of such self-evidently good things as a decent, loving childhood, a stable marriage or family background, regular employment, or cash. The view of crime as a result of being

---

* *Faust Part One*, translated by David Luke.

† 'But how to be morally severe in the late twentieth century?' asks Susan Sontag, in *Illness as Metaphor*. 'How, when there is so much to be severe about; how, when we have a sense of evil but no longer the religious or philosophical language to talk intelligently about evil. Trying to comprehend "radical" or "absolute" evil, we search for adequate metaphors. But the modern disease metaphors are all cheap shots.' She is objecting to the crass and impermissible use of the 'cancer metaphor' in polemics of all kinds, notably political, and adds that those who have the real disease are not helped by hearing its name 'constantly being dropped as the epitome of evil'.

underprivileged has taken a beating of late; in especial, not too many of us are able to perceive exactly what those privileges can be whose lack, whether early in life or later, leads to the rape and murder of children.*

Russell opines that some modern theologians have been motivated by the thought that the subtraction of Devil/Evil from Christianity would 'remove barriers' and 'be ecumenical'. Yet it is barely credible that theologians could soft-pedal Devil/Evil purely as a tactical, popularizing measure: their personal belief in him/it would surely need to have waned already. (Otherwise, one takes it, they would scarcely leave moral damnation to Chief Constables.) To get rid of God will remove barriers, too, and prove even more ecumenical, for it admits convinced atheists into the Church. Why nibble away at such marginal matters as the Immaculate Conception, the Virgin Birth, the loaves and fishes, the Resurrection? As for the Crucifixion, it was all so very long ago, as they say, that by the grace of God it may not be true.

Among the scribes and Pharisees swallowing camels is still accompanied by straining at gnats. The Bishop of London declared that if female ordination was permitted, he would have no choice but to transfer to Rome. The only argument against women as priests is that they are women, whereas Christ appeared in this world in the form of a man. But he had to assume one gender or the other: God would hardly have dispatched us a hermaphrodite. The implication that priests somehow identify themselves with Christ on the grounds of adventitiously shared gender is staggering. For this might be supposed a circumstance in which

> Difference of sex no more we knew,
> Than our guardian angels do.

---

* It appears that some observers regard the 'normal' family—that's to say, not a family in marked financial or other distress—as a primary source of domestic violence ranging from wife-battering to child abuse. I had noticed myself that poorer families often boast (not that they would boast) the best parents. Q. D. Leavis once told me, when I had mumbled a complaint about college dinners, that had I been one of those unfortunates with experience of public schools (as the English call them) behind me, I would have appreciated what I was now being given.

Surely a little effort on the part of theologians, once a nimble enough race, ought to open the way to women. After all, these women positively *want* to be priests.

What is pathetic is the lack of genuine conviction, not among the sheep, whether hungry or lost or otherwise, but among those who make a living as shepherds. A. W. Schlegel sketched out the inevitable sequel to the revisionism touched on by Jeffrey Burton Russell: first the Devil is attacked, then the Holy Spirit, next Christ, and finally God. (No mention here of attacking the male monopoly of ordination.) You will end, in Heine's comparison, with what some people quite like: turtle soup without turtle.

What could more understandably afflict modern theologians are the embarrassments surrounding that ancient crux: how on earth to reconcile evil, man-made or natural, with a merciful, loving God? Over the centuries innumerable explanations have been advanced for the permitted existence of Evil and the Devil, some of them less far-fetched than others. Churchmen ought to hammer away at the problem even so, and even though they are unlikely to come up with anything more cogent than the theory that God elected to limit his omnipotence in order to favour man with free will, freedom to choose virtue or vice. Or of course the argument, misused, distasteful, but irrefutable, that we cannot understand the ways of God and no amount of sublunary enquiry will enable us to. In *Religio Laici* Dryden hints a threat: 'For what could fathom God were *more* than He', but Hardy's Lord, in 'A Dream Question', remains bland or offhand:

> A fourth dimension, say the guides,
> To matter is conceivable.
> Think some such mystery resides
> Within the ethic of my will.

Otherwise, if ecumenism can extend itself so far, we are left with the Manichaean struggle, unending, between the two great and independent antagonistic powers of light and darkness. While obviously curtailing the Almighty's almightiness, in another respect this dualism saves his face; it brings the Father closer to the Son, making that relationship more credible, and it might actually persuade us, through a sense of fellowship, to side with the light.

Many will rate all such speculations as sterile and pigheaded, yet it would be rash to dismiss them as 'irrelevant', and on the theoretical side no patently better justification of the cloth is to be seen. However, in a recent paper in the *Journal of Literature and Theology* Margarita Stocker points out that since the problem of evil arises precisely in the context of belief in a beneficent Creation, God's goodness is a logical pre-condition of the argument, whereas literature caters for those who are not necessarily theists, and 'literary theodicies are therefore (in our time at least) problematically detached from proper theological discourse'. So perhaps it is a subject best left to amateurs after all. And notably to literary people, for 'If evil does not exist, what is going to happen to literature?', a character asks slyly in V.S. Pritchett's comic (and more than comical) novel, *Mr Beluncle*, alluding to a sect which ascribes all set-backs to sensory illusion.

In the meanwhile we are driven back on the sayings of Adrian Leverkühn's polymorphous visitor in *Doctor Faustus*. 'But I hope you do not marvel that "the Great Adversary" speaks to you of religion. Gog's nails! Who else, I should like to know, is to speak of it today? Surely not the liberal theologian! After all I am by now its sole custodian! In whom will you recognize theological existence if not in me?'

Earlier I was thinking of the everyday evil that television news assiduously brings to our attention. But the entertainment side of television has been enriched—oddly, that seems the right word— by the myth-like stories of Dracula and Frankenstein and the questions they raise. Can these, often inane in treatment and incidentals, compete as regards power and persuasiveness with the highbrow dramas we are offered? The answer is: without difficulty.

Dr Frankenstein at least has respectable origins, being the creation of the wife of a famous poet. And the novel carries a reputable Miltonic epigraph on its title-page:

> Did I request thee, Maker, from my clay
> To mould me man, did I solicit thee
> From darkness to promote me?

The story has obvious similarities with that of Faust. 'It was the secrets of heaven and earth that I desired to learn,' says Victor Frankenstein of his younger self. Like Marlowe's Faustus, he has studied Albertus Magnus and Cornelius Agrippa. After years of 'incredible labour and fatigue' he discovers 'the cause of generation and life', and is able to bestow animation on lifeless matter: a new species is at hand, whose 'happy and excellent' members will bless him as their source. Wagner, the erstwhile famulus of Goethe's Faust, contrived to create Homunculus—a sharp, energetic, and endearing little spirit, safely confined within a test-tube—probably after the recipe given by Paracelsus, another author studied by the young Victor. Such homunculi, Paracelsus declared, were wondrous wise in that they had acquired their life through art, and hence art was incorporate and innate in them.

But something went wrong with Frankenstein's art. Wagner's ingredients all seem to have been inorganic ('everything depends on the mixing'), whereas Frankenstein not only collected bones from charnel-houses but also tortured living animals, a means bound to taint the end. The dreary November night on which his creature opens a dull yellow eye is very different from the scene in Wagner's comical medieval laboratory, where the project was to find a mode of reproduction more befitting man's present dignity, the atmosphere further lightened by Mephistopheles' naughty jokes. Homunculus's first words to his creator were 'Well, Daddy, how's things? That was no joke!', followed by an invitation to press him to his breast, but not too ardently because of the glass.

The monster, as we have to call him since Frankenstein omitted to give him a name, is far from brutish. Greeted by his creator, 'Begone, vile insect!', he replies urbanely, 'I expected this reception.' He ought to be Frankenstein's Adam, he observes, but he is 'rather the fallen angel'. He has been reading *Paradise Lost*, in French translation, along with *The Sorrows of Werther*, whose 'lofty sentiments' and account of domestic manners have impressed him, and also Plutarch's *Lives*, among whom, in harmony with Shelleyan principles, he admired 'peaceable lawgivers' rather than famous warriors.

'I was benevolent and good; misery made me a fiend. Make me happy, and I shall again be virtuous.' This is the defence offered by criminals, we note, or more often by their solicitors and caseworkers, though here couched in more resonant terms. Villagers attack him with stones; when he saves a girl from drowning, her companion shoots and wounds him; every man's hand is against him, and in turn he declares everlasting war 'against the species'. A species not his own: he was created by an experimental scientist, not by God, as Adam was, and so is closer to Satan, concerning whose provenance we are less sure. Yet he returns to the comparison with Adam, having derived from Milton the picture of 'an omnipotent God warring with his creatures': Adam, even so, was provided with a companion, whereas the monster has no friends, no relatives, no Eve to soothe his sorrows, and hence—'What was I?'—no identity. Created desolate, by killing Frankenstein's young brother in whom, an innocent and unprejudiced child, he had hoped vainly to find a friend, he proves that he too can create desolation.

And so, he tells Frankenstein, passing from the Byronic mode to the Shelleyan, he must be given a female with whom he can live 'in the interchange of those sympathies necessary for my being'. Reasonably enough, this female should have the same defects: neither miscegenation nor hypergamy is in the monster's mind. What he wants is something approaching normal human life, *mutatis mutandis*. (Homunculus, more overtly allegorical, flings himself into the ocean, where life as we know it began; by due evolutionary process he is to escape from his test-tube existence into something putatively richer.) Again and again the hunger for companionship is expressed; if one sole being would show benevolence towards him, he would make his peace with the whole race: this is a more generous offer than Jehovah's, who finally agreed to spare Sodom could ten righteous citizens be found there.

Given that, as Adam admitted to Raphael,

> For man to tell how human life began
> Is hard; for who himself beginning knew?

the monster's account of the growth of consciousness is discreetly and movingly done. His memories are 'confused and indistinct'; 'a strange multiplicity of sensations seized me, and I saw, felt, heard, and smelt', seemingly all at the same time, without differentiation between the senses. He discovered the moon, with wonder, and birds, and fire, left by wandering beggars; observing the cottagers from hiding, he learned such basic words as 'milk', 'bread', 'wood'. He is a vegetarian, living on acorns and berries. In the Notes on *Queen Mab* the young Shelley held that the allegory of Adam and Eve and how they ate of 'the tree of evil', thus bringing down God's wrath on their posterity, admitted of no other explanation than that disease and crime have come from 'unnatural diet', the eating of *meat*.

God told Adam that it was not good for man to be alone, but Frankenstein rejects the view that a change in family environment will reclaim his creature, asserting that one of the first results of 'those sympathies for which the daemon thirsted'—thirst suggests lust, which is not what we have perceived in the monster—would be offspring, a race of devils bound to endanger the existence of mankind. He is of the opinion that the female of the species, in this instance, might well be more deadly than the male, perhaps ten thousand times more malignant; she could even desert her mate for the 'superior beauty of man'. Mary Shelley has told us of the villagers' cruel treatment of the then innocent and well-intentioned monster, but it is improbable that she was being ironical about the beauty of man; and what she intended by Frankenstein's notion of the greater malevolence and capacity for evil of the female can only be guessed at. And yet her subtitle cannot well be other than ironic: 'The Modern Prometheus'. Much in the novel is plainly in tune with the romantic movement, but essentially it is unromantic, chastened, even-handed in its sympathies, turning the romantic, humanist Greek hero ('Forethought') on his head. This nineteen-year-old girl seems much older, not to say wiser, than her excitable male colleagues and comrades.

Frankenstein destroys the Eve he has been working on, and is appositely warned (despite the words sounding like those of a jilted lover in a different sort of tale): 'Remember, I shall be with you on your wedding-night.' Having murdered Frankenstein's bride, the monster avers, 'Evil thenceforth became my good', almost literally the words of Milton's Satan as he approached Eden and prepared the downfall of man.

Yet the monster's agony is 'superior' to his creator's, in that he feels the bitter sting of remorse. And he makes, one would say, a good end, sailing northwards to build his funeral pyre. 'My spirit will sleep in peace; or if it thinks, it will not surely think thus.' The equipoise of the phraseology, and its restrained pathos, recur in Wilfred Owen's 'Strange Meeting': 'And if it grieves, grieves richlier than here.'

It is a nobler epitaph than mankind is likely to pronounce on itself. We may have thought of Mary Shelley as an enlightened free-thinker and a relatively simple soul, yet in her pleading of the abandoned creature's case against the creator she too is of the Devil's party without knowing it: simultaneously a 'liberal' thinker and a 'devilish' theologian. Milton at least nominally justified God's ways—God gave his creatures freedom of choice, he 'formed them free', whereas Frankenstein's creature hasn't heard of such delights—but Mary Shelley had no intention of doing so. Her husband maintained that the great secret of morals was love, a going out of one's own nature to identify with others—a truth indistinctly but profoundly sensed by the monster—and that 'the great instrument of moral good is the imagination'. Frankenstein is deficient in imagination, an incompetent father; and God is less than adept at putting himself in the place of another. Or he does so only belatedly: 'Account me man,' says Milton's Son of God, as if to warn men that they can always be crucified.

Mary Shelley is a theologian after the Great Adversary's heart, it being conceded that since he has no heart he will esteem her liberal compassion towards man only as it reflects discredit on the other great adversary.

But the story and the suppositions on which it rests, it may be objected, are plain nonsense. And the same will be said, more emphatically and more contemptuously, of vampire tales. The sad thing is not that we don't believe in the factuality of such stories, but that we cannot accept them as fiction, as products of the incited imagination. (If we accept the visitation in Mann, then it is because Leverkühn is insane, prone to hallucinations; or, just possibly, in retrospect, because the author is so persuasive.) Heaven knows, we are prepared to swallow no end of fancy nonsense, and loads of grinding banality, in the name of fiction. What we recognize, and resent, I think, is the presence of myth. Myths are old bullies, still throwing their weight about, what weight they retain, and we would prefer something new, something that is 'ours', never mind if its grip on us lasts no longer than the time it takes for our eyes to pass over the print or the pictures.

Equally old as classical legend and European folklore, in English writing the vampire story began at the same time as *Frankenstein*, and in the same place: in Switzerland, during the wet summer of 1816, when, in competition with Mary Shelley, Byron drafted a tale which his physician, John Polidori, later published as *The Vampyre*.

The idea of the vampire, Clive Leatherdale states in *Dracula: The Novel and the Legend*, is founded on two concepts, 'the belief in life after death, and the magical power of blood'. Other factors could easily be added: the destructive power of sexual desire; parasitism in diverse forms; the fear of sickness, often mysterious in its causes (*Nosferatu*, the title of F. W. Murnau's 1922 cult film, based on Bram Stoker's *Dracula*, indicates 'disease carrier'). By its openness, and because of its abiding fascination, the theme has lent itself to strange applications and accretions, some of them nervously humorous. A Hammer film featured lesbian vampires (nothing new there); Roman Polanski's comedy, *Dance of the Vampires*, included a homosexual male vampire, given to coffin-hopping, and a Jewish one, gleefully immune to the crucifix; *Blacula* was black throughout. Lusty though dead lady lovers glide through old Chinese and Japanese tales, and Malay legend has the *pontianak*, the ghost of a woman who died in childbirth and returns at night to attack men; I have heard talk of them hailing taxis and vanishing without paying the fare. Practically every ethnic group has been accommodated. On film, where his blend of pathos and rage made Boris Karloff the only possible Frankenstein's monster, Bela Lugosi (said to have been buried in his black cloak lined in blood-red) was the best Count Dracula because he combined piggishness with arrogance, while Christopher Lee has excelled in home-grown libidinous gentlemanliness.

So much is obvious in the story and its various versions and reworkings that there is small need to import significances. This hasn't deterred the exegetes. Leatherdale mentions someone's discovery that the name of the hero of Stoker's *Dracula* (1897), Professor Van Helsing, approximates to 'Hell Singer', and points out that Mina (Harker) spelt backwards is very nearly *anima*, soul. Dracula's 'orality' is illustrative of regressive infantilism (as long as we ignore the fact that drinking blood is the quickest way of absorbing it, and vampires cannot be expected to carry transfusion equipment around); and of course the vampire's teeth are phallic symbols, and likewise—the punishment fitting the crime?—the wooden stake that destroys him. How endearing, compared with these crude formulations, is the discourse of the old-fashioned, old fictional characters themselves. When Carmilla, in Sheridan Le Fanu's story of that name (1872), embraces the innocent young lady, Laura, and kisses her ardently: 'You are mine, you *shall* be mine, and you and I are one for ever', the bewildered Laura asks, 'Are we related?', and 'What can you mean by all this?'

Latter-day political interpretations have run the gamut. *Dracula* represents the eventual victory of the middle classes over the blood-sucking aristocracy. The novel is racist in that the villain is made a foreigner, and said to smell bad. Dracula is a capitalist since he accumulates blood. He is a bloodthirsty Nazi (it appears that copies of the book were supplied gratis to American forces fighting overseas in the Second World War). He is a Communist, hailing from behind the Iron Curtain, an expansionist who subverts others to his way of life (or death). A man for all fearful seasons!

Other commentators have gone so far, such is modern niceness, as to insist on the unethical conduct of the 'good' characters in failing to allow Dracula an opportunity to explain his actions, and in openly admitting that they are responsible for the deaths of a number of alleged vampires. But this is the standard perversity of modern exegesis: Claudius is a pretty stout fellow, really, the stuff of which rulers are made, whereas Hamlet is a pain in everybody's neck. Apropos of those ill-done-by and alleged vampires, someone has pointed out that their bodies have dissolved into dust and hence (habeas corpus?) their killers run little risk of prosecution. More interestingly, Clive Leatherdale intimates that, left to themselves, vampires' bodies do not decay—in this resembling the bodies of saints.

The potency of the legend is commensurate with its ability to elicit multifarious interpretations of itself.* The sexual charge of the vampire legend is undeniable, though the ingenious Mr Leatherdale probably exaggerates when he claims that a careful search of Stoker's novel unearths 'seduction, rape, necrophilia, paedophilia, incest, adultery, oral sex, group sex, menstruation, venereal disease, voyeurism'. Enough, as he concludes, to titillate the most avid sexual appetite. Yet there is no evidence, as far as I know, of anyone reading that very Victorian novel specifically for the sake of sexual titillation, albeit *Dracula* has been said, correctly or otherwise, to be the second-best-selling book of all time. The same statistician has the Bible standing at number one in the charts.

Goethe's Mephistopheles admits, quite cheerfully, that

> Devils and spirits have a law, as you may know:
> They must use the same route to come and go.
> We enter as we please; leaving, we have no choice

—to which Faust replies pertly: 'So even hell has laws?' Indeed its agents are of necessity subject to conventions, rules of conduct, circumscriptions, and vulnerabilities. No more than Mephistopheles, no more than Mary Shelley's monster, is the vampire a mere *lusus naturae*. He is preternaturally cunning, and as strong as twenty men, he can transform himself into a wolf or a bat, he can see in the dark, he can change his size, he can vanish altogether. 'He can do all these things, yet he is not free,' Van Helsing, the authority, comforts his unnerved confederates. 'He who is not of nature has yet to obey some of nature's laws.'

Given that everyone who succumbs to a vampire's attentions becomes a vampire in turn, obviously some limitations and restraints have to be built in. To begin with, the vampire's poten-

---

* Praise of another and contradictory nature, negative yet heartfelt, has been accorded films on the subject, which not fairmindedness alone moves me to record. A letter in a recent *Radio Times* quoted Christopher Lee on old Hammer films—they afford 'terror without risk'—and added: 'When you see a Hammer vampire or zombie you know that when the film ends you're safe because such things don't exist, unlike many of today's horror films which feature things that do exist, like madmen armed with dozens of nasty-looking weapons.'

tial victim must evince a degree of complicity, at least to the extent of inviting it (here we can easily avoid gender embarrassment) into the house on the first occasion. It doesn't have to be asked twice. Coleridge's Geraldine and Le Fanu's Carmilla appear as damsels in distress, to whom help and hospitality are naturally extended. Mephistopheles, although taken home in the shape of a frisky poodle, tells Faust that he must leave and then be invited back three times before they get down to serious business. Heathcliff in *Wuthering Heights*—'Is he a ghoul or a vampire?' Nelly Dean asks herself—has been adopted by Mr Earnshaw, a starving orphan picked up in the streets of Liverpool: '. . . a gift of God; though it's as dark almost as if it came from the devil'. This is the obverse of entertaining angels unaware.

Then, according to some versions, in its various enterprises the vampire is obliged to use names that are anagrams of one another: Carmilla, Millarca, Mircalla. Less troubled by this formality, when negotiating a lease in Piccadilly Dracula introduces himself to the house-agents as Count de Ville, thus echoing Jonson, whose Pug, a junior demon, is given in polite London society the prettier name of De-vile, which 'sounds as it came in with the Conqueror'. Unsubtle slapstick of this sort, though it won't do in serious television drama, is common in mankind's central myths.

The vampire's ascendancy ceases with the coming of day, it is devitalized by the 'Sun of righteousness', and must retreat to its coffin, lined with earth from the creature's native place. That a cross made of the thorns of wild roses will detain it in its grave is a Christian touch, as is its fear of the crucifix. And that it is averse to garlic appears to be an old Transylvanian belief; garlic is a preventive against disease, and it might be that one bad smell is thought to drive out another. Some say that it cannot endure fire, others that it can pass over running water only at the slack or the flood of the tide. Another penalty laid on the vampire is that, if it is so forgetful as to pass in front of a mirror, it can be identified by the absence of a reflection: it can have no reflection because it has no soul; its immortality is a soulless one, at best only of the body, which still requires nourishment and sleep.

There are several set ways of dispatching a vampire; the favourite, after the manner of St George impaling the dragon, is to thrust a stake through the heart, ideally a stake made of the wood used for the Cross, and in one blow, as if to prove conviction, or prevent resistance. In the struggle between good (no matter how inept) and evil (however tawdry) there must be a minimum of observed conventions, conventions more binding than the laws pertaining to secular warfare.

Julian Birkett has remarked of *Frankenstein* that 'the novel's passionately religious and metaphysical themes are even more out of favour today than the rhetoric that Mary Shelley employs to deal with them'. Nevertheless, having noted that the novel's concern is with the purpose of creation, he opines that the many popular spin-offs—he cites thirty-five films and some 2,500 plays, musicals, stories, comics, etc.—might paradoxically be said to flourish 'precisely because they touch secretly upon metaphysical anxieties'. The paradox stems from the simple truth that what is out of public favour can always be present in the private mind.

What this phenomenon, this secret perturbation, has to do with *belief*, to what extent believing is involved, is hard to say. The postulation of a half-way house between belief and disbelief is the best we can manage; that famous 'willing suspension of disbelief for the moment' doesn't fill the bill, nor does the 'hoping' (or fearing) 'it might be so' of Hardy's poem, 'The Oxen'. We can agree with William James that what keeps religion going is 'something else than abstract definitions and systems of concatenated adjectives, and something different from faculties of theology and their professors'. And we shall probably find it easier to assent to Octavio Paz's summing-up: 'Although religions belong to history and perish, in all of them a non-religious seed survives: poetic imagination.' Yet the relationship between imagination and belief remains an indecipherable mystery.

Despite lacking an author as well connected as that of *Frankenstein*, the vampire stories too are highly theological. Here the concern is with eternal life, but an eternity passed on earth, a shameful immortality thrust on the vampire's victims. Love will have its sacrifices, and 'No sacrifice without blood,' Carmilla pronounces. 'Whoso drinketh my blood hath eternal life' is the Christian promise. The vampire could say, widdershins, He whose blood I drink dwelleth in me, and I in him. When describing one of Dracula's victims, Lucy Westenra, as she was before and as she is after her release at the hands of her lover, Van Helsing invokes a pair of related opposites: 'the devil's Un-Dead' and 'God's true dead'.

Dracula, we understand, chose to be a vampire; like a suicide—primal vampires were believed to be people who had killed themselves—he took matters into his own hands, he was not infected by others. Those he has bled to death, to untrue death, are to be pitied—especially when they haven't as yet brought further vampires into the world—and delivered, though by the same grisly means, from their miserable travesty of a life after death. The distinction between hunter and prey parallels that between Satan and his victims, in whose exclusion from Eden he found solace for his exclusion from heaven. Stoker may merely have set out to write a hair-raising story, but he ended by doing much more. In his introduction to the World's Classics edition of the novel, A. N. Wilson makes the excellent observation that Stoker's 'classic distinction is not artistic, but mythopoeic':

He reflects the very bewildered sense, still potent in a world which was (even in 1897) preparing to do without religion, that mysteries can only be fought by mysteries, and that the power of evil in human life is too strong to be defeated by repression, violence, or good behaviour. Virtue avails the characters in *Dracula* nothing. It is the old magic—wood, garlic, and a crucifix—which are the only effective weapons against the Count's appalling power.

In part, he adds, posterity will be able to judge us by our continuing interest in the book.

Bram Stoker shows little pity for his Dracula, and endows him with little that could arouse compassion in us. And yet, as Jonathan Harker administers the *coup de grâce*, Mina sees on the vampire's face 'a look of peace, such as I never could have imagined might have rested there'. Slightly more of Satan's equivocal dignity, and of the fleeting compunctions inspired by the sight of Eve, whose innocence

> overawed
> His malice, and with rapine sweet bereaved
> His fierceness of the fierce intent it brought,

111

is briefly visible in *Varney the Vampyre*, published in 1847, fifty years before Stoker's novel, and attributed variously to James Malcolm Rymer and Thomas Peckett Prest, both of them diligent churners-out of penny dreadfuls. Sir Francis Varney explains that he is subject to laws, like any other being. He did not choose to be what he is; he must endure a fate laid on him as a punishment for accidentally killing his young son in a fit of anger.

Flora Bannerworth, you are persecuted—persecuted by me, the vampyre. It is my fate to persecute you; for there are laws to the invisible as well as the visible creation that force even such a being as I am to play my part in the great drama of existence. I am a vampyre; the sustenance that supports this frame must be drawn from the life-blood of others.

He brings to mind Frankenstein's monster when he declares: 'Even at the moment when the reviving fluid from the gushing fountain of your veins was warming at my heart, I pitied and I loved you. Oh, Flora! even I can now feel the pang of being what I am!' And similarly when he tells her that it is a condition of his 'hateful race' that 'if we can find one human heart to love us, we are free'. Flora can give him pity, but love is out of the question. 'I am answered,' he says, for once laconically. 'It was a bad proposal. I am a vampyre still.'

While this turgid, rambling and interminable novel (876 double-columned pages) doesn't have much to recommend it, Varney comes out well in comparison with most modern fictional villains and their declarations, indeed with many modern heroes. 'Even I can now feel the pang of being what I am!' If a participant in a talk show or an 'intimate' interview so far departed from the contemporary brand of rhetoric as to voice a half-way noble sentiment, the cameras would crack from side to side.

Reverting to Jeffrey Burton Russell's question, we ask ourselves whether a belief in evil might not reduce the amount of what looks like evil active in the world, for at least it would endow our behaviour with some sense of seriousness. The 'dedemonization' of life has clearly failed to do what it professes. But we see only the outward face of things, the official side, and the media, like governmental departments, are predominantly secular. We really don't know very much about private states of mind, despite the current outpourings and public baring of tailored breasts. We have become a society of actors, yet the majority of us, I think, would still rather play the clown, or keep our mouths shut, than pretend to some petty, partial Hamlet, stripping off selected veils.

A thought from George Steiner's book, *In Bluebeard's Castle*, provides a felicitous if grim conclusion.

Much has been said of man's bewilderment and solitude after the disappearance of Heaven from active belief. . . . But it may be that the loss of Hell is the more severe dislocation . . . . The absence of the familiar damned opened a vortex which the modern totalitarian state filled. To have neither Heaven nor Hell is to be intolerably deprived and alone in a world gone flat. Of the two, Hell proved the easier to re-create.

There *may* be heaven, one of Browning's characters conjectured, but there *must* be hell. And in that case, we had better re-create it, such snatches of it as we decently can, in our arts and even our entertainments. Vulgarities and absurdities, frequently found in the most elevated company, are a small price to pay for a release from triviality.

The Third Place

At first sight it seems odd of Chateaubriand to think Purgatory a richer theme for poetry than Heaven or Hell, yet the reasons he gives carry some weight. The place of purification offers gradations of suffering, a confusion of happiness and misery, and above all it supposes a future, its inhabitants are going to move on. Thus it escapes Yeats's objection that passive suffering is not a theme for poetry, which might be thought to rule out much richness in Hell.

As a *tertium quid*, Purgatory has always posed a particular problem: while the majority of those sent there would be expected to advance to Heaven in due course, it couldn't well be represented as a health farm or after-dinner sleep, and hence its landscape has partaken more of Hell. Belief in it, Jacques Le Goff says in *The Birth of Purgatory*, 'requires the projection into the afterlife of a highly sophisticated legal and penal system'. Purgatorial fire really hurts, its pain exceeds anything known on earth; Lear's 'wheel of fire' has been attributed to both Purgatory and Hell. And in Eliot's 'Little Gidding', the 'familiar compound ghost' might be thought a native of Hell (like Brunetto Latini), but for his closing reference to 'that refining fire/Where you must move in measure, like a dancer'.

The question of who invented—or discovered—Purgatory is a vexed one, and Le Goff proposes a number of possible 'fathers'. The original begetter, one might reckon, was the notion or instinct of natural justice: not all sins are equal, and in gravity the punishment should fit the crime. Or possibly the conception of God as, after all, a merciful being.

Le Goff dates the establishment or coming of age of Purgatory between 1150 and 1200. A mass of ideas and urges and images went towards its piecemeal building-up. Among them, despite its function in Hell, the redeeming, refining quality of fire, and the legend of the phoenix; the coupling of water and fire, two modes of baptism; the ancient imagery of the bridge, as in the 'Lyke-Wake Dirge', where Brig o' Dread leads to Purgatory fire; contributions from Indo-European folklore; volcanoes ('men roamed

Sicily between Stromboli and Etna hoping to compile a map of Purgatory'); the feeling in Plato that lesser sins warranted lesser chastisements, and in the *Epic of Gilgamesh* that men of rank deserved choicer accommodation in the underworld; the various categories of sinners awaiting diverse punishments in apocryphal texts, and the Jewish concept of Gehenna as shared between permanent and temporary residents; and the distinction drawn by the third-century Alexandrian theologians, Clement and Origen, between educative and retributive punishment, and elaborated by Augustine, who was zealous not to underestimate the pains of Purgatory.

Moreover, the Church would find Purgatory a powerful instrument in strengthening the links between the living and the dead, and a source of profit as well. There was little point in praying for the souls of those in Hell, or for those in Heaven, but a strong incentive existed to pray for those believed to sojourn in what, since it wasn't mentioned in the Bible, Luther termed 'the third place'. Also it constituted a base from which spirits of the dead could reasonably visit the living with their complaints or warnings: Hamlet's father, for instance, though in a Protestant country his credentials had to be left uncertain. By making the salvation of usurers possible, Le Goff ventures, Purgatory contributed to the birth of capitalism. Influences could conceivably have operated in the reverse direction, the growth of a middle class prefiguring a middle state in the afterlife proper for people of middling spiritual capital.

A thirteenth-century anecdote is especially pleasing. Seduced by a priest, a nun died in childbirth, her sin so hopelessly grave that no one bothered to pray for her. The soul approached an abbot and asked timidly for a few masses, whereupon all joined in the task of intercession, relatives and clergy alike. That her name was Mary may not have been totally immaterial. Le Goff, who cites what seems practically every single medieval reference capable of being read as evidence, is undeterred by another exemplum, concerning a Portuguese friar who was educatively castigated for taking an undue interest in manuscripts.

Purgatory began as a shabby-genteel suburb of Hell, sharing what looked like the same fire, but shifted gradually towards Heaven; and its duration in time for the individual soul has varied from between death and the Last Judgement to a handful of years or days, albeit measured by standards different from ours. It found its apotheosis in Dante's *Purgatorio*: that second kingdom, between two others, that third place, 'where the human soul purifies itself and grows worthy to ascend to Heaven'. Some precise locations have been mooted: a hot and cold Roman bath (Gregory the Great), and a tall mountain (Bede and Dante), and—since Sicily, specifically Mount Etna, suffered from a long association with Hell—a favourite spot has been the cavern described in *Saint Patrick's Purgatory*, written in Latin in the late twelfth century by a monk known only as 'H'. Christ revealed the cave, or exemplary dark hole in the ground, to Patrick when the latter was labouring to convert the natives. This purgatory in miniature is on Station Island in Lough Derg, Co. Donegal; it was blocked up by order of Pope Alexander VI in 1497, but a church dedicated to St Patrick was built there in 1931 and the site is a popular place of pilgrimage.

Dante had a care for limbo too, the double-purpose 'edge' of Hell assigned to pre-Christian good men—the beginnings of ecumenism—and unbaptized babies. This we might expect to lie even closer to Heaven, a broadening of Abraham's bosom, in that theirs were not even venial sins but accidents of circumstance; however, doctrine must be obeyed or else heresy incurred. By the end of the thirteenth century, Le Goff claims, Purgatory was ubiquitous, figuratively speaking. *Vox populi* had done much in fostering the vogue.

Raising his head from the manuscripts, Le Goff asks himself nervously whether, in drawing near to Heaven, Purgatory didn't shrink into a mere antechamber; and, worse, whether in the Church's eyes the point of Purgatory wasn't chiefly to make the inextinguishable flames of Hell appear all the more dreadful. Yet there ought to be room in our dreams for subtlety, justice, measure, reason, and mercy. It is curious that Purgatory holds no appeal for our English bishops, with their taste for the middle way; but then, they have their hands full, subtraction is the order of the day, not addition. Still, some of us will end, as Le Goff's book does, with the hope that 'it will be a long while before it can truly be said of Purgatory that its time is past'.

Hell's Angels

The authorized version has it that Lucifer fell through pride, having set himself up as the equal of the Almighty, and thereafter sought revenge by seducing God's newly created favourites, mankind. In *The Wandering Jew*, Stefan Heym has come up with an alternative reading, according to which Lucifer and his associates, among them the archangel Ahasuerus or Ahasverus, whose name means Beloved by God, were expelled because they refused to bow down before man, that curiously arbitrary invention. Lucifer declined on the not unreasonable grounds of superior birth (created on the first day, not the sixth) and superior qualities, and Ahasverus out of pity for man. For both of them saw how man would turn out. 'It was such a great hope,' sighs Ahasverus as they fall, seemingly without the hideous ruin and combustion reported by Milton, towards the depths. 'Such a beautiful world! And such a beautiful man!'

What is made of dust, Lucifer points out, must return to dust; and so they bide their time, Ahasverus fretted by his 'Jewish impatience'. A 'little angel', Lucifer calls him, 'a regular saviour of mankind', unrest personified, driven by the desire to change things. Whereas he, Lucifer, insists—as would any expert in dialectical thinking—that every thesis carries within itself its antithesis, and one simply has to wait for things to change in their own time, 'their own, God-given time', as he expresses it.

In time, and in accordance with the medieval legend, Jesus, bearing the cross, pauses wearily outside the house of the cobbler Ahasverus. Heym's Ahasverus, eager to redeem the world through action, tells Jesus that he possesses a sword of God, whereby the guards can be put to flight and Christ lead the people of Israel to victory, 'as is written in the book'. But Christ will not listen: his kingdom is not of this world, and the meek shall inherit the earth. In anger and despair, Ahasverus, although he loves Reb Joshua, as he calls him, drives Christ from his doorstep: 'Get going, you idiot!' Christ then speaks the words which initiate the legend of the Wandering Jew: 'You shall remain here and tarry till I come.'

In Heym's brilliant theological fantasy, at once profound and farcical, spiritual and fleshly, we meet Ahasverus in different guises, at various times and in various places, including the Warsaw ghetto, where he suffers death without dying. For the greater part the narrative shifts back and forth between the sixteenth century and the present. As is generally the case, the devil has the best tunes, and the liveliest passages concern a mysterious, scruffy, but powerful club-footed hunchback named Leuchtentrager, which translates into Latin as 'Lucifer'. He takes under his wing a dim but zealously self-seeking young cleric, Eitzen, whose career, by virtue of his knowledge of the future, he promotes with outstanding success. Eitzen can never tell whether his friend is being serious or not when he advances unorthodox opinions. Thus,

But I have a liking for the snake. The snake saw that God had equipped man with two hands to work and a head to think with, and to what good purpose might man have used those in paradise? In the end they might have withered like any thing not being used, and what, my dear *Studiosus*, would under these circumstances have become of the likeness of God?

But Eitzen knows which side his bread is buttered. By means of magic, Leuchtentrager sees to it that he passes the examination in divinity. Having managed a question about *angeli boni*, he finds himself (or is it someone else?) discoursing eloquently on *angeli mali*:

And behold, the power of the bad angels is greater than any which humans possess, for it derives from divine force, and is but a whit less than the power of God. And their lord is the angel Lucifer . . . and another of them is Ahasverus who wants to change the world as he believes it can be changed, and man along with it. And no one knows how many of them there might be and what shape they will take.

The gentlemen from the city council like the sound of this, in so far as they understand it: it lets them off the hook. The chief examiner, Doctor Luther, is uneasy but impressed. This young fellow, he thinks, is worth watching.

We are on familiar (and fertile) German ground. Eitzen rises to fame and fortune as Luther's leading apostle and Superintendent of the Duchy of Sleswick. In the latter capacity he has the Jew

Ahasverus seemingly whipped to death. In due course, in return for services rendered him, his miserable little soul is forfeit to Leuchtentrager, and he is discovered with his head twisted backwards, his tongue hanging out of his mouth, and his eyes staring in horror. In one of the early Faustbooks, Faust's head is twisted back to front. Moreover, Heym has introduced a female demon to stir but not assuage Eitzen's lust: Margriet is ostensibly Leuchtentrager's housemaid, and she much prefers a young Jew, calling himself Ahab, whose hands wander all over her body. Rude knockabout comedy emits theological overtones: souls are made fun of, but souls are in peril.

Finally Margriet turns into a scarecrow made of a bundle of straw and a feather duster, A similar demon appears in the Faustbooks and, in Marlowe's play, as a devil dressed like a woman, bearing fireworks about her: that is, 'a hot whore'. Margriet is no sort of Gretchen, but another source of inspiration (not that Heym stands in much need of it) may have been Goethe's 'Prologue in Heaven', where Mephistopheles jokingly bemoans the sorry condition of mankind and swears to reduce Faust to eating dust 'like my cousin, the well-known snake'.

As if this were not riches enough, Heym interlards the story with letters from an ongoing correspondence, dated 1979/80, between a Professor Siegfried Beifuss of the Institute for Scientific Atheism in East Berlin and a Professor Jochanaan Leuchtentrager of the Hebrew University in Jerusalem, both of them in their different styles specialists in the legend of the Wandering Jew. The Israeli professor is actually acquainted with a Mr Ahasverus, and sends Beifuss a snapshot of him outside his shoe shop on the Via Dolorosa: 'the person portrayed indubitably is a man of character, intelligent, and—if you will look at his mouth and eyes—with a good sense of humour.' 'On principle,' the German professor replies, 'I should like to state that we in the German Democratic Republic do not believe in any kind of miracles, just as we do not believe in spirits, ghosts, angels, or devils.' To accept the longevity of Mr Ahasverus would be tantamount to believing in Christ knows what. In a fit of donnish jocularity, Beifuss permits himself a smile at the idea of almost two thousand years of business carried on by the same proprietor at the same address. 'What capitalist enterprise could claim for itself a record even approximating this one!'

The correspondence preserves the civility of tone ('dear Colleague') we would expect from scholars of integrity and international standing, but the watch-dog at the GDR's Ministry of Higher Education advises Beifuss to concentrate on 'the close interaction of religion and imperialist expansionism, particularly in relation to Israel', and later warns him (an instance of Heym's unobtrusive, effective interlocking) that he had better steer clear of the Lutheran connection in view of the approaching Luther anniversary of 1983, sponsored by the highest representatives of the State and the Party. Beifuss confides to his Israeli confrère that his Institute has promised a paper, to mark May Day, on an allied topic, 'the reactionary character of the myth of the transmigration of the soul'. The soul itself is a myth, of course, unlike the psyche, which is a function of the nervous system and something we are intimately acquainted with through the labours of psychologists, psychiatrists, psychoanalysts, and psychotherapists.

The Israeli academic informs his opposite number in Berlin that Mr Ahasverus has recently encountered Reb Joshua, the alleged messiah, dragging himself along the Via Dolorosa—whereupon he invited the man into his house for a drink of water and to have the wounds on his head cleaned. Professor Beifuss will appreciate his correspondent's happiness at having 'just such a Marxist sceptic as yourself as the first person to be informed by me of so astonishing and cataclysmic an occurrence as the second coming of Christ', even though for the moment only one source vouches for it. Professor Leuchtentrager promises that Mr Ahasverus and he will shortly be visiting East Berlin for a fruitful exchange of views, and Beifuss intimates tactfully that while Leuchtentrager, to all appearances a champion of law and order, might conceivably be allowed in, there is no chance of his friend qualifying for an entry permit. Somehow the fellow makes him think of Trotsky.

Despite which—I am running impatiently ahead—the two of them, later identified as Israeli secret agents specializing in 'ideological penetration', show up on New Year's Eve and make off with Beifuss through a hole inexplicably blown in the wall of his eighth-floor apartment. Two policemen, subsequently disciplined for drinking while on duty, claim to have seen three shapes in the sky, two of them with fiery tails (jet-engine exhausts?) and the third, in the middle, hauled along by the other two. So that was the fruitful exchange of views.

The highest fantasy always has its roots in reality, like some dreams, or some nightmares, but to modulate from fantasy into reality is always a dodgy proposition. Ha, we think, now we are being got at! We think this when we hear of Mr Ahasverus's conversation with Rabbi Joshua in 1980 and the Rabbi's account of Armageddon in terms of nuclear submarines and intercontinental missiles, the 'entire hellish force' in the hands of a few men of limited intelligence:

In his lust for power, paired with fear of his own kind, man had made a grab for the forces of the universe, but without being able to control or regulate these; thus Adam himself, once made in the image of God, had turned into the beast with the seven heads and the ten horns, the all-destroyer, the antichrist.

There needs no ghost, holy or otherwise, come from the tomb to tell us this. Still, it is not something that considerations of literary refinement should forbid us to retell.

And Heym is as artful as the subjects he has set himself are tricky. He ends his book with a touching coda, though for us mere mortals an ambiguously consoling one. Armageddon is fought, and the old earth destroyed. Following Ahasverus's earlier advice to take to the sword, the Rabbi ousts his fainéant father, old and feeble, and announces the imminent creation of a new heaven and a new earth where love and justice rule and the wolf shall lie down with the lamb. As he raises his sword against his father, the old man grows to giant size, reminding the Rabbi that 'your image is also my image because you cannot be seen separate from me, as no man can'. To the echoing laughter of the angel Lucifer, the great champion of law and order, and in a reprise of the fall with which the book began, Ahasverus and the Rabbi merge lovingly into one and then, becoming one with God, into 'one image, one great thought, one dream'.

Beer and onions, bums and breasts, slapstick and horror, metaphysics and damnation . . . This is the composite matter in which the German literary genius is most at home and at its best. Stefan Heym has surpassed himself here, sustaining his imagination and maintaining our engagement in it; and by force of wit holding in check what might be thought—or is it that we are jealous of the love that exists between angels?—a drift towards sentimentality. Heym spent some twenty years in America and writes English with panache and apparent ease; he has a weakness for the progressive form—'I am still seeing the Rabbi's face growing pale'—though such minor eccentricities may be deemed appropriate to the story's time or timelessness.

A character in his previous novel, *Collin*, a writer, gave as his reason for staying in East Germany the opportunities provided for observing so much that was contradictory. And Heym has said *in propria persona* that East Berlin is a fascinating place for a writer to live in because there are so many contradictions. It is perhaps by no contradiction that *The Wandering Jew* is unpublishable in its author's country. Its meaning, or part at least of the fable's meaning, as manifest in Ahasverus's conviction that man is free to make changes and redemption requires revolution, might hold some historic charm for the authorities. But, even if the story's Manichaean implications were glossed over, Heym's metaphors could only appal them. He has arrived at what might just be considered sound doctrine by a distinctly unscientific route. And, what is worse, while his writing is full of vigorous *disputatio*, its deployment of dialectics smacks of the disapproved device, sterile and formalistic, known as parody. It may occur to us that the Devil cited a modern scripture when, in tempting the composer Leverkühn, he dismissed parody as a melancholy form of aristocratic nihilism generating little profit. If you want to be enraptured, impassioned, ravished, then the Devil's your man.

A Doomsday Book

In a brief address delivered in Rome in late 1982, a sombre thank-you for receiving a prize, Günter Grass spoke of the superior staying-power of literature. However mighty the forces ranged against it and its makers, 'sure of its after-effect, it could count on time', even though this took time. Now, however, 'the book, formerly made to last for ever, is beginning to resemble a non-returnable bottle': we can no longer be sure we have a future. Grass closed by saying that the book he was nevertheless planning to write—writers persist in writing—would have to contain 'a fare-well to the damaged world', to all its creatures, including us humans, who in our time have thought of everything, including the end.

The Rat, the book Grass was referring to, is a hectic meditation, darting and diverging in characteristic fashion, a gathering of old obsessions and newer pains, and a recall or roll-call of characters from his earlier works, a roll of honour and of dishonour, an elaborate Last Post for what he has created, and what he loves, for himself, and for all of us. Yet another apocalypse, another busy Last Days of Mankind.

It is Christmas, candles burning low, a festive dinner, the cracking of nuts, happy children. . . In a homely beginning, the narrator finds under the Christmas tree the present he had surprisingly asked for: a rat, a She-rat. Pretty smartly, the She-rat is talking to him, seemingly in his dreams, arguing with him, and getting the better of the argument. When two by two the other animals entered the ark—she tells him—her people were turned away by Noah, in defiance of divine instructions. They were taken into God's hand, where they quickly procreated; and, finding hiding-places for themselves, stopped-up passages under the drowned earth, they were firmly established by the time the waters sank and the ark discharged its coddled cargo. As they survived that great flood, so they will survive the great fire next time. Indeed—for time is elastic here, running freely backwards and forwards—that is what they have done. For this, the She-rat insists, is the post-human era.

The rats have, or used to have, considerable admiration for mankind, 'so lovable, so spontaneous, by definition prone to error'. What most of all distinguished man was that he walked erect, albeit he walked in strange paths; and the She-rat divulges her wish that rats could blush, as man did, though usually for absurd reasons. (This is Grassian whimsy: rats have nothing much to blush for.) How deeply the rats regret that man has finished himself off: for one thing, rats need human beings to tell stories (writers have a purpose!), many of the stories, like the affair of the Pied Piper, featuring rats. The She-rat oozes compassion; her people did their utmost to alert man to the peril he was in, by staging demonstrations in human fashion, scurrying in hordes through city streets, round and round Red Square, the White House, the Champs-Élysées, Trafalgar Square. But all in vain: men were united only in putting an end to themselves.

There was no Noah's ark this time, but one man is left alive, orbiting in an observation satellite. And he, perforce, is the narrator: 'you, full of stories and curly-headed lies, you, our friend, faithfully preserving the image of man for us.' And so the stories tumble desperately out, a little of this one and then a little of that one, as tenuously connected as events and circumstances in a hastily compiled obituary.

Nothing has been heard of Oskar Matzerath since he reached his thirtieth year, since *The Tin Drum*, but now he returns, on the brink of sixty, still small and humpbacked, suffering from prostate trouble, 'a common taxpayer', a prosperous business man with a large office, a villa, and a Mercedes. From making porn videos he has moved on to educational cassettes; he looks forward to the day when, thanks to the media, we shall be able to create reality in advance of its arrival. Covert allusions are made to Oskar's past, for instance his 'glass-oriented exploits'. And his grandmother, Anna Koljaiczek, she of the long and commodious skirts, is still alive. Invited to her 107th birthday party, he is driven by his chauffeur—Bruno, erstwhile his keeper in a mental hospital—to Gdańsk and on to Kashubia, and a family reunion, or a family farewell.

Then there is a largely pointless account of five females, to all of whom the narrator is attached by long threads and short, who are investigating jellyfish infestation in the western Baltic from the *New Ilsebill*, a ship named after the greedy wife of the fisherman who caught a talking flounder. The fish-hero of Grass's novel *The Flounder* rejected the Grimm version of events as misogynistic distortion, and rehabilitated Ilsebill. He surfaces again, but— understandably disinclined to compete with the garrulous rodent —only to inform the women that the end is nigh.

The story of Lothar Malskat, the honest forger of 'Gothic' paintings, is a parable about the currency reform of 1948 (the substitution of the Deutsche Mark for the old Reichsmark, devalued on exchange), prosperity founded on falsification, and the creation of two 'phony' German states, each associated with one of the victorious camps, the Western or the Eastern. Where her kind were concerned, the She-rat notes, 'Germany was never split in two, it was one good feed.' Malskat is sent to prison, whereas, in that 'era of winking, of appearances, of white-washing', Ulbricht and Adenauer, perpetrators of a double forgery, get off scot-free. So angry is Grass about this, a subject touched on lightly in *Headbirths* and *The Meeting at Telgte*, that he begins to bully the reader and to forfeit credibility. What's a bit of forgery compared with a holocaust?

The dislocated and tangled narratives make for arduous reading, more so than in Grass's greener days; and as soon as the narrator finishes an instalment of one of his ongoing stories, or simply stops to draw breath, the She-rat resumes her nagging, armed at times with chalk, blackboard, and pointer. 'You should have learned from your mistakes. You should have this, you should have that.' Mercifully, she seems not to have heard of AIDS. Taking refuge in his tales, or bolstering himself through self-cannibalization, the narrator continues to disbelieve her— 'It's all a pack of lies. There hasn't been any Big Bang'—and to claim that mankind can still save itself. He is under the impression that he is sitting at home in an armchair or perhaps strapped in a wheelchair.

The She-rat advances alternative accounts of how the Big Bang, technically the second one, came about. First: rat-droppings in the central computers of both the Protector Powers, the Western and the Eastern, triggered off the first strikes: a face-saving theory had it that this was contrived by a Third

Power, conceivably the Jews. Second: each side trained laboratory mice to paralyse the other's command computer, but instead the mice started the countdown. Third: it was the rats, after all, who entered the computers through the sewage system and substituted their own countdown programme, later set off by the code word 'Noah'. Fourth: the technically benighted narrator, up there in his space capsule, initiated proceedings by inadvertently feeding footage from end-of-the-world science fiction movies into the Western and Eastern terminals. We can take our pick, though we may find ourselves tempted by a fifth interpretation and attribute the whole business to over-indulgence at Christmas.

As is commonly the case with Grass, there is plenty of what one takes to be bona fide documentation, even though it is the She-rat who states that during 'the last year of human history' breeders in Wilmington, Delaware, produced eighteen million laboratory rats for the domestic and foreign markets, netting a profit of thirty million dollars. And the public issues are present, in profusion: Germany's post-war amnesia, garbage disposal, pensions, the butter mountain, immigration problems, Solidarity, food shortages in Poland, lead in gasoline, expense accounts, unemployment, over-population and undernourishment, pollution and deforestation.

This last distress generates the liveliest and most original of the four main narrative strands. Gathered in the Gingerbread House, characters from fairy-tales are worrying over acid rain and dying trees: Little Red Ridinghood and her Grandmother, the Witch, Snow White, the Frog Prince, the Wicked Stepmother, Rapunzel, Briar Rose (who is forever having to be kissed awake by her young prince, described as 'a kind of male nurse') . . . They are joined by Hansel and Gretel, who make their first appearance as the runaway children of the German chancellor and then merge with the figures of Störtebeker and Tulla Pokriefke, once the wartime *enfants terribles* of *The Tin Drum*, *Cat and Mouse*, and *Dog Years*, and now 'the unripe fruits of lasting peace'.

Hansel and Gretel have made their way through the dead forest with its garbage dumps, toxic-waste disposal sites, and off-limits military installations: no fit place for babes to be abandoned in. A delegation is sent to Bonn, in an old Ford, to meet Jacob and Wilhelm Grimm, respectively minister and under-secretary for forests, rivers, lakes, and fresh air. In a typical flash of sly humour, Rumpelstiltskin, chairman of the 'Save the Fairy-Tales' committee, is careful to sign with three crosses, until Briar Rose reminds him that the gentlemen already know his name. The old Grandmother is presented with Volume I of the Grimms' *Deutsches Wörterbuch* of 1852, a monumental dictionary of beautiful words that are soon to be heard or seen no more. All of this will furnish Herr Matzerath with an excellent educational film, and perhaps, since morals among the dramatis personae are at a low ebb, a mildly naughty one, too.

Among much else we are treated to several fresh explications of the Hamelin legend. It can be read as (*a*) a political fable about people who follow their leaders like sheep; (*b*) a prefigurement of how the Jews were 'piped out of town and exterminated like rats'; and (*c*) a heavily euphemized chronicle pertaining to young Gothic punks (as we should label them nowadays) who carried pet rats around on their shoulders or inside their shirts, offended the aldermen sorely, and were enticed into a mountain cave and walled up there. As the narrator reflects, it is always easy to derive a moral from legends. Especially easy if you are Günter Grass, who was never one for passing up an opportunity to fantasize, to improvise and extrapolate in all directions, to turn traditions upside-down, to switch from one scenario to another.

The She-rat tells of quaint life-forms emerging after the Big Bang, flying snails (hardly the kind who keep a diary) and viviparous bluebottles; later she asserts that she made them up just to amuse her human protégé; still later she resuscitates them as authentic phenomena. Either way they have little significance, literally or allegorically. And to complicate matters further, blond, blue-eyed rat-people arrive in Gdańsk, aboard the *New Ilsebill*, with little curly tails yet walking erect. They are 'programmed to start from zero and burdened with no guilt', like our first parents. The female of the species is dominant; the offspring are obedient; they reproduce with gusto and they eat likewise; there is 'something gratifyingly Scandinavian about their behaviour, as if a certain Social Democratic quality were embedded in their genes'. These 'Watsoncricks' shall inherit the earth, or so we might think, but—in what resembles a replay of human history—they are wiped out by plague and hunger, and by the rats 'entrusted' to their care. The hominoids were a little too human.

Blind alleys and red herrings abound; nothing is allowed to stay put; subversion is itself subverted; nothing can be taken as certain. One of the poems scattered through the book raises the question,

> Could it be that both of us,
> the She-rat and I,
> are being dreamed, that we are the dreams
> of a third species?

Of God? The Almighty, less almighty than he claimed to be, according to the She-rat, seems to have given up the ghost after the affair of the flood. Grass's inventiveness, like his ability to squeeze the last drop out of whatever turns up, remains unsurpassed, but it can also strike us as an inability to leave well alone, to know when to stop. We gasp with astonishment and admiration, we groan with dismay, and on occasion, I fear, we yawn out of boredom. If we are to be frightened in time—'in the end,' the She-rat declares, 'humans were too cowardly to be afraid'—this isn't the ideal way to go about it.

Inconsequence, we are aware, is a distinguishing mark of genuine folklore. And no one wants to be seen complaining of complexity in a literary work. And, yes, order and organization may be deemed trifling virtues when compared with a crowded and multifarious canvas. Yet if a book have not clarity, what does it profit us? Grass's teeming eschatological phantasmagoria, if it does not wholly appal, clouds the poor, overburdened mind. These warnings—if indeed they are warnings and not obsequies—tend to create confusion, cripple rational thought, and foster despondency. Like other prophets of calamity, Grass contributes his little shove downhill. If that's the game, the game is up; great fun for the author, and—let's admit—for the reader as well, so long as the reader doesn't take it too seriously. And, after all, I suppose by now we have learned not to take books too seriously.

Yet most of the time our leaders, whose duty it is to be serious, seem less reluctant than the rest of us to contemplate the Big Bang, the End, or at any rate those 'losses' which no doubt computers have already determined as being 'acceptable'. When Grass's narrator begs to be allowed to assume that, in spite of everything, some humans have survived, or will survive, and asks, 'this time let us live for one another and peacefully, do you hear, gently and lovingly, as nature made us', the She-rat replies, in the last words of the book: 'A beautiful dream'. If we are to be buried before we are dead, and while we can still in some degree enjoy the ceremony, then Grass is the man to undertake the job with acumen and gusto, wild and gritty humour, a mercifully numbing bitterness, traces of pathos, and more than a touch of ireful regret.

Master of Horror

Apart from a vague impression that some people think Karl Kraus a guardian of language and morals of super-Confucian proportions while others consider him an intemperate destroyer of reputations by means as foul as fair, all that most of us anglophones know about the Viennese satirist (1874–1936) is that his writings are unamenable to translation. Erich Heller, whose essay on him in *In the Age of Prose* is a capital introduction, has declared that Kraus's peculiar way with the German language simply isn't reproducible outside that language, while Harry Zohn, although the editor of the Kraus reader *In These Great Times*, concludes by modestly exhorting us to learn German. The translator's task is certainly more than commonly hazardous in the case of an author who maintained that after his death he would worry more about a misplaced comma than about the actual dissemination of his works. For much of the time Kraus was dealing in the German language, idiosyncratically, with usages and perversions of the German language. In translating, we are told, what gets lost is the poetry. But in not translating even more can get lost. And it is true that, for much of the time, Kraus's concerns, like those of any satirist or polemicist worth his salt, are universal and timeless in their nature.

Kraus's conception of the direct relation between language and behaviour is unique only in its unyielding intensity, its thrusting to extremes. 'Psychopathologists now concern themselves with poets who arrive for their check-up after they are dead. It serves the poets right. They should have raised mankind to a level where there could have been no psychopathologists.' Nothing is seen as fortuitous or free from consequences, not even a printing error. He was remote from those of our contemporaries who regard words as workaday signs of no greater inner consequence than the painted arrow directing us to an exit. For Kraus, corruption of language entailed corruption of thought, and hence of action, public and private. His habit of establishing guilt by induction and association has naturally drawn obloquy—'When a man makes personal polemics into a way of life,' Idris Parry has commented, 'he runs a serious risk of error'—but there is a curious logic to it. You can tell a man by the words he uses, so you can tell the words by the man (assuming you know him) who uses them—and there's an end to it.

Getting style and tone right or wrong doesn't much affect Kraus's reflections on contraceptive advertisements in the daily press: the only decent, sensible, and tasteful contributions consistently found there, their propriety marred solely by the highly moral front pages disavowing gratis what is presented, against payment, on the back pages—and by the accompanying picture of an officer 'who, in order to make things more palatable, strokes his moustache'. On a similar theme, 'The World of Posters' starts with the straight-faced proposition that art and intellect have been removed, much to their advantage, to the realm of advertising, and cultural ideals now manifest themselves in the wrappings of a patent clothes-hanger.

The piece grows increasingly phantasmagoric. 'Is there life beyond the posters?' We lie there helplessly and suffer the torments of Macbeth—'What, will the line stretch out to the crack of doom? Another yet?'—as they pass before us: the Button King, the Soap King, the Carpet King, the Cognac King, the Rubber King (whose eyes 'remind us of our sins, but his features bespeak the untearability of human trust'). William Tell enters as the trade mark of a chocolate firm; a snatch of song approximating to a line of Heine's as set by Schumann—*ich liebe alleine / Die Kleine, die Feine, die Reine, die Eine*—heralds a brand of lozenge . . . We might recall the more explicit judgement of Robert Musil, Kraus's fellow Austrian and contemporary: 'What this age demonstrates when it talks of the genius of a racehorse or a tennis-player is probably less its conception of genius than its mistrust of the whole higher sphere.' Nothing of this is outdated; rather the opposite, in view of the more sophisticated television commercials of our day.

Translation doesn't fatally harm the elaborate and more bitter comedy of 'The Discovery of the North Pole'. This was the great American event of 1909 (the glory shared by Germany since the discoverer was Frederick A. Cook, formerly Koch), all the greater in that it compensated for the miscegenetic scandals arising in New York's Chinatown that same year (the shame also shared by Germany since a murdered white woman bore the name Elsie Siegl). The great dream of Christian civilization was to conquer the Pole, virgin nature. But when the dreamer realizes his dream he behaves like a suitor to whose advances a virgin has at last surrendered. 'I was disappointed,' said Mr Cook. Kraus interjects: 'For the only valuable thing about the North Pole was that it had not been reached.' The argument grows more complex when he comes to the rival claims of Commander Peary and the question, 'What is truth?' Certainly 'it is not the midnight sun which brings it to light'.

And what does the Zeppelin bring to light? The newspapers gaily print the headline 'Conquest of the Air' alongside other headlines announcing the deaths of hundreds of thousands in earthquakes, typhoons, and floods. 'What good is speed if the brain has oozed out on the way?' The ice-fields of the abused intellect have gradually killed reason and imagination, and the piece ends: 'We who thought, died.' Harry Zohn duly notes the parallel with the 'conquest' of the moon and with other developments in the ice-fields of applied science.

Irony cannot save the fighting satirist and moralist, with his sense of being a voice in the wilderness, from sounding much like a prig at times. Despite its celebrated opening, in which the inaugural cliché is elegantly whittled at from all angles, and despite its expressing Kraus's central beliefs at their keenest and most persuasive, the essay 'In These Great Times' (late 1914) is repetitious and uneven in force, omitting to differentiate between sins and peccadilloes, and treating honest disagreement and inveterate viciousness with equal contempt: those who were not a hundred per cent with him were a hundred per cent against him. (In this we may be reminded of the later writings of F. R. Leavis, a figure Kraus resembles in others ways as well.) Rilke remarked that he distilled a very pure poison; he could also lay about him with a rather blunt instrument.

A common misfortune of cultural historians, scholars who offer to supply the background to the work of writers, is that the writers have already supplied not only a foreground but, by implication, a background as well, a peculiarly intimate one. We know medieval England through Chaucer, and Victorian

London through Dickens; we know Habsburg Austria because of *The Man Without Qualities*, and because of Karl Kraus.

Kraus's magazine, *Die Fackel* ('The Torch'), ran for thirty-seven years and 922 numbers, and more than the writers mentioned above, possibly more than any other writer, he occupied himself with the minutiae of the local life of his time, the personalities and practices of what Schoenberg called 'our beloved and hated Vienna'. Edward Timms's task in *Karl Kraus: Apocalyptic Satirist*—to trace his subject's literary career and personal life up till the founding of the Austrian Republic in 1919—would seem to be more supererogatory than usual. Except that Kraus is little known to the larger English-speaking public: interest in him has been mounting for some time now, and hence Timms's book arrives opportunely. It is no great matter that it makes heavy weather of describing the fragmented condition, ethnic, social, political, and religious, of Austria-Hungary and especially of Vienna. More could have been left to the reader's imagination, itself capable of feeding on Kraus's imagination. But we should be grateful for the lively illustrations: a literary coffee-house; the Kaiser kitted out in medieval armour, fearing God but nobody else; a repulsive grinning male face advertising the virtues of something called Lysoform, 'the most perfect disinfectant. Indispensable for ladies.' And for such insights as the quotation from Arthur Schnitzler, to the effect that before one joined a cycling club one would need to ascertain whether it was a Progressive, or Christian Social, or German Nationalist, or anti-Semitic organization.

Erich Heller wrote on Kraus in *The Disinherited Mind* (1952), and honour should also be accorded Frank Field's early study, *The Last Days of Mankind: Karl Kraus and his Vienna* (1967), and Thomas Szasz's *Karl Kraus and the Soul-Doctors* (1977). The latter deals entertainingly with Kraus's attitude towards Freud and his followers, though Timms insists that Kraus's strictures were directed against the followers rather than Freud himself. Szasz cited not only the famous epigram, 'Psychoanalysis is the disease of which it claims to be the cure', but also Kraus's fundamental principle, 'Language is the mother, not the maid, of thought', as well as that useful distinction, 'The agitator seizes the word. The artist is seized by it.'

The greatest step forward was Harry Zohn's selection, *In These Great Times*, published in Canada in 1976 and in Britain in 1984. Untranslatable—that high yet equivocal accolade—often means that the right translator hasn't come along, or that for one reason or another few people desire a translation and hence publishers evince no interest. In Kraus's case the situation seems to have been aggravated by the discomfort felt among German-speaking critics: he doesn't fit into any 'school', any of the prime, well-founded, well-thought-of categories—and that, where taxonomy has ruled so long, is a sin. English-speaking Germanists have tended to follow suit, or else, as with J. P. Stern, their thoughts have been chiefly confined to academic circles, where popularization or vulgarization (which includes translation) is itself a solecism. An exception is an essay by Stern, printed in *Encounter* in 1975, in which he mentions a professor of German literature at an Austrian university who knew of Kraus only as 'one of those typical querulous coffee-house literati, who is said to have waged a peculiarly quixotic linguistic campaign lasting more than forty years against his fellow journalists'.

Paradoxes are fairly easily come by; we can pluck them out of the air once we have the knack. They are virtually bound to surface where people commit themselves to opinions and causes, and they serve the critic and the commentator as faithful stand-bys. Paradoxes and contradictions flourish in Timms's commentary. Kraus attacked ideological thinking in all its shapes: while his campaign for reforms could only be implemented with political support, 'his intransigence towards organized factions effectively precluded it'. Politics is said to be the art of the possible; Kraus's art was that of the truth as he saw it, and we cannot honestly regret that he forfeited the power which political affiliation would in theory have supplied. Had he enrolled in a party, it would have been the end of him, or more likely of the party. In a breezy piece calling for the demotion of tourism in Vienna, he mentioned a female tourist who asked if what she had heard was true and he was incapable of being constructive. After some hesitation he admitted it, 'but not without at the same time boasting of a positive ability: that I am capable of being destructive'.

Timms quotes Kraus's remark that if scoundrels cannot be

improved then it is still an ethical aim to vex them, and juxtaposes it with Swift's objective: 'to vex rogues though it will not amend them', adding truly if tritely, 'Both formulations reflect the difficulties inherent in any attempt to set the world to rights by means of the pen.' Not even the consciousness that no one is going to read him can stop a writer writing; Günter Grass will be busy at his desk while the debris from the Big Bang is falling about him. Related is 'a paradox which runs right through Kraus's writing': that's to say, he desired to raise the standards of Austrian journalism, and yet he proclaimed that the press was irretrievably corrupt. The theory that the satirist must be optimistic (or at any rate not pessimistic), since otherwise he wouldn't go to the trouble of mounting his assaults, has never convinced me. One could as well maintain that no optimist would ever bother himself with satire since he knows that time or some other benign agency will rectify whatever is amiss.

Brechtian *avant la lettre*, Kraus asserted that he did not want 'performance' to overpower the intellectual understanding of the text. 'When I give public readings, I am not making literature into a performance.' Yet contemporary reports of his recitations —there were some seven hundred of them, from Shakespeare, Goethe, Offenbach's librettos, Johann Nestroy, and (mostly) his own work—dwell on his declamatory and histrionic style. This paradox, Timms says, 'can only be resolved by seeing his public role as a quest for authentic identity'. It could be that, to Kraus's way of thinking, when he did it, it was right, and when others did it, it was wrong. But that, too, might be taken as questing for identity.

A more engaging paradox emerges from Kraus's dealings with women, or with women and Woman. His public emphasis was on women as the brainless but bountiful vehicles or vessels of sensuality, in contrast with men, whose strength and purpose lie in ideas. 'The sensuality of woman', he wrote, 'is the primal spring at which the intellectuality of man finds renewal.' In private, however, his taste was for intelligent women, such as the actresses he loved, and the blue-blooded and cultivated Sidonie Nadherny. A man may well apotheosize the pure (in one sense, at least) and elemental *Weib* or Earth Mother, while in personal matters preferring a woman, a lady even, whom he can converse with as well as embrace in bed. Intelligence, it might be reckoned, is more likely to stimulate or enhance sensuality than to deter it. Not infrequently one is oneself the great exception to the rule one is promulgating, possibly the exception that proves it.

There is no compelling reason for surprise when we hear that, according to his acquaintances, in private life the fierce and unforgiving battler was sociable, charming, relaxed, and kindly. But George Steiner touched on another oddity when reviewing Kraus's letters to Sidonie Nadherny (*Encounter*, 1975), though he was too wily to invoke the word 'paradox':

One may, in one's public writings and utterances, be a ferocious rationalist, contemptuous of human lies and illusions. But one is privately, and almost obsessively, involved with a graphologist and clairvoyant whose interpretations of Sidonie's handwriting and of the handwriting and horoscopes of her friends seem 'miraculously accurate' and fill numerous letters.

The best comment on the phenomenon occurs in Johnson's *Rasselas*, when Imlac, asked why his father desired to increase his wealth when he already had more money than he could enjoy, answers: 'Inconsistencies cannot both be right, but, imputed to man, they may both be true.' This isn't much of an explanation, but some things can only be described. The rationalist tells you that why he doesn't walk under ladders is purely because a brick or a pot of paint might fall on him. Instead, he steps off the pavement and risks being run down.

So marked were Kraus's attempts to discard his Jewish identity that he has been associated with the notion of 'Jewish self-hatred'. He no more wanted to be categorized as a Jew than Heine did. Jews were prominent in commercial, financial, and journalistic spheres, and hence among the enemy, but when Kraus described himself as 'Aryan' he set the word inside inverted commas: 'arisch'. He meant he was unaligned, and therefore uncompromised; or, *tout court*, 'ethical'. He embraced Catholicism in 1911, seemingly without much passion, and remained within that faith for twelve years, though always silently; 'baptized Jews' was another category to be avoided. There was little trace of Christianity in his writing. Perhaps the point was not so much entering one religion or community as extricating himself from another. (There is a faint suggestion of leaning over backwards in these 'liberating' manœuvres.) As Timms notes, it is not the redeeming Christ who informs his satire, but rather the retributive and Judaic Jehovah.

'If the roles of satirist and Christian are incompatible, what of those of satirist and lover?' Incompatibles, or what look like them, are a more extreme form of paradox, equally handy as a trellis on which critics and biographers weave their deliberations. To understand a love-affair from inside is hard enough; to assess it from outside can be impossible. Timms is properly circumspect. Kraus fell in love with Sidonie Nadherny, a Catholic and an aristocrat, in 1913; between that date and his death in 1936, although the decisive break came in 1918, he addressed nearly eleven hundred letters, postcards, and telegrams to her. Their love was clandestine, less because satirists are forbidden love than because Sidonie needed to make a socially acceptable match. Kraus was well off: he inherited an income from his father, a paper manufacturer, and—another paradox here?—*Die Fackel* prospered, its first number, published on 1 April 1899, having sold around 30,000 copies. But affluence alone wasn't sufficient qualification. In 1914 Sidonie wrote in her diary, 'He is the only man living . . . K.K. shall always remain the *glory & crown* of my life!', yet apparently she felt she couldn't stay faithful to one man, even the only man living, and an entry of 1918 reads, 'the greater his love grows, the less I can return'. The relationship made little impression on his published writings; disguised, his love for Sidonie evinces itself in his poetry, in poems that are elegiac in mood. In this respect love resembled religion: satire seems to rule out, as themes, the very matters you would expect to inspire it. But then, inspiration can work in roundabout ways.

Apropos of Kraus's 'mythopoeic imagination', Timms points out that you don't need to know anything about the Viennese journalist, Felix Salten, to appreciate the authority of Kraus's portrait of him. Historically accurate though the portrait is, the individual has become a type, Kraus has moved from the particular to the general while retaining all the cogency that the particular carries. 'Am I to blame', he asked, 'if hallucinations and visions are alive and have names and permanent residences?' Every great satirist must be a great creator, a myth-maker as well as a realist. The proponent of Swift's *Modest Proposal* takes on mythic stature as we listen to him. He is a counsel we would eagerly hire for our defence were we guilty as charged; he is politically sophisticated; as an economist he cannot be faulted; he is a skilled demographer, a sound psychologist (his plan will secure pregnant wives from being kicked by their husbands), and not a bad butcher (he knows about salting meat). A veritable Nestor, a Daniel come to judgement! If there is nothing in Kraus that reaches this level of reasoned insanity, then it is not to be wondered at.

Kraus is a superb aphorist. 'A school without grades must have been concocted by someone who was drunk on non-alcoholic wine.' Very timely; my local school has banned competitive sports such as running because someone might win, ergo others might lose, and this would offend the golden rule of equality. 'Sex education is legitimate in that girls cannot be taught soon enough how children don't come into the world': that's up to the minute too. And pertinent in an age of revisionist bishops is this: 'It is a mystery to me how a theologian can be praised for having brought himself to disbelieve dogmas. I've always thought that those who have brought themselves to *believe* in dogmas merit the true recognition owing a heroic deed.' There hasn't been so much change since Old Vienna: 'If something is stolen from you, don't go to the police. They're not interested. Don't go to a psychologist either, because he's interested in only one thing: that it was really *you* who did the stealing.'*

An example of Kraus's rather fearsome extrapolation, his turning of individual offence into universal disgrace, was prompted by the case of a young man who had been acquitted of a *crime passionnel*—murdering his wife because she sought a divorce— and was seen some months later dancing in public. (He had shot himself too, but clearly without doing much damage.) Writing about the affair in a poem, *Tod und Tango*, Kraus deduces from it the moral bankruptcy, indeed the living death, of the world at large. 'Guilty is the age, not to perish at such sport!' In defence of the poem, the feminist point has been urged that it exposes the

---

* These examples come from the excellent selection, *Half-Truths & One-and-a-Half Truths*, edited and translated by Harry Zohn. As is, of course, 'An aphorism never coincides with the truth: it is either a half-truth or one-and-a-half truths.'

double standard of Austrian justice: coming from a 'good family', the man got off whereas, Kraus notes, a woman who killed her husband during her menopause was condemned to death. So much is valid. Only a cad would bring up Kraus's aphorism, 'I am not for women but against men.'

Kraus runs the risk of being branded an aesthete. In the piece 'Interview with a Dying Child' we may think him more angry about callous and exploitative journalism than pitiful towards the victim, and, when he is contemplating the war, on occasion more indignant about the crass or disgusting reporting of the slaughter than on the subject of the slaughter itself. He was too ready to equate a badly written sentence with moral degeneracy, and a good literary style with truth and moral virtue—even reasoning (though we should allow for coat-trailing) in the reverse direction: 'A poem is good until one knows by whom it is.' A tendency to take short cuts is understandable in one who was always on the go. But it is central to Kraus's mode of operation that, as Timms puts it, apocalyptic conclusions are drawn from apparently commonplace and trivial symptoms. Heller's gloss is apposite here: 'It was Karl Kraus who discovered to what satanic heights inferiority may rise.'

Two essays in Elias Canetti's *The Conscience of Words* are very much to the purpose. In the second of them, a lecture given in Berlin in 1974, Canetti asserts that

what annoys today's reader of the *Fackel*, what makes it unbearable for him over long stretches, is the evenness of assault. Everything happens with the same strength, everything is drawn as equally important into one and the same language. One senses that the attack is an end in itself, a superior strength is demonstrated where absolutely no strength would be necessary; the victim vanishes under the incessant blows, he is long since gone, and the fight continues.

None the less Canetti insists on Kraus's place as the greatest German satirist, largely by reason of the vast drama, *The Last Days of Mankind*, a war against war, against World War I, conducted by one man, the most belligerent of pacifists, concurrently with World War I, without the benefit of hindsight.*

---

* Kraus's views at the time may not have been as simple and unqualified as this suggests. Another paradox detected by Timms is that of 'the loyal satirist': Kraus

In the earlier and more personal essay, dated 1965, Canetti tells of the first time he heard Kraus lecture, in 1924. Kraus's law was certain and inviolable, it '*glowed*: it radiated, it scorched and destroyed'.

These sentences, built like cyclopean fortresses and always carefully dovetailing, shot out sudden flashes of lightning, not harmless, not illuminating, not even theatrical flashes, but deadly lightning. And this process of annihilatory punishment, occurring in public and in all ears at once, was so fearful and dreadful that no one could resist it.

Canetti became a devoted and passionate follower of Kraus's dictatorship, for a while. Gradually he rebelled against it, against the ever-extending Chinese Wall of relentless judgements, against 'the general shrinkage of the desire to do your own judging' which set in after a brief exposure to *Die Fackel*. A man so rigorously and comprehensively 'responsible' left little responsibility to his followers. Yet Canetti acknowledges his indebtedness—Kraus opened his ear to a new dimension of language—and his account of 'the master of horror', the man's energy, his gift for condemning people out of their own mouths, his courage and relish, the sheer necessity of him, is eloquent.

A deft breaking of a butterfly happens in a short item inspired by the announcement in a St Gallen newspaper of 1912 of a forthcoming performance at the municipal theatre of what must have been a hitherto unknown tragedy by Shakespeare—*King Lehar*. The printer wasn't trying to make a joke. 'The word that he was not supposed to set, the association that got into his work, is the measure of our time. By their misprints shall ye know them.' Nearer the knuckle is an advertisement spotted in the *Neue Freie Presse* in 1900: 'Travelling companion sought, young, congenial, Christian, independent. Replies to "Invert 69" poste restante Habsburgergasse.' Again Kraus's design was to bring out the discrepancy between the paid ads and the Pharisaical editorials.

was on fairly good terms with the Austrian authorities and with the censorship during the war, though decreasingly so as time went by. He was (a self-description) 'a word-fetishist'; it was the press, the propagandists, the profiteers, and the armchair warriors whom *Die Fackel* attacked, rather than the military men, some of whom had a respectable literary style. *The Last Days of Mankind*, begun in 1915, was not published in its final, book form until 1922, and not produced on the stage before 1962.

A more sustained, and quite irresistible, instance of his humour and light-heartedness is the story of his beaver coat. It has been stolen, the whole of Vienna knows about his loss, people pity him, they forgive him, they admire him, they stop him in the street to condole with him. 'I wrote books, but people understood only the coat.' His life has been transformed; the solitary and estranged satirist is suddenly 'in the thick of it, the earth has me again'. (*Die Erde hat mich wieder*: the words come towards the end of the first scene of Goethe's drama, when Faust's superhuman aspirations have been knocked on the head and only the sound of Easter bells dissuades him from drinking poison.) But all this solicitude, this unwonted solidarity, is too much for him. Next thing, the tax collectors will realize he was rich enough to own a fur coat. 'But I still had one hope left: by publishing a new book I might manage to make the Viennese forget me.'

Harry Zohn's selection also demonstrates the grimmer side of Kraus, where the indignation and the punishment truly fit the provocation and the crime. As in parts of *The Last Days of Mankind*, which (its prologue admits) would take ten evenings of earthly time to perform and was meant for a theatre on Mars. In it news reports are seen to 'stand up as people, and people wither into editorials', phrases walk on two legs while men make do with one. The villains of the piece are what we would expect: demagogues and militarists, arms manufacturers and other profiteers, fire-breathing churchmen ('the miracle of the U-boats', etc.), propagandists and culture-mongers (freely adapted: 'They call us Huns and Krauts, and killers— / Where are their Goethes and their Schillers?'), and of course the ladies and gentlemen of the press. Fury conduces to frenzy, and at times it is hard to disentangle the anti-rant from the rant, but Kraus's alertness to linguistic mayhem provides light relief from the glut of denunciations. Some patriots persuade the owner to change the name of the Café Westminster to Westmünster (it means the same, 'and it's German. Perfect'), but on parting so far forget themselves as to wish one another *adieu* and *addio* and *au revoir*. In another scene the waiter in a restaurant needs to identify the dish 'Fatherland mutton with Valhalla nectar' as the pre-war English mutton with Worcestershire sauce; in the original, the waiter explains that *Butterteighohlpastete* is what used to be known as a *Volavan*.

The Last Days of Mankind ends with the Voice of God echoing the words attributed to the dying Austrian Emperor in 1916, *Ich habe es nicht gewollt*: he did not will it. Some late words of Kraus were *Mir fällt zu Hitler nichts ein*: on Hitler he found nothing to say. The disclaimer is ambiguous, in the manner of irony, but hardly affects one as a confession of feebleness. Words, as the saying goes, did fail him.

On the subject of the press—and, now, on television—the key text is the essay or oration, 'In These Great Times'. Progress, with the brand of logic at its disposal, claims that the press serves an existing need: in short, it is nothing other than 'an imprint of life'. In reality it is increasingly the case that life is only an imprint of the press. 'Is the press a messenger? No, it is the event itself. . . . Once again the instrument has got the better of us.' (Marshall McLuhan anticipated.) If we had any sense, then—like Cleopatra —we would beat the messenger. It's too late for that, however: through decades of practising his trade the reporter has 'produced in mankind that degree of unimaginativeness which enables it to wage a war of extermination against itself'.

Perhaps most forceful—and nearest to Swift's *Modest Proposal*—is an extract from *The Third Walpurgis Night* (the first two came in *Faust*), written in 1933 but not published until 1952. In neighbouring Germany, according to press reports, unusual events are happening. Despite efforts to save them, people taken into protective custody are dying, because—the doctors say— they have lost the will to live. Others are so perverse as to inflict wounds on themselves while in transit to a camp. (A camp of the kind defined in the press as 'a temporary curtailment of liberty with an educational aim'.) A Polish workman 'died of heart failure; in any case, he was stateless'. Many of these people are sickly, no doubt as a result of regrettable habits, and liable to have fainting-fits while standing near open windows on upper floors. Nevertheless great things are expected, and indeed claimed, in the way of spiritual rehabilitation, but unfortunately— Kraus interjects—the patients themselves cannot testify to this because their astonishment leads to speech disorders, or because 'the spiritual transformation which often occurs at a stroke not infrequently results in unconsciousness or at least an impaired memory'. Here the subject-matter is heavy, the writer's hand light. Fortunately for him, Kraus's heart failed three years later.

As for paradoxes, Kraus provided one for himself, along with an explication, in a poem entitled *Mein Widerspruch* ('My Ambivalence'):

> Where lives were subjugated by lies
> I was a revolutionary—
> where norms against nature they sought to devise
> I was a revolutionary . . .
>
> Where freedom became a meaningless phrase
> I was a reactionary—
> where art they besmirched by their arty ways
> I was a reactionary . . .

The Executioner Himself

Our attitude towards the great European thinkers and writers of the late nineteenth and early twentieth centuries can be a distinctly mixed one. In their high seriousness and sombre admonition they seem to have said virtually everything of importance there was to say, charting the disintegration of values and prophesying the doom that promptly followed. History set its seal on them. Indeed, so thorough and authoritative were their diagnoses and prognoses that we begin to wonder whether in some way they weren't partly responsible for what they described and foretold.

Having this shameful thought in mind, I should have been gratified rather than disconcerted by what Elias Canetti says on the first page of *The Play of the Eyes*, his third volume of memoirs, relating to the years from 1931 to 1937. In his novel, finished during that time, and later known in English as *Auto da Fé*, he had burned the books before Hitler got to work on them. His hero's library, which contained everything of account to the world, had gone up in flames. 'All that had burned, I had let it happen, I had made no attempt to save any part of it; what remained was a desert, and I myself was to blame.' He continues, not in self-aggrandizement but in tribute to the power of words:

For what happens in that kind of book is not just a game, it is reality; one has to justify it, not only against criticism from outside but in one's own eyes as well. Even if an immense fear has compelled one to write such things, one must still ask oneself whether in so doing one has not helped to bring about what one so vastly fears.

Such is human perversity that one wishes to console him: no, sir, please don't take on so! *Auto da Fé* is only a book, no matter how chilling, only a novel about a crazy sinologist who failed to keep his ivory tower in good repair . . .

Of all those stern, erudite, apocalyptic Europeans—to whose elevated company he has been admitted rather late in the day—Canetti impresses me as the most difficult to assess, even the hardest to describe. How genuine is his originality, how deeply is he indebted to Kraus and Broch? (Certainly not cripplingly.) There is no doubt about his seriousness, the depth of his thought; yet one might have hoped for a firmer incisiveness; we assent, or are ready to assent, to his statements, but we may be disappointed by his exposition and development of them, by the kind of rhetoric he employs. Fairly plainly, this is no grandiloquent or notably supple rhetoric, being blunt, assertive, four-square, and at times portentous, rather than exploratory as in Czeslaw Milosz, or nimble and witty as in Robert Musil, or protean and mischievous as in Thomas Mann. We want to be borne along, we have no misgivings about his sincerity, yet he is not wholly persuasive; his solemnity of tenor and his intensity promise—or threaten—more than they deliver. As we pass through his book, *The Human Province*, we feel we are being steamrollered even by aphorisms no more than a line and a half in length. 'God as a preparation for something more sinister that we do not yet know.'

Canetti explains that the 'jottings' which make up that book served as a safety-valve during the years spent on his *Crowds and Power* (1962) and well beyond its completion, in fact from 1942 to 1972. They saved him from paralysis, and from suffocation. Death and religion are recurrent themes, often found in conjunction. 'The fact that the gods die makes death more brazen'; 'No one should ever have had to die. The worst crime did not merit death; and without the *recognition* of death, there could never have been the worst crime.' Among lighter *aperçus* are 'A love letter from Sweden. Strindberg on the stamp', and 'He kept turning the other cheek until they stuck a medal on it.' And there is an entertaining list of eccentric societies, including one in which every man is painted and prays to his own picture, and another—so much for crowds—in which it is unthinkable for more than two people to stand together, and when a third party approaches, the two of them, 'shaken with disgust', quickly separate.

The majority of these jottings are considerably less playful. 'My greatest wish is to see a mouse devour a cat alive. But first she has to play with it long enough' and 'Oh, for a stethoscope to identify the generals in their wombs!' belong to the year 1942; and an anecdote about people living underground because the earth's surface is uninhabitable—'War has moved into outer space, earth is heaving a sigh of relief before its end'—is dated 1945. Looking on the brighter side, however, 'as long as there are any people in the world who have *no power whatsoever*, I cannot lose all hope'.

Mann twists and turns, Musil ironizes in all directions, while Canetti looms. Canetti is not an entertainer; he is too stern and cold and unforgiving for that. Perhaps in the end he will be adjudged a major thinker rather than a major writer; or a thinker who has some difficulty in writing. Yet in his 1976 speech, 'The Writer's Profession', printed in *The Conscience of Words*, he speaks nobly on the true profession of the true writer, reproaching both those who use the solemn word *Dichter* (writer or poet) and those who scoff at it. A poet worthy the name would wince away from the name, but true poets do exist. 'If I were really a writer, I would have been able to prevent the war': when Canetti came across this anonymous sentence, dated 23 August 1939, his first inclination was to spurn it as an example of 'the blustering that has discredited the word *writer*'. But it haunted him, for there seemed to be more to it than that. Albeit an admission of complete failure (and in a sphere where few would expect anything other), it expressed, however irrationally, 'the admission of a *responsibility*'. After all, if words can lead to war, why can't words avert war? (As one might ask, if great literature can elevate, why can't pornography debase?) No condition is closer to events, more profoundly related, than feeling responsible for them, however 'fictively'. A kinship with Kraus displays itself here, as in Canetti's aphorism, 'Literature as a profession is destructive; one should *fear* words more.'

This responsibility is developed in his concept of the writer as the keeper and practitioner of 'metamorphosis', or the ability, explicit in myth, to become anybody and everybody, 'even the smallest, the most naïve, the most powerless person'. In this process, which embraces an acceptance of chaos and an effort to overcome it, the writer is spurred on by an inexplicable hunger— unlike the seeker after success, who always knows what, among his chances and choices, he should exploit and what he should throw overboard. The writer pursues nothingness only to find, and to mark for others, a way out of it. His pride is to fight against death and, using means other than theirs, against 'the envoys of nothingness, who are growing more and more numerous in literature'. True enough, the last days of mankind are always about to arrive; but we are not obliged to welcome them.

That Canetti has his own brand of humour, signally his own, is illustrated in the short, impassive character sketches, falling uncertainly between typology and fable, published under the title *Earwitness*. The Self-giver lives by taking back her presents; she gave them only in order to take them back: how painful it is if her present was edible and has been eaten up! Other subjects are more easily recognized as types, almost conventional 'characters', such as the God-swanker, 'a handsome man, with a voice and a mane', who can always find a passage in the Bible to endorse him, or if the first doesn't, he finds another that does; and the Blind Man, a traveller who, back home, looks at his photographs of places he has visited without seeing them at the time: the camera never lies, it *proves*.

The more comical these sketches, the more pertinent they are. The Tear-warmer relies on sentimental movies since people won't always oblige by dying when you feel like a nice weep. The Paper Drunkard reads books that others haven't even heard of; he avoids speaking about his seven doctorates and mentions only three. And the Sultan-addict is a rare, or rarely heard from, species of feminist, yearning for harems because they offered women the chance to be truly feminine and outstrip men. 'The one thing that only a woman can do is to bear a prince, who kills all the other princes and eventually the sultan too when the sultan gets too old.' She feels sorry for Turkey, which has lost its former greatness and is now a modern country like any other.

The Damage-fresh Man needs no gloss; he thrives on the accidents of others, sniffing them out before they happen and looking them bravely in the face. So many bad things befall other people that there simply isn't time for any misfortune to happen to him. The Water-harbourer hoards water, even asking to fill bottles with it from his neighbours' taps. By revealing that there were no humans on the moon and also not a drop of water, the moon landings have confirmed what he always knew—that the people up there all died from wasting the precious liquid. Bizarre though the man is, he exhibits the knack we all have of conscripting logic to prop up our irrationalities, of fattening our fancies on selected facts. Then of course there is the Earwitness himself, who hears everything, forgets nothing, and in due course comes out with it all. On occasion, as if he were on holiday, he claps 'blinders' on his ears and is so friendly and trustworthy that people fail to realize they are speaking with 'the executioner himself'. One of Canetti's autobiographical volumes is called *The Torch in My Ear*, and he has related how Kraus, that constant listener and tireless executioner, opened new perspectives on language and its capacities for good and ill.

Good fun though these character sketches are, or intriguing, one feels that there must surely be something more momentous, larger of implication, hovering in the shadows, something about to be revealed, about to be. It is in his memoirs that Canetti's habit of observation and ruthless report operates at its peak. Compared with the portraits on display there, these miniatures are fleeting and insubstantial, as it were the playful (if chilly) products of a novelist's spare hours.

Therese, the housekeeper of *Auto da Fé*, is the creation of a major novelistic talent, comparable to (though more dreadful than) Frau Stöhr in Mann's *The Magic Mountain*; you can hear the starch crackle in her skirt, you can smell the starch. And yet the novel is essentially static, loaded, cut and dried from the start: in the course of a self-fulfilling prophecy a born hater of mankind is brought down by hateful men and women. There is an over-bearing determinedness about it, a ferocity and contempt at which even Kraus, from whose sway Canetti had recently disengaged himself, might have flinched.

The novel, a final distillation of eight potential novels, was originally called *Kant Catches Fire*, but was published, in 1935, under the more austere title *Die Blendung* ('blinding' or 'bedazzlement'), and with the protagonist's name changed on Hermann Broch's insistence. Kant became Kien ('pine-wood'), thus retaining something of the man's combustibility, as Canetti has observed in a rare flash of everyday humour. When Broch read the manuscript, 'You're terrifying,' he told the author: 'Do you want to terrify people? . . . Is it the writer's function to bring more fear into the world? Is that a worthy intention?' At the time

Canetti must have thought it so. Not that he was, or is, deficient in self-awareness, or awareness of other people's views of him and his work. In *The Play of the Eyes*, when he is doubting his ability to do full justice to Broch, and with his preparations for a life-work on the psychology of crowds also in mind, he writes:

He could not help recognizing my tendency to include *everything* in my plans and ambitions as an authentic passion. What repelled him was my zealotic, dogmatic way of making the improvement of mankind depend-ent on chastisement and without hesitation appointing myself executor of this chastisement.

It may be that the 1981 Nobel Prize was awarded to Canetti more on account of *Crowds and Power*, but *Auto da Fé* is to say the very least a unique work, and we would not be without it. 'It's good such a book exists,' the proprietor of a Strasbourg news-paper affirmed, adding that 'people who read it will wake up as from a nightmare and be thankful that reality is different'.

Canetti visited Strasbourg for a music festival in 1933, in the course of a refuse collectors' strike which brought out the city's medieval character. Suddenly, without warning, he found him-self in the fourteenth century, a period that had always interested him because of its mass movements, the flagellants, the burning of Jews, the Plague. As he walked through the reeking streets he saw everywhere, both outside and inside behind closed doors, the dead and the despair of those still alive.

What in Germany, beyond the Rhine, was felt to be a fresh start struck me here as the consequence of a war that had not yet begun. I did not foresee—how could I foresee?—what lay ten years ahead. No, I looked six hundred years back, and what I saw was the Plague with its masses of dead, which had spread irresistibly and was once again threatening from across the Rhine.

Only when he climbed the Cathedral spire and took a deep breath did 'reality' reassert itself, and it appeared to him that the Plague had been thrust back into its proper century.

Canetti's eyes match the 'thirsty eyes' he attributed to Isaac Babel in the preceding volume of memoirs, *The Torch in My Ear*. They are hyperactive throughout *The Play of the Eyes*, although 'play' is not always the right word for what they are engaged in. While his idols generally have a toe or two of clay, his fools and

bêtes noires are formed of something worse than mud. Franz
Werfel had pop eyes and a mouth like a carp's:

Since he took any number of important ideas from others, he often held
forth as if he were a font of infinite wisdom. He overflowed with sentiment, his fat belly gurgled with love and feeling, one expected to find
little puddles on the floor around him and was almost disappointed to
find it dry.

It isn't hard to see why Canetti despised him and his ' "O Man!"
rubbish', but all the same the author of *The Forty Days of Musa
Dagh* deserves better than this. Emil Ludwig, the once acclaimed
biographer, 'wrote a whole book in three or four weeks and
boasted about it'—perhaps he oughtn't to have boasted—while
Richard Beer-Hofmann, the surviving leader of the Viennese *fin
de siècle*, whom Canetti met on the same occasion, 'wrote no
more than two lines a year'. (We wonder whether he boasted
about that.) And grim and grotesque fun is made of those artistic
relicts, the widows of Gustav Mahler and Jakob Wassermann.
Displaying her daughter by Walter Gropius, Alma Mahler (now
married to Werfel) asked Canetti, 'Beautiful, isn't she? . . . Like
father, like daughter. Did you ever see Gropius? A big handsome
man. The true Aryan type. The only man who was racially suited
to me. All the others who fell in love with me were little Jews.
Like Mahler. The fact is, I go for both kinds.'

Canetti met James Joyce once, in Zurich in 1935, and rudeness,
on Joyce's part, ensued. The incident, of which he makes what
seems rather too much, occurred during a reading of his play,
Komödie der Eitelkeit ('Comedy of Vanity'), a reading which
fell disastrously flat—except in the eyes of the author. Reporting
an earlier reading of the same play, when Werfel shouted 'This is
unbearable' and walked out, he comments, 'It is defeats of such
catastrophic proportions that keep a writer alive.' He has always
been a doughty fighter.

The larger and more intimate set pieces bear on the novelists
Broch and Musil, the conductor Hermann Scherchen, and—
unequivocally affectionate in tenor—the sculptor Fritz Wotruba
(on whom he has published a monograph), the composer Alban
Berg, and one other and mysterious person. Canetti speaks of the
indelible impressions people leave on him, not surprisingly in

view of his close and pitiless scrutiny of them. These portrayals are indisputably brilliant, the work of a novelist, a dramatist, as well as an unremitting watcher. That there is a trace of resentment in his hero-worship of Broch and Musil, and that elsewhere an incidental tinge of self-praise shows through, is understandable given the history of his reputation, its curiously sluggish growth. And the fact that for the greater part of this period nothing of his had been published, and he had only manuscripts to show for himself in the small, prolific world of Vienna, would have made him (in a phrase he applied to Musil) touchy in his self-esteem.

Just as their conversation had grown fascinating, Broch would announce, 'I must go to Dr Schaxl's now.' That the man who had written *The Sleepwalkers* should break off to go and confide in a female analyst! 'I was filled with consternation. I felt ashamed for him.' Looking back, Canetti admits the possibility that Broch was running away from his avalanche of words, that he couldn't have endured a longer conversation and therefore arranged to meet him just before his appointment with the analyst.

Musil, who was 'a man of solids and avoided liquids and gases' and who possessed 'an unerring instinct for the inadequacy of the simple', he worshipped as greatly as he worshipped Broch. Musil was competitive, and 'his touchiness was merely a defence against murkiness and adulteration'. He wasn't in the least pleased to feature as one of the much trumpeted and (Canetti's words) 'odd triad', Musil, Joyce, and Broch. When he heard that someone had spoken highly of *The Man Without Qualities* he would at once ask, 'Whom else does he praise?' In 1931 Canetti sent the manuscript of *Auto da Fé*, in three heavy tomes, to Thomas Mann, who returned it with an apologetic note: he didn't have the strength to read it.* With what looks like convoluted humour, Canetti now acknowledges that Mann's letter declining to read the manuscript was 'probably not unjust, for he had not read the book'. But after its publication, four years

* It is never easy to be serious about important matters without sounding portentous or self-important. In an essay on Confucius, Canetti has talked of the sage's distaste for oratory and 'the weight of chosen words': he took death so seriously that he declined to answer questions about it. Incidentally, it was the shade of Confucius—'To see the right and not to do it is to lack courage'—who inspired Kien to marry Therese. Weighty words, those.

later, he received the letter he had hoped for, making amends. Musil had launched into his own and eagerly awaited praise of the book when, excited and befuddled, Canetti interrupted to say that he had had a long letter from Thomas Mann. Musil's face went grey. 'Did you?' he said, and turned on his heel. (A case of 'Who else has praised you?') It was the end of their friendship. 'He was a master of dismissal. He had ample practice. Once he had dismissed you, you stayed dismissed.' This is saddening to read—a premonition of the kind of literary biography so popular today: by their frailties ye shall know them—and, aware of Canetti's own edginess, we can be forgiven for wondering whether it is true, the whole truth.

It is Scherchen, the conductor, a lesser person, who gets the roughest handling: a man of indestructible will, voluble in self-praise ('hymns of triumph, one might say, if it didn't sound so dull and colourless'), with never a commendatory word for others, stage-managing a circus of cowed protégés. For Canetti, he was 'a perfect specimen of something I was determined to understand and portray: a dictator'. Only when Scherchen fell in love with a Chinese girl whom he had seen conducting Mozart in Brussels, and cancelled all his engagements to rush off to Peking to marry her, did Canetti soften towards him. For once, instead of issuing orders, the man had voluntarily submitted to one.

The most glowing tribute is that paid to a man Canetti had watched in a café for a year and a half before being introduced to him. Dr Sonne, who lived in retirement, looked like Kraus but showed none of Kraus's anger, and spoke as Musil wrote but had none of Musil's purposiveness or urge to prevail. Sonne's was a spiritual influence, his charisma hardly to be conveyed in cold print; Canetti thought of him as 'the angel Gabriel', and served a four-year apprenticeship to him. He heard from somebody else that in his youth Sonne had written, under the name of Abraham ben Yitzhak, a few consummate poems in Hebrew, perhaps fewer than a dozen. They never discussed this, and for a time Canetti was faintly shocked to discover that his 'perfect sage', his peerless model, had *done* something; but then he admired him the more for turning his back on it and disparaging fame—whereas he, Canetti, was busy fighting for a reputation. According to T. Carmi's *Penguin Book of Hebrew Verse*, Avraham ben Yitshak printed only eleven poems during his lifetime (1883–1950), was rediscovered when his collected poems came out in 1952, and is considered by many to be the first truly modern Hebrew poet.

'She despised her sex. Her hero was not some woman, it was Coriolanus.' In the first of his autobiographical volumes, *The Tongue Set Free*, Canetti had much to say about his mother, the raging contradictions in her character, her intolerance and her magnanimity, possessiveness and scorn, wildness and implacability. At ten years old, he had equated her with Medea, encountered in a book about classical myths. Now, in her eyes, he had sold his soul to Vienna, he had even married, in secret, a Viennese woman, and she never wanted to see him again. *The Play of the Eyes* ends with the end of the long, tormented struggle between mother and son, or more accurately with her death, in Paris, in 1937. The account of her last days is totally unsentimental, as we would expect, and weirdly affecting. He brought her roses, from her childhood garden in Ruschuk, he told her, the Bulgarian town where he too was born. 'Her earliest memory was of lying under a rosebush, and then she was crying because she had been carried into the house and the fragrance was gone.' Coming straight from Vienna, he had actually bought the roses on the spot, in Paris. But she believed him. 'She accepted my story, she accepted me too—I was included in the fragrant cloud.'

Is God an Endless Orgasm?

Isaac Bashevis Singer's novel *The Penitent*, originally serialized in the *Jewish Daily Forward* in 1973, offers a handy introduction to his cast of mind or soul and serves as a gloss on his memoirs. Three volumes of these, covering his early years, have been gathered together, with a new preamble, in *Love and Exile*. In that the memoirs, albeit animated in the extreme, are somewhat clotted, the reader may care to draw on Clive Sinclair's *The Brothers Singer* for directional aid.

Joseph Shapiro, the penitent of the novel, is a Polish Jew, now an American citizen, who accosts the author at the Wailing Wall and recounts the story of his life. In his tirade against the modern world and pre-eminently the modern Jew (including his former self), Shapiro is sweeping, circumstantial, unsparing, and often acute. Students of sociology become experts on saving the world while they are busily fouling it; students of literature—he has suffered at the hands of this sort too—take some bad writer and find in him meanings he himself had never dreamed of. So-called good writers are no use either: among those who trade in violence and fornication are Tolstoy (see *Anna Karenina*), Homer, Dante, and (because of *Faust*) Goethe. All the kitsch novels in the world, he complains, have already been translated into the Holy Tongue. But then, modern Hebrew is a hundred per cent worldly: 'A language used to build ships and airplanes and to manufacture guns and bombs cannot be a Sacred Tongue.' As for women, they certainly aren't the Jewish wives their grand-mothers were.

The turning-point in Shapiro's life came when by pure coinci-dence he stumbled on the Sandzer Hasidim study house, and hence on his future wife, Sarah. But 'coincidence is not a kosher word': like everything else, the encounter was destined. In his new father-in-law's eyes Shapiro runs to excess: he is a vegetar-ian. No one who has seen people being eaten can ever again eat an animal. It is vain for Reb Haim to tell him that one doesn't need to be more compassionate than the Almighty, for Shapiro has long been at odds with the Almighty on this score. The Evil Spirit whispered in his head, 'What did God do for us Jews that we should love him?' To which he has no reasoned answer and can only reply that he would rather speak to an unjust Creator than to the KGB. By now Shapiro has accepted everything; he has grown a beard and earlocks and wears a long gaberdine, on the principle that if you comport yourself in a Jewish fashion then faith will follow. Either you are a fundamentalist or you are a pseudo-Gentile, there's no half-way house.

In the concluding note the author declares that, unlike Joseph Shapiro, he hasn't himself made peace with the cruelty of life. 'I still say to myself that there isn't and there cannot be a justification either for the pain of the famished wolf or that of the wounded sheep.' You can serve God and question his justice notwithstanding. Like the angry Shapiro, he was brought up among extremists, but he cannot agree that there is any final escape from the human dilemma; in fact 'a total solution would void the greatest gift that God has bestowed upon mankind—free choice.' Faith coexists with doubt, despair with hope, and you fight your battles as they arise.

In the memoirs Bashevis shows himself an assiduous questioner right from the start. 'Mama, does a horse have a soul?' His father the rabbi writes commentaries on the Torah; his brother Joshua (I.J. Singer), eleven years older, is keen on 'worldly books', among them Tolstoy's; Bashevis reads Yiddish story-books about imps, dybbuks, and vampires. The boy's questioning extends from the sufferings of flies, chickens, and fish, to cover all people and all animals in all lands at all times. How can God permit and, in the matter of ritual sacrifice, even encourage such horrors? Joshua, who has become a non-believer, comes up with the ready answer—there is no God, only nature, and nature knows nothing of pity. This satisfies Bashevis no more than it satisfied Shapiro, for along with the cruelty there is wisdom too in evidence. Freedom of choice, say the theologians. But, Bashevis muses, does a cat have a choice? Does a mouse? In him there is something of his father, a pious, mystical, and good-natured man, and something of his rational, sarcastic, and biting mother.

'I stem from generations of rabbis, Hasidim, and cabbalists. I can frankly say that in our house Jewishness wasn't some diluted formal religion but one that contained all the flavours, all the vitamins, the entire mysticism of faith.' He soon rejected modern Jews and their (generally Communistic) schemes for world improvement, his own unorthodoxy lying in his inability to resign himself to the unjustness and agonies of God's universe, and also, as he grew up, in his urgent sexuality. Later in the story, when his father visits Warsaw to consult a medical specialist, or rather a 'healer', the father is amazed to see a column of young people parading through the streets, and actually carrying sticks. Bashevis explains that they want to emigrate to Palestine, but his father cannot begin to comprehend: good Jews should stay put where they are, lambs surrounded by wolves, and wait for the Messiah to come. 'Jews are tired of waiting,' the son says. The father replies, in the spirit of Joseph Shapiro: 'Those that grow tired aren't Jews'; and he asks the way to the nearest house of worship.

'I liked women,' the author states, or understates. From the outset he shocked Yiddish readers by the freedom with which he wrote about sex. His first lover was Gina, perhaps twice his age, a holy woman and a whore, whom he hated as well as loved; their relationship was thoroughgoingly physical and intensely metaphysical, as hectic and tormented as anything in his fiction. A voice in his head—his father's? his grandfather's?—told him he had desecrated his soul: 'You are defiled! You've copulated with Lilith, Naamah, Machlat, Shibta!' His ideal was always 'a decent Jewish daughter', but in real life, like Shapiro, he kept meeting a different sort of woman. He appears to have enjoyed himself far more than Shapiro ever did, and his lovers, no matter how light on morals, had one thing in common with the Almighty—they never calculated the results.

Whatever Bashevis believed or disbelieved, he was sure he wasn't meant to be a soldier, and having received notice of his call-up, he starved himself in order to fail the medical. He had supposed this would weaken him sexually, but it had the opposite effect. The sexual urge, he discovered, is linked with spiritual rather than physical strength: 'Love and sex were functions of the soul.' (One of his stories, 'Moon and Madness', quotes the Talmud as pronouncing that the greater a man is, the greater is his passion.) Early in life, passages in the cabbalistic books had captured his imagination—God copulating with his wife, the Divine Presence—despite the authors' warning against taking their metaphors literally. Marx and Freud were merely mechanical in their theories; philosophy, though he persevered with it, disappointed him; and no more than Shapiro could he attach any real significance to sociology. Even sex, for all its strange intimations, didn't advance him very far in wisdom. The narrator of his story 'A Day in Coney Island' was to speculate on the nature of God: 'Can he be sex, as the cabbalists hint? Is God an orgasm that never ceases?', but as Bashevis lay in bed he had a dream, a formulaic solution to the mysteries preying on him—death was life, and life was death, life was a scab that grew on old planets, 'the earth suffered from an eczema of its skin'. Then Gina woke him up to announce that she wanted a child by him.

While he couldn't see it himself, being conscious of his ugliness, uncouthness of attire, and general incompetence, Bashevis was a great sexual charmer, and the ancestral voices in his head rarely succeeded in holding him back. Even though, when the affair seems to be ending, they are dying of consumption or about to commit suicide, or even though they vanish wordlessly into thin air, his lady-friends bear him no ill will. On the contrary, they often crop up later on and lend a hand. In this sphere, as in some others, coincidence works to his advantage; but coincidence is not a kosher word.

In the busy midst of an exceptionally vivid love life, the author does at times display the self-righteousness of Joseph Shapiro, as when complaining about the groupies who frequented the Yiddish Writers' Club in Warsaw; professing to love Yiddish literature but making do with Yiddish writers, these girls were known jokingly as 'literary supplements'. Perhaps what he holds against them is less their avidity for 'illicit affairs' than their being fellow-travellers of Communism or Zionism. He himself, as he puts it, stole love, but was always caught in the act. One girl-friend, Lena, was an ex-Stalinist now turned Trotskyite, on the run from the police, and disposed towards lesbianism. She railed at him as a capitalistic lackey 'even as she clamped her lips on to mine', and accused his mystical, supernatural tales of helping to perpetuate Fascism, but nevertheless she too wanted to have a child by him. And she did.

The Yiddish papers in which he published his tales were on the brink of collapse. His novel *Satan in Goray* (1935) first appeared in one such magazine; not only was he not paid for it, he had to contribute towards the cost of printing and paper. A cheque for ninety dollars for a story printed in the American *Jewish Daily Forward*, where his brother Joshua worked as a staff member, came as a life-saver. In great part his themes grew out of the stories he had read of demons and prodigies, or had heard his father telling as a prophylactic against Joshua's infection by logic and science and modernity. A particular attraction was that these topics, though they didn't explain, at least *illustrated*, whereas philosophy did neither. Contemporary Yiddish writing he deemed sentimental or naïve, or else Zionist or radical. In his own stories he remained rooted in the Middle Ages, in folklore, magic, dreams, and fantasies. 'Instead of fighting in my writings the political leaders of a decadent Europe and helping to build a new world, I waged a private war against the Almighty.' That couldn't be done in abstract, theoretical terms. *The Magic Mountain*, which he translated into Yiddish, he considered a long essay spiced with description, something for intellectuals on the lookout for 'a purpose, a sum total', and lacking in suspense and vitality, although he admired *Buddenbrooks* because of its zest for life. Thieves, whores, freaks, charlatans, holy fools, miraculous happenings, the living dead, possession by demons—they really did have to do with life as it is lived. No need for explanations or messages.

The news is always bad, Shapiro maintained, it poisons your life, but men today cannot live without this venom. And Bashevis's father had warned his family that to start the day by reading the newspapers was tantamount to breakfasting on poison. Yet later, in America, Bashevis decided that a writer could learn much from the papers, in particular the so-called yellow press, 'a treasure trove of human idiosyncrasies and quirks', surpassing and mocking the findings of philosophers, sociologists, and psychologists. He has never been concerned with literary style, linguistic innovation, or deliberate originality; his interest lies in the manifold situations thrown up by life, the impossible that occurs every day. He 'must have a story'.

'I denied the existence of Providence, yet I awaited its dictates.'

It dictated in his favour, and in April 1935, having fought off the women with whom he had conducted 'semi-, quarter-, or might-have-been affairs' and who judged the eve of his departure just the time to go the rest of the way, he left for America, on a three-months' visa to visit his brother. Officials wearing swastikas showed no interest in him, and the worst that happened to him was forgetting his cabin number out of Cherbourg and throwing the ship into confusion and himself into near-starvation by insisting on vegetarian meals. In one of his tales a ritual slaughterer who could no longer live with himself is saved from being judged a suicide by the rabbi's ruling that he must have been raving mad.

Although welcomed warmly by the Jewish community—for all its many miracles and pseudo-coincidences Singer's life appears to have been peculiarly wanting in goys—he felt lost in the United States. He itched, he sneezed, his ears rang, he was constipated. He couldn't master the Yiddish typewriter donated by his brother, his pen began to leak, his new novel was going badly. The transition from the Middle Ages into the New World had thrown him; it was as if he had become an absolute beginner all over again, in writing, in love, in his struggle for independence. Things looked up in one department when he took a lover in Nesha, a Russian Jewess and widow of a suicide. 'We fell upon one another with a hunger that astounded us both'; she found her husband's spirit in Bashevis's body, he recognized the dead Gina within Nesha. He might have married her except that it would have seemed—even to him—that he had done so for the sake of acquiring American citizenship.

Instead he left for Toronto to negotiate a permanent visa, taking along Zosia, a devotee of Baudelaire and another refugee from Polish Jewry, whom he proposed to relieve of her unwanted virginity. God, however, disposes. For, as he charmingly puts it, 'our genitals, which in the language of the vulgar are synonyms of stupidity and insensitivity, are actually the expression of the human soul, defiant of lechery, the most ardent defenders of true love.' Or else, another thought that struck him, an anti-sexual dybbuk had taken hold of him.

Love and Exile ends with Bashevis at his most dejected, bereaved of fruitful 'coincidence', and—like Shapiro before he came to accept everything—accepting nothing. People have abandoned him; or, an inveterate non-joiner, he has abandoned them. He has forgotten his brother's telephone number. He yearns for simple devotion and old-fashioned love, but there isn't any of it in the vicinity. At its best, art is no more than a means of forgetting the human disaster for a while. The *Jewish Daily Forward* has stopped printing his column. A cable comes from Lena, stranded in Athens ('What was she doing in Greece?') with his child, asking for money to be sent at once. He has presented creation with an ultimatum: 'Tell me your secret or let me perish.' And it looks as though creation has chosen the second course.

But God hasn't stopped writing *his* column. And the evil spirits are busy, too . . . On the bright side, Bashevis is still in his thirties, practically all his future fiction will be printed in the *Forward*, and further forward a Nobel Prize is waiting.

Signs and Wonders

It helps if you are Jewish, but you don't have to be. Robertson Davies has for long been dealing in mysteries and magic, and always with clarity and—which is essential to any mystery worth its name—a solid, exciting story. However widely his branches spread, he is rooted in material reality, even in the provincial, often Canadian as it happens. Like Borges, he carries coolness and common sense into realms supposedly inimical to or irreconcilable with those qualities, and he sees what is called 'chance' as part of the intricate phenomenon of causality. Coincidence, says a supernatural commentator in his *What's Bred in the Bone*, is 'a useful, dismissive word for people who cannot bear the idea of pattern shaping their own lives'. And the Jungian analyst in *The Manticore*, the second novel in Davies's 'Deptford Trilogy', contends that mythic pattern is common in modern life, but few people still know the myths and fewer can detect the pattern under all the detail. More open, or more metaphorical, less theosophical or credal, than Isaac Bashevis Singer, yet Davies is at one with him in rejecting the word 'coincidence'.

Everything, things done or left undone, means something; what reveals itself in the flesh is what has been bred in the bone. This is nothing so simple as the doctrine of predestination, for a fair share is left to 'free will', the great gift of choice prized by Singer. The same card may be dealt out to various people, but how they play it or fail to play it depends on their individual attributes. A delicate balance of forces obtains, perceptible in its effects but barely analysable. Towards the end of *World of Wonders*, the third part of the trilogy, an authoritative character says this:

God wants to intervene in the world, and how is he to do it except through man? I think the Devil is in the same predicament. . . . It's the moment of decision—of will—when those Two nab us, and as they both speak so compellingly it's tricky work to know who's talking. Where there's a will, there are always two ways.

During *What's Bred in the Bone* we overhear at intervals a conversation between the 'Angel of Biography', a member of the Recording Angel's staff, known as the Lesser Zadkiel, and Maimas, the personal daemon of the central character, Francis Cornish. The Lesser Zadkiel is a compassionate soul and even, someone says, an angel of mercy, 'though a lot of biographers aren't',* whereas the Daemon Maimas states that as a tutelary spirit it is not his job to coddle softies; he is 'the grinder, the shaper, the refiner'. In one of their brief, pithy chats, and with the young Francis in mind, the milder angel deplores the breaking of hearts, but Maimas insists that what matters is to break the heart in such a way that when it mends it will be stronger than before. His job is to nudge Francis in the direction of the destiny he may have: he's not a guardian angel (sniff!) but a daemon, and his work is bound to seem rough at times. Like the Lesser Zadkiel, Maimas is a metaphor, he remarks towards the end of the book, a metaphor in the service of the greater metaphors that have shaped Francis's life: 'Saturn, the resolute, and Mercury, the maker, the humorist, the trickster'. His task was to see that these, the Great Ones, 'were bred in the bone, and came out in the flesh'.

But this makes the novel sound more, or more explicitly and exigently, philosophical or theological than it is. The author is that rare bird, an intellectual entertainer, and the story he tells is tightly organized, never drifting into inconsequence, its literal narrative and its figurative signals constantly in step, as with the best poetry. Or, a more germane parallel, the best painting.

The plot is complex, packed with incident and 'coincidence'; to attempt to summarize it would be foolish. 'I also was what was bred in his bone, right from the instant of his conception,' says the Daemon Maimas. And since nature and nurture are inextricable —'only scientists and psychologists could think otherwise,' the Lesser Zadkiel mocks, 'and we know all about them, don't we?'— the reader follows Francis's life from his birth into a wealthy, patrician Canadian family, through schools and Oxford, his training as a restorer (and rather more) of old paintings, a shadowy career in the British secret service (not much myth left

* A sentiment prefigured in *The Rebel Angels*, with which this novel is lightly linked: 'We're not hyenas or biographers, to pee on the dead.'

in the Great Game by now!), an unfortunate marriage and a
happy though short-lived love-affair, up to the moment of his
death. If death is the right word: 'Where was this? Unknown, yet
familiar, more the true abode of his spirit than he had ever known
before; a place never visited, but from which intimations had
come that were the most precious gifts of his life.' Perhaps the
strange words of the angel in that *Marriage at Cana*, a painting by
some Old Master (actually a creation of Francis's, undetected by
the experts), were true. 'Thou hast kept the best wine till the last.'

Whoever is concerned with the ineffable must be liberal in
adducing the effable, and firm and exact in portraying it. The
way to the infinite, Goethe instructed, is by following the finite in
as many directions as you possibly can. No excursion into mystery
will be more than merely mystifying in the absence of clarity and
cleanness of expression, and the authority they confer. In turn,
these qualities rest on knowledge, simple knowledge it may be,
but sound knowledge. In *Fifth Business*, the first volume of the
'Deptford Trilogy', there is much out-of-the-way (but material)
history and hagiology, along with technical insights into stage
magic and illusionism; in *The Manticore*, a sound grasp of
Jungian theory and more than a passing acquaintance with
the workings of the law; in *World of Wonders*, an informed
and colourful chronicle of a travelling carnival, its freaks, con-
tortionists, conjurors, its hypnotist, knife-thrower, sword-
swallower, its Card-Playing Automaton.

We have educated ourselves into a world from which wonder, and the
fear and dread and splendour and freedom of wonder, have been banished. Of course wonder is costly. You couldn't incorporate it into a
modern state, because it is the antithesis of the anxiously worshipped
security which is what a modern state is asked to give. Wonder is marvellous but it is also cruel, cruel, cruel. It is undemocratic, discriminatory,
and pitiless.

Merged with minor triumphs like the counterpointing of
Catholics and Protestants in the Ottawa Valley town of Blairlogie,
the dominant feature in *What's Bred in the Bone* is art, and the
underworld of art, conjured up with what one would term expertise
were it not that the experts make a sorry showing here. Francis is
able to prove that a *Harrowing of Hell* purportedly executed by

Hubertus van Eyck is a later forgery: the monkey hanging by its tail from the bars of hell is not the traditional *Macacus rhesus* but a *Cebus capucinus* from the New World, and monkeys with prehensile tails were unknown in Europe in van Eyck's day. If 'chance' had led Francis to the local zoo on the afternoon before the experts met in The Hague to sit in judgement, it was still his innate perceptiveness that made the connection.

Francis's early training consisted in drawing the corpses at the Blairlogie undertaker's establishment, which doubled as the local bootlegger's. Later he apprentices himself to the brilliant and shady Italian, Tancred Saraceni, a master restorer of old paintings, who is keeping the Renaissance 'in repair'. The two work in Germany, tarting up boring old canvases on Germanic themes, which are then sent to a London wine merchant, and subsequently acquired by high-ranking Nazis, patriotic connoisseurs, for the proposed national collection—in exchange for Italian and other non-German works of far greater artistic value. When war breaks out, Francis's role in MI5, besides vaguely investigating questionable refugees, is to track the movements of looted works of art. Two of his own unsigned paintings will turn up in Goering's private collection.

A keen cinema-goer in his youth, Francis didn't care for Charlie Chaplin: 'he was a loser.' And Saraceni, like other unworldly figures in the novel, has a sharp eye for money; prudently he keeps it in numbered accounts in Switzerland. Once he had a wife, an Englishwoman, but she found his Roman apartment impossible to live in, cluttered with objects of art, and told him he must choose. 'My dearest one, the collection is timeless and you, alas that it should be so, are trapped in time.' She laughed, and removed to Florence, where she married again, more comfortably.

Saraceni becomes Francis's earthly daemon, or in homelier terms his guide, instructor in forgery (passages here amount to an art forger's handbook), and scurrilous oracle. The Daemon Maimas comments that a great man like Saraceni is necessarily rich in spiritual energy and not all the energy finds a benevolent outlet; an expert who has just crossed swords with him falls downstairs and breaks a hip. Though far less sinister, in his manner he recalls Leverkühn's visitant; Francis observes that when he is in Saraceni's presence, and particularly when the Italian is holding forth on art's heedlessness of conventional morality, he feels like Faust listening to Mephistopheles:

The Kingdom of Christ, if it ever comes, will contain no art; Christ never showed the least concern with it. His church has inspired much but not because of anything the Master said. Who then was the inspirer? The much-maligned Devil, one supposes. It is he who understands and ministers to man's carnal and intellectual self, and art is carnal and intellectual.

Saraceni's views on modern art are shared by Francis, and by the author too, one surmises, for they point up the novel's 'tendency'. In earlier times the inner vision which is the business of all honest painters presented itself in a coherent language, the language of mythology or religion, but now both of these have lost their power to move the mind. And so

the artist solicits and implores something from the realm of what the psychoanalysts, who are the great magicians of our day, call the Unconscious, though it is actually the Most Conscious. And what they fish up—what the Unconscious hangs on the end of the hook the artists drop into the great well in which art has its being—may be very fine, but they express it in a language more or less private. It is not the language of mythology or religion. And the great danger is that such private language is perilously easy to fake. Much easier to fake than the well-understood language of the past.

Like Mann's, like Henry James's, Robertson Davies's people are both dismayingly and inspiringly intelligent; we may feel humble before them, but we don't resent them. It helps that they 'embrace the gamut between eschatology and scatology'—an attribute of the best fiction, Anthony Burgess opined in his review of *The Rebel Angels*. They have no need of streams of consciousness or other latter-day devices to impress their high seriousness upon the reader, or to make up for a poverty of story. Where the Unconscious is concerned, and other mysteries factitious or genuine, they are able to be perfectly and unselfconsciously conscious. Their author offers both pleasure and instruction. And of course that extra dimension in which the Anglo-Saxon arts have been deficient of late.

More than Mere Biology

On its title-page Josef Skvorecky's novel, *The Engineer of Human Souls*, describes itself as 'an entertainment on the old themes of life, women, fate, dreams, the working class, secret agents, love and death'. All that in slightly under 600 pages. In the event we witness a miracle of narrowly achieved organization, helped out by the gusto Skvorecky communicates and the reader's reluctance to lose his way for longer than a paragraph or two.

Like the author, the narrator is a Czech writer who emigrated in 1968 and is currently a professor of English in Toronto: at Edenvale College in his case, at Erindale College in the case of the author. His books are published by a small *émigré* press in Toronto, while the author's books, in their original language, are published by an *émigré* press run by Professor and Mrs Skvorecky. Danny Smiricky, the fictitious professor, specializes in American writers (plus Conrad), and the novel's scaffolding comes from the texts he is teaching. A modern story hangs by every ancient tale: in *Heart of Darkness* Kurtz prefigures Stalin, in Poe the Raven's 'Nevermore' applies to more lost things than one, and Lovecraft (H.P.), similarly of broad application, requires no gloss.

First of all, then, an entertainment, almost to excess, in humour ranging from slapstick to high wit, and in humankind from the utterly wicked to the virtually saintly. The novel also comprises a history of Czechoslovakia from the Nazi occupation through the subsequent sovietization with its various phases. And it also amounts to a Bible of exile. In each respect it accomplishes this by means not of generalizations but of particularities, as promised in an epigraph from Blake and confirmed towards the end by a line of Czech poetry: 'the poet's fleeting heart beats strongest in small stories.' Sir Philip Sidney's preference was similar: the poet 'coupleth the general notion with the particular example'.

In his youth Danny Smiricky embarks on a hero's career by sabotaging the Messerschmitt ammunition drums he is obliged to work on; in large part he is moved by desire for the girl Nadia, whose father has been killed by the Germans. His efforts are worse than futile, and his mates have to work overtime to restore the botched parts since they would never pass testing and because more important activities on another front would be jeopardized. In this, to Danny's astonishment, they are aided by the Oberkontrolleur, a former member of the German-American Bund who 'came home' in error. At the end of the war he is disposed of before Danny can testify on his behalf. Danny is soon cured of his taste for heroism, which can cost innocent lives, and at one stage thinks of entering a seminary in the hope of avoiding the gallows.

Other small stories crowd the generally hilarious account of the Czech community in Toronto. The exile's fate is a complex one, but Danny himself is happy enough. Although the Communist Party exists in Canada, it has no power 'as yet'; there is nothing to fear in the literary line since he writes in Czech and the professional critics leave him alone, indeed he goes unreviewed apart from occasional idle flatteries in the *émigré* press, 'sandwiched between harvest home announcements and ads for Bohemian tripe soup'. Moreover he is tolerant by nature, more amused than shocked by his students' ineptitudes—'This novel is a novel. It is a great work, for it is written in the form of a book'—and likewise Canada's 'blessed ignorance'. This ignorance or innocence infuriates many of the *émigrés*: the feather-bedded rebels, the easy contempt for democracy (the grass is never very green on one's own side of the fence), the sight of male prostitutes skipping about in the streets: 'They deserve a dose of Bolshevism!' And how galling that Leni Riefenstahl's *Triumph of the Will* should suddenly erupt into fame and fashion as the first art film entirely made by a woman and hence of central significance to Women's Studies! Danny admits to himself that 'the real religion of life, the true idolatry of literature' cannot flourish in democracies, 'those vague, boring kingdoms of the freedom not to read, not to suffer, not to desire, not to know, not to understand'. (Milan Kundera has commented, with pardonable exaggeration, that 'if all the reviews in France or England disappeared, no one would notice it, not even their editors'.) But one should take the smooth with the rough, and he notes that there is some progress—women's bottoms are now a third of the size they were in his parents' time.

Émigrés of an older generation wrangle over whether they should describe the projected National Liberation Army as *Incorporated* or *and Co.* or *Limited*: 'Of course it always makes a better impression in business circles if your company's incorporated.' One tenacious character plans to set up a radio transmitter in Ethiopia and by this means exhort the citizens of Czechoslovakia to buy ten boxes of matches each and break them to form a Churchillian V for Victory, an exercise that will both ruin the five-year plan and demoralize the Party bosses. In a version of art for art's sake, the State Security Police go on spying after all reason has long disappeared, and agents, professional or amateur, turn up in Canada with alleged messages from old friends and colleagues. One way of unmasking them is to get them drunk and enquire after certain supposedly well-known personalities who don't actually exist: they are bound to know them intimately.

Not all is sweetness and light—or drinking and love-making—in the Czech community; some of its members are sick of home, some sick for home, and some both. One of them denounces another to the Czechoslovak Association of Canada as a former Party member while someone else is rumoured to be a Fascist. Yet in these generations of immigrants, one layer set on another, Danny sees a close humanity: 'Pauperized, re-established, industrious, hungry for money, sentimental, hungry for freedom, limited, intellectual, mean, merciful. All kinds. Indestructible.' Veronika, the second-finest character in the book, wants Prague and freedom but knows she can't have both. She chooses Prague, and the last we hear of her is a cable to Danny: 'IM A FOOL STOP VERONIKA'. She would have done better—could she have brought herself—to marry the playboy admirer who has a vague idea that *Nineteen Eighty-Four* was a satire on America, probably on McCarthyism. Milan, unable to settle down in Toronto, buys a ticket home, sees a smiling 'comrade' at the embarkation gate, and turns tail—returning white-faced in time for the later stages of his own farewell party. As for Danny, he will—in Veronika's admonitory word—stop; he can return to his native Kostelec as easily in Canada, 'in the safety of a decadently anti-police democracy', as in Prague. He carries his homeland in his heart, just as it is carried within this novel.

The narrative shifts back and forth in time and place, and at one point, in the course of a few lines of print, we dart from present-day Canada to Danny's father's leg and how it was shattered at Zborov during the First World War and he died when it was amputated fifty years later, and then to 1948, when he was led off to prison by a Comrade Pytlik, exactly as the Gestapo had led him off five years earlier. The alternating of Danny's Czech past with Professor Smiricky's Canadian present has its purpose—everything is happening here and now—and the cost in extra attentiveness is not too high to be borne. We cannot expect hard living to make easy reading. That 'abominations tend to repeat themselves in variations that are embarrassingly similar' is a thought arising during an academic seminar, but its pertinence is far from academic. We hear how Nadia saved Danny and herself from having to sign a mass petition condemning the assassination of Reichsprotektor Heydrich: she fainted and he carried her off to the first-aid room. One of Danny's correspondents reports, ten years later, that during the signing of a petition denouncing a traitorous gang of Titoist-Zionist-revisionists a young woman faints and is helped to the first-aid room by a member of the Union of Youth.

Jazz, loved by both narrator and author, gives offence equally to Nazis and Communists, as demonstrated in Skvorecky's novella, *The Bass Saxophone*. There, a band got away with playing 'Tiger Rag' under the Third Reich by calling it 'The Wild Bull'; here, the number appears in the programme as 'Red Flag'. Danny's earnest friend Jan, who strives to reconcile literature with the demands of socialism and is eventually found hanged, mentions a picture in an exhibition of Soviet art called 'The Defence of Sevastopol'; it shows a handful of idealized Russian soldiers resisting a horde of villainous Germans. He remembers that he has already seen a specimen of Nazi art in which a scattering of noble German soldiers were dispatching a mob of degenerate Russians; the title was 'The Conquest of Sevastopol'. *Plus c'est la même chose* is heaped on *plus ça change*, and the last instance, at least, may be thought both banal and inartistically neat: embarrassing, you could say. Yet banality and inartistic neatness (and untidiness) are part and parcel of the story. Such exempla contribute to the dense texture of the novel, and it is hard to say what we would really rather be without.

Personally I could dispense with some of the lavatory scenes and smells—including an absurd and protracted episode in which a smuggled manuscript is surreptitiously handed over in a Toronto comfort station—and the tall horror-stories with which a youth regales the Messerschmitt workers. Švejkian, all too Švejkian! And in addition much of the what-abouting that passes between native Canadian intellectuals and Czech *émigrés*: what about Angela Davis? What about the Rosenbergs? What about Sacco and Vanzetti? Once democracy insists that people must be free to express opinions, then express opinions they will.

Skvorecky's novel rivals *The Good Soldier Švejk*, another sprawling canvas, in scatology but easily outdoes it in sexual zest. His slogan, one thinks at times, could well be Sex Conquers All—or comes nearer to doing so even than jazz. (In George Konrád's novel, *The Loser*, a narrower Hungarian Calvary, the narrator jokes with Imre Nagy: 'You will admit that a good fuck is worth more than ten revolutions'—while the one may lead to an unwanted pregnancy, the other is bound to end in rows of coffins.) But love is here as well: in the refusal to despair, characteristic too of Milosz's poetry of Poland and its memories of good things as well as of bad, and specifically in the figure of Nadia, the book's finest character, truest love of the great lover Danny, the factory girl who died young of tuberculosis.

How she would lick her lips with her unfussy little tongue, how she was simple as a clarinet counterpoint in a village band and yet full of surprises . . . how she had displayed the wisdom of a beautiful mayfly who is crushed under foot before she can fulfil the one meaning her life has. But no. Nadia's life had a different meaning. It was more than mere biology.

'Every serious novel is *à thèse*,' the Professor tells his distrustful students. 'But the thesis is always the same, except in novels *à thèse*.' And the thesis is: *Homo sum; humani nil a me alienum puto*. All the same, some things strike us as more alien than others. We may doubt that Goethe was wholly sincere when he said, of his *Wilhelm Meister*, that a rich manifold life brought close to our eyes ought to be sufficient without any express tendency. Granted, it is the sort of challenge a writer does well to toss at the feet of the thesis-hunter. And decent writers will veer away from roles laid down for them; as, for example, prescribed by Stalin: to build, like some engineer, the soul of the New Man. However, one way of suggesting an implication, if not a thesis, is to invoke another literary work whose tendency is itself not so very express. *The Engineer of Human Souls* brings to mind an authorial intervention in *Middlemarch*: 'There is no general doctrine which is not capable of eating out our morality if unchecked by the deep-seated habit of direct fellow-feeling with individual fellow men.' What better check on general doctrine can there be than the poet's and the novelist's 'small stories', told with verve and generosity?

'A Bad Man, my Dears':
Heine in English

As Jeffrey L. Sammons has indicated in his judicious 'modern biography' of 1979, Heine's critics and biographers have re-created their subject in the image of their own tastes or (he has latterly become a hot political property) their doctrines; in this they have been encouraged by Heine's protean self-projection or production. The phenomenon, not so very rare, isn't necessarily the sign of a difficult, sophisticated, or recondite author. When Sammons judges that Heine is 'a complex but not really a profound writer', he is conveying a truth about him, though we might want to substitute 'obscure' for 'profound'. He can always be understood, with reasonable immediacy, though this isn't to deny that we are grateful for the notes Hal Draper appends to *The Complete Poems of Heinrich Heine: A Modern English Version*, for Heine was a great namer of names and instancer of instances. What is truly hard to come to terms with is the overall paradoxicality, the unnerving juxtaposition of opposed and seemingly incompatible attitudes and feelings, and the unheralded switching from one to another.

Heine habitually introduces himself as a man of sorrows and acquainted with little but grief ('For me the world has been a torture cell'); and the next moment he is thumbing his nose at the respectful reader: 'Usually you're not such a donkey, / Dearest friend, in such affairs!' Or more often at somebody or something else; after what sounds like a stirring night spent on the Drachenfels, scene of Siegfried's slaying of the dragon, 'What I brought back with me was a cough and cold', while in a poem about the Devil as a professional diplomat we come across the lines

> He's somewhat pale—no wonder, I vow,
> For he's studying Sanskrit and Hegel now . . .
> He'll put reviewing on the shelf
> And do that job no more himself.

The only English poet he can be likened to is Byron: all those ready and often rough rhymes, the gentlemanly casualness attending a blow to the solar plexus, or lower down . . . In which case, we must agree, Heine is a proletarian model of that lord, or (to avoid an adjective which would arouse his wrath) a much less lordly one. And more intelligent, in that you couldn't say of him, as Goethe said of Byron, that as soon as he reflects, he is a child. Heine is at his best when he sobers up and reflects; to do this, it appears, he needed strong draughts of fairly violent excitement in advance.

Hal Draper has a shrewd passage in his foreword on the subject of Heine as 'freedom fighter' and in relation to Marx: 'He was against oppression because he thought the people should have *good* masters, the benevolent type. He preferred that society be controlled by bankers he could scorn than by a democratic mass movement he would fear.' The sight of complacent burghers made a crusading socialist of him; when he considered the grey masses at his back he turned into an intellectual élitist. (Which he more whole-heartedly was.) 'We are all brothers, but I am the big brother, and you are the little brothers, and I am entitled to a more substantial portion.' In a similar spirit, although baptized a Christian, he could summon up his Jewishness when it provided extra momentum in attacking Christian hypocrites. Some have seen this as itself hypocritical, as opportunism, egotism, play-acting; to me it seems part of a free-ranging individual's survival kit.

Varying Heine's own self-description, Matthew Arnold termed him 'if not pre-eminently a brave, yet a brilliant, a most effective soldier in the war of liberation of humanity'. One may wonder why 'brave' has yielded to 'brilliant', that suspect epithet; surely not because Heine failed to get himself killed on active service (the Continent was a more dangerous place for intellectuals than England, then as later), or because he conducted himself with prudent obliqueness. That was clearly not the case, nor would Arnold have thought along those lines. To be brave in Arnold's sense it was necessary to be less intemperately susceptible (to offence, to female charms), less 'unscrupulous in passion' (whatever the passion), less given to 'incessant mocking'—and to possess a larger or less adulterated share of 'self-respect', of 'true dignity of character', 'moral balance', and 'nobleness of soul and character'. Rather more explicitly, and more lightly, George Eliot spoke of Heine's great powers serving to give 'electric force to the expression of debased feeling', and recommended the use of a 'friendly penknife' before handing his works to immature minds. *

After that summary of what Arnold saw as Heine's 'crying faults', it is necessary to remind ourselves that he considered him the chief successor to Goethe. All the same, when he pronounced Heine 'profoundly *dis*respectable' he was not simply getting in a dig at Carlyle for overlooking Heine in favour of the romantic school. He meant it as a distinct reproach; for him, as he makes plain, 'respectable' was too valuable a word to subvert through ironic usage. But his views on the subject were remote from the feelings of Charles Kingsley; according to the story, when Kingsley was asked by his children who Heine was, he replied: 'A bad man, my dears, a bad man.'† In fact '*dis*respectable' is a fair description of Heine, and one to bear in mind when forging through Draper's bumper volume, sometimes suppressing and sometimes admitting its pejorative connotations.

Heine delighted in rhythms—and in jingles—and in playing with them, often disconcertingly, in a variety of poetic forms. His translator has to be correspondingly nimble and versatile, coping with ballad, folk-song, narrative, the tremulously yearning, the heroic-rhetorical, the *Hiawatha*-stutter, and the low-life (verging on doggerel, yet scanning and rhyming nattily no matter

---

* 'German Wit', *Westminster Review*, January 1856. In this article, published a month before Heine's death, and seven and a half years before Arnold's essay, George Eliot is highly amusing on the topic of German humour and finely perceptive about Heine's prose: in his hands 'German prose, usually so heavy, so clumsy, so dull, becomes, like clay in the hands of the chemist, compact, metallic, brilliant; it is German in an *allotropic* condition.'

† And he wouldn't have known this poem, uncollected until the *Sämtliche Schriften* of 1968–76:

> Last night, in a dream—too bad, too bad!—
> I enjoyed the dirtiest girl yet seen:
> Yet for the same price I could have had
> The loveliest princess or fairest queen.

Most un-Goethean? No; see Goethe's 'un-Goethean' *Venezianische Epigramme*. One difference is that Goethe hived off his naughtinesses.

what the diction is up to). Other problems stem from Heine's application of solemn or pensive-promising metres to light-hearted or deflationary material, as when a poem evokes the springtime sun, flowerets, moon and stars, and 'two beautiful eyes', and terminates thus:

> Wie sehr das Zeug auch gefällt,
> So macht's doch noch lang keine Welt,

which Draper translates:

> No matter how much you like such stuff,
> To make a world they're just not enough;

or as in a three-stanza poem which begins in trite distress—'once you were mine only/In body and in soul'—and modulates into this:

> I still want your body, the merry
> Tender young body I know;
> Your soul you can go and bury—
> I've soul enough for two.

Such sudden reversals of tone or—when generalized meditation shifts into specific abuse or debunking—of matter are found cheek by jowl with the dark-side 'romantic' paraphernalia of faithless loves, belles dames sans merci, funeral bells, hauntings, wounded knights, howling winds, the Devil, and (more often than not figurative) prison cells.

In the opening poem of the early sequence, The Homecoming, Draper rhymes more royally than his original, which has one pure rhyme and one approximate (e.g. Dunkeln/bannen) in each stanza:

> In my life so dark and jaded,
> Once a vision glistened bright.
> Now the vision's dim and faded—
> Once again I'm wrapped in night.

> In the dark a child, dissembling
> While the fearsome phantoms throng,
> Tries to cover up his trembling
> With a shrill and noisy song.

> I, a frantic child, am straining
> At my song in darkness here.
> What if the song's not entertaining?
> Still it's freed me of my fear.

This involves a slight misrepresentation in that the 'I' is 'straining' instead of simply singing, and Draper makes the song 'not entertaining' rather than not delightful. But one wouldn't quarrel with this latter shade of difference: 'entertaining' (less private in suggestion) carries us on from the child singing to keep up its spirits to the poet singing to entertain—perhaps—other people.

Alas, the following poem—and one so famous—collapses at the very outset:

> I do not know what it means that
> I am so sadly inclined;
> There is an old tale and its scenes that
> Will not depart from my mind.

The original sings itself:

> *Ich weiss nicht, was soll es bedeuten,*
> *Dass ich so traurig bin;*
> *Ein Märchen aus alten Zeiten,*
> *Das kommt mir nicht aus dem Sinn.*

Draper follows the rhythm closely, except for the second line, and 'means that'/'scenes that' is a purer rhyme than *bedeuten/Zeiten*, but the loss of the end-stopping and the inapt stress given (twice) to 'that' turn a sweetly grave lyric into something approaching a pop song. The translation rises from the dust in its final verse:

> I think, at last the wave swallows
> The boat and the boatman's cry;
> And this is the fate that follows
> The song of the Lorelei.

The third line, submitting (with fairly good grace) to rhyme's importunity, sounds like a warning against harmful practices, yet the second line has a nice synecdochic variation on the original's boatman and boat, and Draper too contrives to leave the naming of the fatal siren until the very last.

In Heine, as in Goethe, the 'pure' lyric, with its bare, fragile but precise simplicity, has generally proved impossible to carry over into another language. A notable exception here is the third poem in the group entitled *In der Fremde* ('Abroad'):

> Oh, once I had a lovely fatherland.
>   The oaks grew tall
> Up to the sky, the gentle violets swayed.
>   I dreamt it all.
>
> I felt a German kiss, heard German words
>   (Hard to recall
> How good they rang)—the words *Ich liebe dich!*
>   I dreamt it all.

Draper's departures are minimal: the initial 'Oh'; the harmless 'grew tall up to the sky', compensating for the discrepancy in length between *Eichenbaum* and 'oak', instead of the undecorated 'grew so high'; and, to preserve the essential rhyme, 'Hard to recall' for the literal 'One can hardly believe'.

Heine's translators are faced by an extra problem, one not encountered in Goethe outside the squibs and parts of *Faust*. The poet is frequently slapdash and (to put it mildly) over-hearty. We may not altogether admire such behaviour in him—*dis*-respectable indeed!—but we know that it is wholly deliberate, whereas when we are reading a translation we may well ascribe such effects to the translator's inadequate resourcefulness in the face of formal exigencies. The expression 'dizzy dame' affects us as just *too* American, or stage-American, for *tolle Dirne* (not that 'whimsical wench' would sound much better); in fact the immediate context goes far to condone it, but it still looks odd in the vicinity of so many a 'lo' and 'ere' and (which isn't quite the same as *Und sieh!*) 'Behold!' Vulgarity, sincere vulgarity, is the most difficult of styles to carry convincingly into another tongue; or the next trickiest after simple sincerity.

Similarly, in translation self-caricature can easily emerge as evidence of near-imbecility, unless the reader is already fairly intimate with the poet. An instance of this form of parody—and also of the poet's mixed mode—is the poem from *Lyrisches Intermezzo* which begins:

> *Ich steh' auf des Berges Spitze,*
> *Und werde sentimental.*
> *'Wenn ich ein Vöglein wäre!'*
> *Seufz' ich viel tausendmal.*

177

> I stand on the mountain summit
> And sentimentalize.
> 'If I were a birdie, dearest!'
> I say with a thousand sighs.

Draper renders this virtually word for word, except that 'senti-mentalize' tips us off rather more forcibly than does the German expression. The second and third verses appear wholly conventional and well-meaning, untouched by irony: 'If I were a swallow', 'If I were a nightingale' . . . The final verse, however, runs:

> *Wenn ich ein Gimpel wäre,*
> *So flög' ich gleich an dein Herz;*
> *Du bist ja hold den Gimpeln,*
> *Und heilest Gimpelschmerz.*

> If I were a boobybird, dearest,
> I'd fly to you straight as a dart;
> You're partial to boobies and able
> To heal a booby-heart.

The traditional accessories, swallow and nightingale, have slumped into boobybird. The original *Gimpel* is a bullfinch, but the word also means 'ninny'; Draper's boobybird—albeit a marine species not, as far as I know, notable for stupidity—speaks for itself, and the designation takes on a further felicitousness if we think of the probable derivation from *balbus*, stammering.

Here Draper has scored a triumph, improving on Heine. It is all the stranger, then, that in his dealings with another poem in this collection—

> *Aus meinen grossen Schmerzen*
> *Mach' ich die kleinen Lieder;*
> *Die heben ihr klingend Gefieder*
> *Und flattern nach ihrem Herzen . . .* —

he should rest content with a sad travesty of those famous lines.

> Out of my great unrest
> I make little songs and things;
> They lift their tinkling wings
> And flutter off to her breast.

The more tolerant may allow 'unrest' to pass for *Schmerzen*, and accept that Heine's songs do sometimes tinkle—but 'songs and things'! What sort of things? Just things that happen to rhyme with other things.

Yet Draper displays considerable brio in such darker items as 'The Silesian Weavers', a poem which was banned in Germany and led Engels to claim that 'the most eminent of all living German poets has joined our ranks':

> A curse on this false fatherland, teeming
> With nothing but shame and dirty scheming,
> Where every flower is crushed in a day,
> Where worms are regaled on rot and decay—
>   We're weaving, we're weaving!
>
> The shuttle flies, the loom creaks loud,
> Night and day we weave your shroud—
> Old Germany, at your shroud we sit,
> We're weaving a threefold curse in it,
>   We're weaving, we're weaving!

And in general he copes pretty well with Heine's rather fearful fluency, or facility of imagination, in those many lyrics that promise to tell a story and then tail off into banality or vague longings and regrets—though not without offering fine incidentals, like this, from 'The Shepherd Boy' in *Die Harzreise*, done into English faithfully and well:

> At his feet the sheep are lying,
> Fleecy flatterers, prinked with red;
> Calves are cavaliers, and pertly
> Strut about with legs outspread.

Draper cannot be held responsible for the poet's glib or reiterative cynicism, neatly replicated in

> Friendship, love, philosophers' stones—
> These are praised in reverent tones;
> These I praised and sought to get—
> Ah, but I've never found them yet,

or for his crude self-dramatization (a posturing which later was transmuted into something more authentic and moving), his zestful but hammered-in moralizing on the degeneracy of the age, or the sitting ducks he scuppers. Or his gratuitous outbursts, as when chiding some harmless woman for possessing a tepid soul (unlike his adventurous one) and wanting to lead a life

> Hanging on your husband—cosy,
> Just a proper pregnant wife.

Pregnancy—rather common among wives at that time—was one of the trials that, though he suffered many, Heine didn't have to endure.

From 1848 till his death eight years later, Heine was paralysed by a disease of the spinal cord. Written from his 'mattress-grave', the *Lazarus* poems and those in the supplementary group, *Zum Lazarus*, are sardonic yet spirited, bitter but humorous, and even affectionate, less evidently personal than the mass of his verse and yet more deeply so, originating in 'self' but invulnerable to Arnold's charge of insufficient self-respect and dignity of character. They are relatively modern in sensibility, closer to current poetic preferences and practice, and have been reproduced in English quite brilliantly by Alistair Elliot. More relaxed, more idiomatic, Elliot generally has the edge over Draper, but the *Lazarus* poems are a fraction of Heine's output. Far harder to make readable, though Draper does his swashbuckling best, are the two early verse tragedies. The production of a tragedy, George Eliot remarked in this connection, is the 'chicken-pox of authorship'. *Almansor* is an exercise in the Spanish/Arab exotic, and *William Ratcliff* an attempt at Scottish Gothic. Both are largely claptrap, while both display the sudden trenchancies typical of their author. 'Here within my breast I bear my turban,' declaims Almansor, a Moor disguised as a Spaniard, to which the faithful old Hassan ritually replies, 'All praise to Allah! Allah's will be praised!' But when Almansor reports the burning of the Koran by the Inquisition, Hassan speaks the celebrated, reverberating words: 'Where men burn books, they will burn people too in the end.'

Other stumbling-blocks for the modern reader are the mock epics, *Atta Troll: A Midsummer Night's Dream* and *Germany: A Winter's Tale*, long, ambitious works, over-long and ambitious to cram rather too much in. Heine, one inclines to feel ruefully, was more a force of nature than a force of art. For the well-disposed reader the famous 'problem' settles into the simple and sheer difficulty of distinguishing with much assurance between verbosity and vivacity. Both these works, I suspect, are more significant as documents in the 'case' of Heine than as poetry. In *Atta Troll* the radical poets are satirized in the figure of a clumsy, sententious bear,

> Atta Troll: bear with a cause.
> Moral, pious. Ardent husband.
> Led astray by our Zeitgeist,
> Primitive sansculotte of the forest.
>
> Dancing: bad. But strong opinions
> Borne within his shaggy bosom.
> Sometimes also stinking strongly.
> Talent, none; but character, yes!

Elsewhere Heine averred that artists who busy themselves with the great idea of freedom are themselves customarily unfree in spirit.

In *Germany*, another banned work, which George Eliot found 'exquisitely humorous', the main thrust of the satire is directed against German feudalism and nationalism and the absolutist state, with Heine present in person ('My head is a twittering nest of books /Good enough to be confiscated') as a radical or at any rate forthright poet, advising the Prussian King: 'Offend the gods both old and new/ . . . But the poets—don't offend them!'

> A little girl was playing the harp
> and singing with genuine feeling
> and out of tune, but still the song
> she sang was most appealing.
>
> She sang of love and sacrifice,
> of pain and a tomorrow
> when all shall meet in a better world
> beyond this vale of sorrow . . .
>
> I know the tune, I know the words,
> I know every single author;
> I know they tippled wine on the quiet
> while publicly preaching water.
>
> A different song, a better song,
> will get the subject straighter:
> let's make a heaven on earth, my friends,
> instead of waiting till later.*

---

* These four stanzas are taken from a more recent and splendidly rollicking translation by T. J. Reed: *Deutschland*, 1986.

In the end, from the beginning, the party Heine belonged to was a 'party of one'.

To sum up, Draper handles satire, polemic, and abuse proficiently, at times with an ingenuity approaching genius, but is (understandably) less at ease with the elegance and the plangency of Heine at his more delicate and lyrical. This generous volume is the outcome of some thirty years' labour; it is not as perfect as it is courageous, but then, it is breath-takingly courageous.

'My Muse, Mnemosyne'

Unity in a book is a comforting thing: we know where we are, whether or not we like where we find ourselves. In Czeslaw Milosz's *The Separate Notebooks*, made up of verse and prose written at various times between 1940 and 1980, the contents hang together precariously, but precariousness, the equal poise of some fell war, is the condition of the book. The author himself proves to stand more firmly than one could possibly have expected.

'Where is the truth of unremembered things?' The star called Wormwood has fallen, a third part of the rivers has become wormwood, and many have died of the bitter waters. Rather than crying 'Woe, woe, woe' like the angel, the Polish poet follows with acts of piety, an offering of memories, utterly unsentimental,

> stench, shit frozen into clods.
> And those centuries
> conceiving in the herring smell of the middle of the night,

scenes from childhood, memories of ways of life, of ousted customs, of objects and incidents and persons, a pearl button on a glove, the burning of Giordano Bruno, a death in Auschwitz, someone lighting a pine chip soaked in resin, apples rolling across tables, the round bottom of a passing girl, a bird 'propped on your grey lizard legs, on cybernetic gloves'. And evocations of

> Ladies of 1920 who served us cocoa.
> Grow strong for the glory of Poland, our little knights, our
>   eagles! . . .
> Ladies from the Polish Circle, ladies from the Auxiliary Corps,

of Aunt Florentyna, Lithuanian-born like Milosz, who, being a good Catholic and a landowner, had to accept a 'tacit change' in her habits, and of an anonymous woman in an undatable gown: 'By whom is she to be seen / If she is deprived even of her name?'

The narrator wonders at his 'reluctance to indulge in fiction, as if I believed that one could faithfully reconstruct what once was'. All those phenomena were prefaces, he had thought, temporary things, but no, they were prefaces to other prefaces, other temporary things. Wormwood has fallen, 'bitter rivers flowed', and 'no sign of divine care shone in the heavens'; the recollections and evocations are sometimes attended by icy comments from 'the Powers above the Earth', who know of human pain but feel no compassion: 'Why should we care about living and dying?' The creatures who 'traced their origin to the dinosaur / And took their deftness from the lemur's paw' are those who

> tied the hands of man with barbed wire.
> And dug shallow graves at the edge of the wood.
> There would be no truth in his last testament.
> They wanted him anonymous for good.

In 'Magpiety', a light-hearted piece in his *Selected Poems*, Milosz declares himself amazed that his Muse, Mnemosyne, has in no way diminished his amazement. Amazement is the enemy of anonymity. Rather than unacknowledged legislators of the world, poets are sometimes noticed memorialists.

Not that there is any suggestion of 'I only am escaped alone to tell thee', of the messenger bringing evil tidings. Nor does Milosz work in the mode of the ornamental stonemason or the obituarist. He is more of an anecdotist or a one-act playwright; at times smilingly so, as in 'A Book in the Ruins', dated Warsaw 1941:

> You pick a fragment
> Of grenade which pierced the body of a song
> On Daphnis and Chloe. And you long,
> Ruefully, to have a talk with her,
> As if it were what life prepared you for.

The poem is a gloss on Blake's proverb, 'Eternity is in love with the productions of time', while adding that immortality is in love with the present, and 'is for its sake'. A short prose story, deriving from a family chronicle, tells of Pan Eugene, who lived in a castle at the turn of the nineteenth century and spent most of his time playing the piano. He continues to play after his death, besides walking abroad, and for a moment we might think we are in

Dracula country. But his posthumous activities cease precisely when his brother dies in 1914: the concluding question is 'whether philosophy is really of any help against the passion of life?' What is wisdom worth, if petty feelings and family quarrels are so potent and durable that they force us to walk after our death?

The present is commemorated too, proleptically; future generations will stumble on our writings in some forgotten cave, and be amazed that 'we knew so many of their own joys, / Though our futile palace has come to mean so little'. But there is more to it than 'attempts at naming the world' or, in Macduff's words, remembering that such things were. There is also celebration, difficult as this must seem: 'How can laments and curses be turned into hymns?' Despite the speaker's bitter and confused life, despite his 'knowing better',

> the lips praised on their own, on their own the feet ran;
> The heart beat strongly; and the tongue proclaimed its adoration.

The following poem reinforces this celebration: the Earth is like no other place—

> What continents, what oceans, what a show it is!
> In the hall of pain, what abundance on the table.

It is, exactly, the life he has lived that makes him feel unable to write accusingly; 'joy would spurt in amid the lamentation'. No easy, sustained flow, but a 'spurt', by reason of the pressure of its opposite. (Milosz has observed, in an essay, that truly Christian writing comes from countries where Christians are persecuted.) The poem ends ambiguously:

> So what, if in a minute I must close the book:
> Life's sweet, but it might be pleasant not to have to look.

As regards the individual, death ends the succession of 'prefaces'; whether it is itself a preface—in which case what follows may quite possibly prove a disappointment compared with earthly life—is another matter, closed to the expectation which properly belongs to living.

Part of the ironic advice to a 'Child of Europe', in *Selected Poems*, runs:

> Love no country: countries soon disappear.
> Love no city: cities are soon rubble.
>
> Throw away keepsakes, or from your desk
> A choking, poisonous fume will exude . . . .
>
> Do not gaze into the pools of the past.
> Their corroded surface will mirror
> A face different from the one you expected.

Elsewhere Milosz has stressed his distrust of ironic or sarcastic writing, which can speedily decline into nihilism and acquiescence, and his disapproval of sterile anger at the world, and of the 'mandatory style' of much modern literature, with its servile courting of the counterfeit 'demonic', cheap and shameful when set against the power of true evil as so many have experienced it.

Possibly the key poem—assuming that one has found the right lock—is 'Counsels', also in *Selected Poems*. If he were a young poet, says the speaker, he would prefer not to describe the earth as 'a madman's dream, a stupid tale full of sound and fury', though he grants that he didn't himself happen to see the triumph of justice. God appears to be strictly neutral, certainly not favouring the virtuous and innocent; or else, which comes to much the same, he is in hiding. 'And yet, the earth merits a bit, a tiny bit, of affection.' Not—he hastens to say—that he takes too seriously the consolations of nature, the moon, those clouds, the wild cherries on the banks of the Wilia . . . Indeed, one ought to keep well away from such 'persistent images of infinite space, of infinite time'. These things are not the proper study of mankind; maybe, like irony, they conduce to nihilism and acquiescence. In its unabstract manifestations, 'black earth and rye', nature is prominent here, part and parcel of what is to be praised and remembered. But nature is no loving mother. More to the point, as Donald Davie has recently proposed in *Czeslaw Milosz and the Insufficiency of Lyric*, is the poet's sympathy with Manichaean ways of thinking. In *The Land of Ulro* Milosz mentions how the obligations of a teacher brought him into conflict with his students in America: he 'openly acknowledged the existence of good and evil, a stance they dismissed as irredeemably reactionary'. The poem 'Counsels' ends with an unfinished sentence:

There is so very much death, and that is why affection
for pigtails, bright-coloured skirts in the wind,
for paper boats no more durable than we are . . .

Milosz is more to be envied than mocked for his conviction that
'human reason is beautiful and invincible', 'an enemy of despair
and a friend of hope', and that Philo-Sophia and poetry, 'her ally
in the service of the good', will prevail over their foes. But perhaps it is a spurt of confidence, rather than a spate, as all poems
are spurts: in some sense good will prevail, in some place, in some
time, and for a time.

Milosz's hunger—though never a hunger for ease of mind—can
sometimes look like Whitman, or like greed:

Every day and in every hour, hungry. A spasm in the throat, staring at
the face of every woman passing in the street. Wanting not her but all the
earth. Desiring, with dilated nostrils, the smells of the bakery, of roast-
ing coffee, wet vegetables. In thought devouring every dish and drinking
every drink. Preparing myself for absolute possession.

A kind of correction comes promptly, in a verse spoken by a
woman and addressed to poets, philosophers, 'contrivers of
romances', and other great talkers:

Not all creatures have your need for words.
Birds you killed, fish you tossed into your boat,
In what words will they find rest and in what heaven?

You received gifts from me: they were accepted.
But you don't understand how to think about the dead.
The scent of winter apples, of hoar-frost, and of linen:
There are nothing but gifts on this poor, poor earth.

To excerpt as I have done, perching here and there on what
Davie calls 'particularities and angularities', may be—if not to
force a false unity upon the compilation—at least to exaggerate
here and understate there: to be, as criticism can hardly help but
be, more explicit than the text, cramped and contrived. What a
reader manages to understand—and in this case, for me, what he
manages to understand from a translation—is bound to carry
most weight with him; and then, as the poet observes here in a
rather different sense, 'What is pronounced strengthens itself.'
But to be moved, again and again, is something.

LANGUAGE

Vulgar Tongues

Observing that the word 'literate' once denoted the ability to read and write, whereas nowadays reviewers praise authors for being literate as if it were an extraordinary state of affairs, Jacques Barzun opines that this shift is the result of the prevalence of bad prose and (more cheeringly) of a new worry about the state of the language. Two causes of decline in all modern European languages, he surmises, are the influence of 'experimental' art and the doctrines of linguistic 'science': 'modern grammarians have thundered against rules and fought the idea of correctness.' Logically, this process should lead to the extinction of modern grammarians, but we cannot always rely on logic.

Strange monsters rear their heads in Barzun's *A Word or Two Before You Go. . . .* Not just *conscientization*, the developing of a social conscience, and *acerbic*, brought in because 'acerb' didn't sound like an adjective (notwithstanding 'superb'), but *roentgenogram* (noun and verb), replacing the 'X-ray' that some hospitals and medical journals have banned. *Fundament* is edging out 'foundation', even though, Barzun says, 'those who look up the accepted meaning of this impostor will be shocked to the bottom of their souls'. Dr Johnson caused titters when he allowed that some woman had 'a bottom of good sense'; whereupon he slowly pronounced: 'I say the *woman* was *fundamentally* sensible', and, Boswell records, 'We all sat composed as at a funeral.'

When Barzun places the sentence 'She was convinced to buy' under the rubric 'Verbs To Turn Right Side Out', I can't tell whether it is the structure he deplores, or the passive voice, or the word *convinced*. The latter, I hope, since the (American?) employment of that word in place of 'persuade' has made great strides backwards in this country. A valuable distinction is thus blurred, and something more than a nuance lost; 'persuade', with its etymological sense of 'advise' and its hint of 'suave', is gentler than 'convince', cognate with 'conquer'. Quite possibly the conflation results from the euphemistic or ironic use, fostered by television, of 'persuasion', 'persuader', to connote something more drastic even than 'convince'.

On the subject of language, outwardly rocklike, always shifting, inherently public, intimately personal, we can well be in general agreement while differing on particulars. Barzun spurns *workaholic* and *breathalyser* because '-aholic' and '-alyser' are meaningless, yet the coinages serve a need, are comprehensible and pronounceable, and here to stay. The British expression *all that*, as in 'They say it's a good movie but it's not all that good', he considers 'one of those imports that this country could do without'; I don't myself think it's all that bad. An import we British could do without is *whitewash*, meaning to beat an opponent so thoroughly that he fails to score at all. On seeing the headline 'Australia whitewashes England', I thought for a moment the old colony had gone soft. But it's too late to do anything; 'US colloq. 1884', my dictionary says.

He also disapproves of *palimony*; for one thing, those concerned were more—and are now less—than just good friends. 'If we were really as clever as we suppose, we would coin true novelties, as Eastman did with *kodak* and Van Helmont with *gas*.' Granted, these terms possess the patina of age and custom, but what, we might still ask, has gas got to do with 'chaos', or a camera with a bear—and one with an 'i' missing, at that? Besides such witticisms as 'the ubiquitous -*wise* guys' and 'wall-to-wall carping', Barzun comes up with some handy neologisms of his own: *addictionary*, denoting addictedness to dictionaries, and *aristocattiness*, apropos of Nancy Mitford's attitude to Americans.

The finest of the essays here is in defence of a common language. Without disrespect to dialects, which have their particular attractions and validities, the standard tongue is the truly democratic form of the language, whereas jargon, dialect, and slang are 'exclusive by nature'. The standard language is 'a creation over time by a whole people, an achievement kept in being by its speakers and in order by its literature'. (The definition indicates why such a language will be no more—perhaps we should say no less—than relatively standard.) Barzun professes amazement that professional groups of teachers of English are found attributing some kind of pre-eminence to dialects,

Hispanic, or Black, or whatever. It is precisely such groups, with their commitment to the relevant (i.e. the *outré*), who would be doing that—less so their pupils, and certainly not the Hispanic business man, cited here, who saw Standard English as a right that no one should be denied.

Earlier on, Barzun has reflected on the absurdity of a biographical note in an encyclopaedia: 'Hating cruelty and suffering as he did, he could never have been satisfied by a life entirely in scholarship', asking whether campuses were such vicious places as to be bearable only on a part-time basis. It may be that the sentence makes better sense than he perceived.

But credit where credit is due. The *Quarterly Review of Doublespeak*, published by the (American) National Council of Teachers of English, has gathered in a fine crop of linguistic perversions. An Army spokesman describes the accidental explosion of a Pershing missile as 'an unplanned rapid ignition of solid fuel'. A bank announces that its '24-hour banker machines' will be open almost eight hours a day. The Air Force reports that a missile which went out of control and crashed had 'impacted with the ground prematurely'. And a boys' camp advertises that it was 'deliberately designed with individual attention for the minimally exceptional'.

Charles Earle Funk's *Horse Feathers* and *Heavens to Betsy!*, books first published some thirty years ago, are given over to fun and games, with a little instruction thrown in. *Horse Feathers* supplies not only the dictionary explanation of *Darby and Joan* but also an extract from the source, a ballad printed in *The Gentleman's Magazine* in 1735, entitled 'The Joys of Love Never Forgot':

> Old Darby, with Joan at his side,
>   You've often regarded with wonder:
> He's dropsical, she is sore-eyed,
>   Yet they're never happy asunder.

It is pleasing that, despite their age and disabilities, the couple have lived on till today in the name of a widespread club (seemingly not an American institution). *Brewer's Dictionary of Phrase and Fable*, agog to outdo its rivals, claims that the French equivalent is *Saint Roch et son chien*; this denotes 'inseparables', but a closer match is the even more ancient *Philémon et Baucis*. The author, who was editor-in-chief of the Funk and Wagnalls Standard Dictionary Series, has spared himself the old colloquialism, *funk* (probably from *fumus*, 'smoke': figuratively, to stink through fear), his own name coming no doubt of nobler stock: 'spark' or 'scintillation'. The author of *A Dictionary of Slang and Unconventional English* did not hesitate: '*partridge*. A harlot: low: late C.17–mid-18.'

Under *belladonna* Funk gives the origin favoured by lexicographers—the Venetian use of the plant's juice as a cosmetic—and adjoins the theory that the name came from a different application, by an Italian called Leucota who specialized in killing beautiful women. Having indicated the etymologies of 'butter' and 'scotch', dictionaries tend to fall silent concerning *butterscotch*, though *Collins English Dictionary* ventures, 'perhaps first made in Scotland'. Funk throws light: this variety of candy or toffee has no connection with Scotland, or with its whisky; 'scotching' (scoring, marking with shallow cuts) is what is done to it as it is cooling. (Cf. lines marked on the ground in hopscotch.) Even so, a link persists with the well-known Scotsman, Macbeth: 'We have scotch'd the snake, not kill'd it; / She'll close, and be herself.' Rather than commemorating the creature's jaws, *monkey-wrench* more probably derives from its inventor, whether a Britisher, Moncke, or a Yankee, Monk. *Caterwaul*, however, is indeed the wauling produced by cats; whereas *farthingale*, a garment which Funk, displaying a curious animus, hopes will never come into fashion again, has to do neither with farthings nor (despite Marilyn Monroe's wafting skirt) with gales. The word is a corruption, via the French, of the Spanish *verdugado*, from *verdugo*, 'rod', alluding to the framework supporting the garment.

Entries like *sadism*, *moonstruck*, *hamlet* (no tie-up with hogs), and *Frankenstein* seem supererogatory, but Funk is addressing people who may suppose that *taciturn* has to do with turning and *fanfare* with either a fan or a fare. While Americans talk of *exclamation point* or *mark*, the British—so he alleges—are content with a reticent *exclamation* 'or occasionally with the older terms, *ecphonesis* or *epiphonema*'. He flatters us.

The first ventriloquist, we hear, was a witch—no vulgar

péteur or *péteuse*—out of whose belly strange voices spoke. (Pepys records of a woman in 1663 that 'her speaking in her belly' does not take him as it once did, 'because I know it and see her mouth when she speaks, which should not be'.) *Love-apple*, described by modern dictionaries as archaic, has no connection with Eve or Eden, although Funk confides that his mother, a virtuous woman, avoided the article since it was reputed to possess aphrodisiac properties. The name, and hence the properties or improprieties, arose from a misunderstanding in translation. The tomato began life in South America, and was introduced via Spain and then Morocco into Italy, where it was called *pomo dei Mori*. Finding its way to France, the apple of the Moors became naturalized as *pomme d'amour*. (The current appellation comes from Mexican *tomatl*.) A similar accident accounts for our *Jerusalem artichoke*, not a native of the Holy City but a corruption of Italian *girasole*, sunflower: the vegetable is the edible tuber of the North American sunflower. *

Coconut or *nut* as slang for 'head' is virtually a return to the source, in that the coconut was named after its resemblance to a head, or a face, or at any rate a facial expression: *coco* in Portuguese (it was they who discovered the fruit in the Indian Ocean) signifies 'grimace'. For *hock* and *hockshop* dictionaries refer us to Dutch *hok*: 'hutch, prison, debt'; more picturesquely, Funk prefers to believe that the words relate to Hocktide, an old festival kept on the second Monday and Tuesday after Easter (*hock* here being of unkn. orig.). On one of these days the village women seized and bound the men, demanding a modest ransom for their release, and on the other the men did the same with the women; the proceeds from this innocent merry-making were handed over to the churchwardens for parish work.

Heavens to Betsy! is the mixture as before, but in slightly larger doses, sayings instead of words. Thus the entry on *to play fast and loose* treats us to an excerpt from a book of 1847 entitled *A Dictionary of Archaic and Provincial Words, Obsolete Phrases, Proverbs and Ancient Customs, from the Fourteenth Century*. The cheating game at issue, played at fairs (nothing to do with playing fair), involved a stick and a belt or length of string 'so arranged

---

* Linguistic cosmopolitanism is not always so felicitous: a French sports footwear chain thought fit to christen itself 'Athlete's Foot'.

that a spectator would think he could make the latter fast by placing the stick through its intricate folds, whereas the operator could detach it at once'. The game may be archaic and obsolete; not so the idiom. One theory has it that *mad as a hatter* is a distortion of 'mad as an adder', but Funk agrees with *Brewer* that hatters had more reason for madness: the mercury used in the making of felt hats eventually caused an uncontrollable twitching, akin to St Vitus's dance, which was interpreted as a sign of insanity. (There is no question of the hatter experiencing the throes of sexual excitement *à la* mad March hare.) *Deaf as an adder*—'that stoppeth her ear', says the Psalmist—is a different story, springing from an oriental belief that snakes would try to thwart charmers by thrusting the tip of the tail into one ear and pressing the other firmly against the ground. Incidentally, the Australians have a saying 'as mad [angry] as a cut snake', where 'cut' intimates not merely scotched but castrated.

Shangri-la needs no gloss, but it is of interest to know that for security reasons Roosevelt jocularly informed reporters, during the Second World War, that bombers heading for Tokyo had taken off 'from Shangri-la'. (Come to think of it, if we should need a code-name for Britain, there's a pretty one.) *All my eye and Betty Martin*, however, has aroused much speculation but found no definitive answer, nor any better conjecture than the old one: that the phrase was brought back from abroad by a British sailor who strayed into a Catholic church and misheard the words, *O mihi, beate Martine*, an invocation to St Martin. The fact that no such Latin prayer can be traced, Funk comments, casts doubt on the theory. This objection can't easily be brought against an alternative derivation proposed in a book called *The Phoenician Origin of Britons, Scots, and Anglo-Saxons* (1914) and cited in Eric Partridge's *Dictionary of Slang*: from *O mihi, Brito Martis*, 'Oh (bring help) to me, Brito Martis', the lady being identified as the tutelary goddess of Crete, associated with the sun-cult of the Phoenicians. Brito Martis—whose name Spenser chose for his chaste Welsh female knight, Britomart, perhaps because it suggested Briton and martial—was a companion of Artemis and the inventor of hunting-nets; pursued lustfully by Minos, she flung herself into the sea, and was hauled out by fishermen. Her name, meaning 'sweet maid', occurs as that of the Moon-goddess in Eastern

Crete, according to Robert Graves. Here is another explanation: Betty Martin was the name of one of the diarist's lustfully pursued mistresses, and 'eye' is a covert allusion to Pepys. Inventing etymologies is a harmless hobby for the elderly to pursue.

Partridge lists a Cheshire dialect expression, *all my eye and Dick's hatband*, seemingly related to *as queer* (or *tight*) *as Dick's hatband*, which both Funk and *Brewer* trace to Richard Cromwell, 'Tumbledown Dick', the ineffectual son of Oliver, and the crown he never wore. Apropos of Cheshire, in his *Catlore* Desmond Morris elucidates *grinning like a Cheshire cat* thus: a kind of Cheshire cheese once had a grinning feline face inscribed on one end of it, a trade mark inspired by the saying 'to grin like a Cheshire Caterling', Caterling (cf. 'caterwaul') being a dedicated protector of the Royal Forests under Richard III, and renowned for the wicked grin he wore while decapitating poachers. More picturesque than Partridge's guess: that *cheeser*, a cat very fond of cheese (cf. 'mouser'), became *cheeser cat*, then turned into *Cheshire cat*, and grinned out of gratification.

Whoever *Betty Martin* was, she is no relation to the lady of Funk's title; *Betsy* is a mystery he has failed to solve—Betsy Ross, maker of the first American flag? Betsy, pet name of the frontiersman's rifle?—although he has met countless people who have used the expression all their lives. Another Americanism, *up Salt Creek without a paddle* (incorporating words from a campaign song of 1884, 'Blaine up Salt Creek'), can well be the original of the better-known and coarser locution. This latter was glossed by Wentworth and Flexner in their *Dictionary of American Slang* (1960) as 'originally from homosexual usage'; Partridge appends the note: 'which may or may not be true of US usage, but is not, I believe, true of British usage'. There's a loyal, right-minded New Zealander!

Randolph Quirk's *Words at Work* is altogether more earnest, and thoroughly pragmatic, as behoves public lectures given in Singapore (where only the best, or the most useful, is good enough) by the Lee Kuan Yew Distinguished Visitor. Not that the book is devoid of lighter moments. It recounts the story of a customer in a bookshop who said to the assistant: 'I've come for T. S. Eliot's *Family Reunion*', and was told: 'Well, I don't think it's being held here, madam.' The interchange demonstrates how hard it is to communicate when you fail to co-operate with, or for some reason fail to elicit co-operation from, the other party. The customer ought to have said something like 'I've come for a book, written by T. S. Eliot, and entitled *The Family Reunion*', preferably adding the name of the publisher. It was foolish of her to assume that, since she was in a bookshop, books would be known about. More recently the *Daily Telegraph* has alleged that a customer who asked for F. A. Hayek's *The Road to Serfdom* was referred to the Travel section.

As a telling example of 'strategies of beginning' Sir Randolph cites the opening of Patrick White's novel, *The Twyborn Affair*:

'Which road this afternoon, Madam?'
'The same, Teakle—the one we took yesterday.'
'Bit rough, isn't it?' her chauffeur ventured.
'We Australians', Mrs Golson declared, 'are used to far rougher at home.'

We learn at once that Mrs Golson is an Australian, well off since she has a chauffeur, and that the present location is somewhere other than Australia. We also learn the chauffeur's name and we gather, from the employer's mode of address, that he is most probably a he. A lot of information has been conveyed in a short space: the time of day, too, the roughness of the road, the fact that roads are even rougher in Australia, and the chauffeur's considerateness (either for his employer or for the car). All this with the very minimum of co-operation demanded from the reader.

Style, Swift said, means proper words in proper places. On propriety of style Sir Randolph provides a bad, browbeating example, a passage from an insurance policy—'If the Insured submits to the X Insurance Company a written proposal . . . and if the particulars therein set forth are accurate, and if the Insured pays to the Company the premium for insurance . . . '—and a good, ringing example, from the charter granted to a College within the University of London. Beginning 'Elizabeth the Second by the Grace of God . . . ', this reads in part: 'NOW THEREFORE KNOW YE that We by virtue of Our Prerogative Royal and of Our especial grace, certain knowledge and mere motion have

willed and ordained . . . ', and concludes: 'BY WARRANT UNDER
THE QUEEN'S SIGN MANUAL'. However exotic ('there are the
French grammatical calques, as in the postposed adjective
manual'), however untypical of prose composed in the year 1980,
the text illustrates 'unambiguously the fundamental principles of
appropriacy in language'. Inappropriacy will get you nowhere—
I recall hearing a famously obscure philosopher ordering a particular kind of ice-cream in a university canteen—or into trouble.
Inevitably those principles are open to abuse, as when one language is employed in addressing the rich or powerful or knowing,
and another used for the poor or powerless or ignorant.

On linguistic sexism and the constraints we ought to recognize
and respect, Sir Randolph makes the right-minded noises, taking
to task an entertainer who declared: 'My ambition is to have a
family show. People would bring their wives, mothers and children', thus betraying the unconscious assumption that people are
always male. 'Spouses', though an awkward plural, would be an
improvement on 'wives', but so would 'parents' in place of 'mothers', for why should fathers be discriminated against? Quoting
the statement 'There were two Singaporeans on the plane', Sir
Randolph (or would 'Professor' be more appropriate?) remarks
that, out of context, nationality names will connote males only. I
think I would have guessed at a married couple in this case, but
his point is valid.

The indeterminacy that is a feature of any great and ever-
growing language is illustrated in Fritz Spiegl's *In-Words &
Out-Words*, where the entry on *toilet* describes the word as an
inaccurate euphemism for a lavatory, and the entry on *lavatory*
defines it as an inaccurate euphemism for a toilet. And, apropos
of the 'felicitous' trickiness of the English language, Brigid
Brophy has cautioned would-be reformers: 'A woman who
becomes a school governor enters the same professional area as
but does not risk being confused with a governess.' How easy it is
to fall foul! And foul is what Mr Funk will fall without fail, for in
one of his books he utilizes the pronoun 'she' when elucidating the
expression *back-seat driver*, and in the other he repeats an old joke
about the three ways of spreading news rapidly: telegraph, telephone, or tell a woman.

Nevertheless I would see no sufficient reason to go along

meekly with the 1984 resolution of the Association of University Teachers that in all its future dealings the word *manpower* should be replaced by *work-force* and *man-made* by *artificial*, and that the adjective *manly* should be avoided altogether. To yield to such bullying is unmanly.

Words Deft and Daft

Like us, words are subject to the wheel of fortune. As it turns, some have gone from rags to riches; but rather more, it seems, have travelled in the opposite direction. To begin with, *coition* referred to the conjunction or going together of the planets— from what height fallen now! (At best, down to coming together.) *Bully* (from Middle Dutch, 'lover', perhaps cognate with 'brother') at first meant 'sweetheart' or 'fine fellow', but slipped via 'pimp' to its present unpleasantness, although traces of its origin linger on in 'bully for you!' *Facetious* has slumped badly from 'merry', 'amusing'; John Silverlight reports that *facetiae* is now a bookseller's euphemism for pornographic items.

There's no word good or bad but usage makes it so: this is the message of Adrian Room's *Dictionary of Changes in Meaning*. The intriguing question is how new usages, new senses, come into being, and what lurks in the shadows behind them. *Boy* ascended in the world from Latin 'fettered person' (cf. 'buoy') via 'male servant', a usage long current in the East, albeit in modern Japan *boi*, for a waiter, is redeemed by the addition of *san*. On its way up the word crossed with *knave*, itself on the way down, degenerating from 'boy' (cf. German *Knabe*), to 'male servant', to 'worthless fellow' (Room cites the playing-card, a servant, a common jack of all trades), to its present sense. *Ace* (from Latin 'unit') has risen from the throw in dice of one, the lowest possible, to the most valuable playing-card, and thence to its metaphorical application in 'ace pilot' and so forth. Yet 'within an ace of death' is as small a span as can be imagined, and the word's ambiguity is reflected in the formula 'aces high' or 'aces low'.

Lady has wandered far and wide since its birth as (Old English) 'loaf-kneader', whereas *wench*, from its innocent beginnings as 'child' (OE *wencel*, related to a word meaning 'weak'), plummeted to 'prostitute', having acquired wanton overtones in the fourteenth century, around the time when it came to be used for 'maidservant'. Now, Room says, its overtone is 'naughty', though I would rather have said jocular, as in the case also of *hussy*, from 'housewife' and once, by implication, betokening 'thrifty'. Like *wench*, but unlike *promiscuous* ('of indiscriminate composition, of mixed kinds'), *hussy* is an example of the class of words which fell in moral import and then—perhaps because moral standards had themselves declined—recovered a little lost ground. Mind you, falling moral standards could equally well be adduced as responsible for the upward motion of *luxurious* (formerly 'lascivious') and of *jilt*, defined by the *Concise Oxford Dictionary* as nothing worse than 'person (esp. woman) who capriciously casts off lover after encouraging him', although in the seventeenth century it denoted 'harlot'. Similarly, and seemingly by a very rapid transition late in the same century, *rapture* was exalted— what male chauvinism lay behind this?—from 'carrying off by force' and 'rape' into 'ecstatic delight'. A word that has moved up in another way is *quilt*, earlier, and in accord with its derivation from Latin *culcita*, a mattress, and hence underneath and not on top. In the Anglo-Saxon world *al fresco* preserves its salubriousness (see Sir Denis Forman, p. 69): in Italy, I gather, it is used to intimate 'in prison'. As John Silverlight points out in *More Words*, *to make love* formerly meant 'to pay court, to woo', even as late as 1940, when a singer could innocently propose to 'Make Love with a Guitar'.

A peculiarly lamentable descent was suffered by *jargon*, from Old French and possibly onomatopoeic, originally denoting the twittering of birds, as illustrated nicely in quotations from Chaucer and Longfellow. Since alas we couldn't understand the avian language the word soon came to signify 'meaningless talk', and subsequently the specialized discourse which may convey meaning but lacks the aesthetic appeal of bird-song. A comparable fate befell *silly*, once indicating 'blessed, holy' (cf. German *selig*, 'holy'; *Seele*, 'soul') and also 'innocent', and therefore (this must be where the rot set in) 'helpless'; likewise *daft*, which initially stood for 'meek' or 'mild', and derived from a Germanic word for 'suitable', from which by a parallel process we also took 'deft'.

Possibly the most pathetic intellectual deterioration was that endured by *trivial*, once related to medieval university courses in grammar, rhetoric, and logic: i.e. *trivium*, literally a place where three ways meet, giving the sense of 'common, everyday' in that these liberal arts were held to be the ones talked about on the street corner. (*Quadrivium*, the higher division of the liberal arts, comprised arithmetic, geometry, astronomy, and music: four roads meeting, but presumably in a less popular part of town, perhaps on the campus.) Room cites *Henry VI*, Part 2 (*c.*1590) where the word occurs in its modern sense of 'trifling': 'And yet we have but trivial argument . . . that shows him worthy death', and lines from Keble's hymn of 1827, 'New every morning', which demonstrate the neutral sense of 'everyday': 'The trivial round, the common task,/Will furnish all we need to ask.' The latter passage shows how easy it is—the association with 'common', the lowering 'round', the modesty of the sentiment— for a word to lose its footing.

Except for those who, as Room notes, have lately and happily embraced the designation, *punk* has always been pejorative, albeit diverse in purport, comprehending 'prostitute', 'rotten wood' or 'touchwood', 'rubbish', 'catamite', 'worthless person or thing', 'young hoodlum', and (principally in show or circus business) 'novice'. The origin of the word remains unknown, though some authorities refer half-heartedly to *spunk*, also of unkn. orig. but primarily indicating 'touchwood' and hence coinciding with one of *punk*'s senses.

Change in meaning has a variety of causes, some of which must continue to baffle us. Others are readily perceived. Obeying its etymology, *target* represented a light shield; since a shield was intended to protect what would be aimed at, the word took on its present sense by simple transference. Allied is the sort of poetic borrowing exemplified by the use in printing of 'widow' to indicate a word ending a paragraph at the top of a page—like some old turtle, as Paulina says in *The Winter's Tale*, lamenting her lost mate. Change in place-names is outside Room's brief, but Fritz Spiegl writes that New York was earlier New Amsterdam, and earlier still bore the Indian name, Manhattan, and that Berlin, Alabama was restyled as Sardis during the Second World War— and yet there are still places in the United States called Sodom.

When something new comes along, for example a preventive against smallpox, an old word may be recruited: in this case, *inoculate*, formerly a botanical term denoting 'engraft' (Latin *oculus* is 'bud' as well as 'eye'), since the disease is being engrafted or implanted. Elsewhere pejoration or amelioration sets in as a result of associations, whether deserved or not. *Meticulous* comes from the Latin for 'fearful': we may speculate that eventually it was perceived that fearful people are often very careful people. *Smug* (from Low German *smuk*, 'pretty') stood for 'trim', 'neat', 'smooth', in the sixteenth century, and Room quotes Shakespeare on 'the smug and silver Trent' running 'fair and evenly'; it must have registered in the course of time that trim, neat, and (of course) smooth people tend to be pleased with themselves. *Buxom* ('bowsome', or inclined to submit) moved from abstract 'pliant' to concrete 'plump and comely'—are plump people disposed to biddability? 'Let me have men about me that are fat,' said Caesar—while *bombast* (Latin *bombyx*, 'silk'; cf. *bombazine*) shifted from concrete 'cotton wool', used for padding, to abstract 'pompous, woolly, padded language'. *Icon* was used for any image, picture or statue, until nineteenth-century travellers to Russia virtually cornered the word for their own purposes. And in the fourteenth century a *tippler* was a seller of drink, a tapster; later on the expression was more urgently required for his customers.

Some words grew befuddled, and managed to carry contradictory meanings. *With* expressed 'against' (cognate with German *wider*), but somehow took on its current meaning, perhaps by confusion with Germanic *mid* (modern *mit*), while continuing to mark opposition in 'withstand' and 'withhold' and in such phrases as 'compete with' and 'at odds with'. *Crib* has been propelled backwards and forwards, between 'manger', 'wicker basket', 'hovel', 'lodgings', 'child's bed', and 'steal' (thieves' cant, possibly with an eye on 'basket'), and thence to both 'plagiarize' and 'steal a semblance of knowledge by resorting illicitly to translations'. The history of *snob* is equally tangled; in the eighteenth century it was dialect for 'cobbler', but also Cambridge University slang for a townsman as distinct from a gownsman. It came to encompass people of humble station in general: the reverse of 'nobs', as it were. In the following century, no doubt helped by Thackeray, and via the sense of 'vulgar or ostentatious person', it moved with something of a jolt from 'lower-class person with no pretensions to gentility' to its present mishmash of connotations: 'lower-class person with genteel pretensions', 'person with inordinate and thus vulgar admiration for wealth or social position', someone who flaunts his intellectual or aesthetic superiority, or one who is excessively conscious of his (generally middling) position in the social or professional hierarchy (i.e. 'stuck-up'). Among disgruntled wage slaves at the bottom of the heap I have heard the horrid but pungent epithet 'snot-gobbler' applied to the last-named class of snobs; cf. 'snooty' or, better, 'snotty', (?) ex-'snout', the allusion being to an affected manner of speech, 'intoning in the nose' like Chaucer's Prioress.

Every page of *Dictionary of Changes in Meaning* holds something to amuse, amaze, or bemuse. *Pearmain* is a variety of apple and not a pear, but all the same it was earlier a pear, presumably one coming, like its name, from Parma. A *stationer*, that's to say a bookseller, was so called because he stayed put in a shop instead of hawking his wares; from books to paper and ink is a short step. In the sixteenth century *exaggerate* carried its Latin sense of 'pile up, accumulate', and Room quotes from a Puritan attack on the theatre: 'they exaggerate a mountain of mire.' I have come across 'over-exaggerate' in a political context, perhaps simply analogous to the common solecism, 'more unique', though possibly implying that while all politicians overstate this particular one exceeded excess. Up until the eighteenth century *starve* (cf. German *sterben*) used to mean 'die', and often still does. In the thirteenth century *holocaust* signified a whole (Greek *holos*) burnt (cf. 'caustic') offering, and for long retained the connotation of 'wholesale destruction by fire'. 'Sacrifices of any kind—lives, fortunes, love, remarkably even of a college fellowship—were "holocausts" from the fifteenth to the nineteenth century,' writes Robert Burchfield. Today the term is loosely employed for any sort of massacre, or terrorist killings, or devastation (for example, the chopping down of forests), and, as 'the Holocaust' with a capital H, quite precisely.

Bomb, we gather, was earlier pronounced 'bum': it seems to have come directly from French *bombe*; and Dr Johnson is surely not the only person to have supposed that the first syllable of *bonfire* was the French *bon*: sorry, it is the much less jolly 'bone', either animal or human. *Carouse* may have arrived by way of military contacts from the French, but the French took it from the German: *trink gar aus*, 'drink right up'. No change of meaning there. *Soothe* is a variant of 'sooth', truth, and at first meant 'prove to be true', 'verify', subsequently acquiring such senses as 'encourage' and 'flatter by agreeing' or 'humour', which in turn led to the current meaning, 'calm' or 'mitigate'. Understandably there is no suggestion that the truth shall make us carefree.

Mufti and *effete* are items Room might think of adding to his generous assortment. Coming from the Arabic 'to give a legal decision, decide a point of law', the use of *mufti* to signify a Muslim priest or expounder of Koranic law is self-explanatory, but how did it come to mean 'civilian dress as worn by someone entitled to wear uniform'—when, moreover, those who are engaged in the law often dress up rather quaintly? Dating the sense from 1816, and quoting from Ernest Weekley's *Etymological Dictionary of Modern English* of 1921, Partridge suggests a possible source in representations in the early nineteenth-century theatre of officers off duty wearing vaguely oriental garb, flowered dressing-gown and tasselled smoking-cap. In *The English Language* Burchfield mentions Evelyn Waugh's pleasure at discovering from a dictionary that *effete* (related to 'foetus') primarily signified 'having given birth'; by a natural extension, Burchfield notes, the word came to convey 'worn out by bearing young', and was used of barren farm animals during the seventeenth and eighteenth centuries. In 1796, however, Burke described France as showing 'symptoms of being almost effete'. Currently suggesting someone or some institution unlikely to bear or sire a child or produce anything else requiring effort, the word hasn't strayed so very far.

Though never in the modern sense *flippant* (initially meaning 'nimble', from *fillip*, 'stimulus'), Adrian Room is not averse to a joke. After a first appearance as 'penis', *verge* (Latin 'rod') came to express 'rod of office' (cf. *verger*). Thence it referred to land subject to the Lord High Steward and his wand of office; then to the boundary of such land; and finally—having trudged from the genital to the marginal—to 'border' or 'edge'. Since in French the word can still bear the anatomical purport, Room wonders what French visitors make of the notice put up at soggy roadsides: 'Soft Verges'.

This *facetia* offers a natural passage to Fritz Spiegl's book *The Joy of Words*, allusively subtitled 'A Bedside Book for English Lovers', although a more earnest transition lies in the thought that while

Room could be utilized by permissivists as ammunition against prescriptivists, Spiegl demonstrates the shameful accidents that happen when we relax our attention for an easygoing split second.

The last true English-speaker is bound to be a foreigner. Those who, like Spiegl, have had to *learn* the language instead of plucking it out of the air will notice errors and absurdities where the native speaker remains either oblivious or acquiescent. And, judging by Spiegl, they will be shocked and enraged, rather as refugees from some repressive regime—Skvorecky's Czech *émigrés* come to mind—are bemused and distressed by the wanton liberties they witness in a free democracy. Spiegl is meticulous—in the modern sense, for he shows no sign of fear—in distinguishing between English-lovers and English lovers, and between two pronunciations and two meanings of *conjure*. He instances such ludicrous headlines as FLIES TO HAVE TWINS IN IRELAND and LADY SEEKS COMPANION IN BATH; such unfortunate wording as that of a Radio 4 interviewee, 'My brother's moved to Belfast and started a glazier's shop, and now he's making a bomb'; a *Radio Times* billing of 'Reginald Dixon and his Organ supported by strings'; and, in a radio play adapted from a novel by Mrs Gaskell, 'I rather fancy her dead.' Browning miscalculated badly when he made his cheery Pippa refer to 'cowls and twats, monks and nuns', under the impression that a twat was a species of nunnish headgear. Spiegl conjectures that the poet was led astray by some lines of verse published in 1660:

> They talk't of his having a Cardinall's Hat,
> They'd send him as soon an Old Nun's Twat.

If this is so, then it is a pathetic instance of what we might call *honi soit qui bien y pense*. Or, in the native idiom, pure ignorance.

The mealy mouth, the loud mouth, the misguided mouth, the sloppy mouth ('icelated shahs' and 'gnats it' from the Weather Forecast)—they all stink in Spiegl's nostrils. Black beasts are spotted prowling the jungles of Fleet Street, like 'The Alban Berg Quartet of Vietnam' (*Daily Telegraph*), no doubt playing 'Chiu Bet, Mo Tsat and Hai Dun, not to mention Yo Han, the Vietnamese Waltz King'. Once, when his typewriter misbehaved and he could manage only single spacing, the compositors returned the copy to the sub-editor, obliging him to cut out each line of typing and paste the strips, double-spaced, on another sheet of paper. Consequently it is with glee that he asks whether Sogat 82 is a fine vintage, and cites a press description of the General Secretary as 'Miss Brenda Dean of Sogat, 82'. Acronyms offer further scandalized fun: 'I've got the HOTS for you' can merely indicate that a BBC secretary has the Head of Office Training Services on the line. Perhaps it takes a foreigner to detect an unappetizing flavour in the inscription VOM on the label of a pork pie from the Vale of Mowbray.

Then there is what, though it seems fairly near the centre, we call the lunatic fringe. The Inner London Education Authority advertises for a Mother Tongue Inspector ('say Aah?' enquires Spiegl); the Greater London Council resolves to black the word 'blacked' from its industrial relations vocabulary; an Equal Opportunity Employer states that 'preference will be given to applicants of ethnic minorities'; a social worker, speaking on the BBC, reprimands the interviewer: 'We do *not* call it "baby battering". *We* call it "non-accidental injury" '; Liverpool Catering Training College offers an unambitious Two-Year Sandwich Course in Food Technology; St Andrews University seeks to fill its Chair of Learning Difficulties ('We used to call it the Dunce's Stool,' adds Spiegl's informant).

Hilarious though *The Joy of Words* is in its parts, in its totality it paints an alarming picture of the world we live in. Can it be wholly accurate? We have it on good authority that the name 'Zeppelina' was given to a scattering of girls born during the First World War, but do fond parents really call their children Hernia, Placenta, Gonadia, Positive Wassermann, and (a deadly genus of fungi) Amanita? (True, Candida is a fairly common name, and it too can stand for an unpleasant fungus.) Were Robertson the jam-makers deprived of a £40,000 contract by the GLC because they refused to give up their gollywog symbol? Agatha Christie's play *Ten Little Niggers* was long ago converted into *Ten Little Indians*, but has it more recently become *Ten Little Highlanders*? In the West End, I see, the latest rechristening is *And Then There Were None*: no hint of discrimination there.

Spiegl is a firm believer in 'Laura Norder', a veritable Mirror for Magistrates. Just as he would have kept the imperial weights

and measures and the pre-decimal currency, so he prefers our
English *sp* at the start of his surname. 'Anyone who religiously
uses the correct *shp* is suspected of calling me a Bloody Foreigner.'
Even so, is *lib*, as in Women's Lib, genuinely an old English term
meaning to castrate? The dictionary says yes; and Spiegl subsequently had a letter confirming that Scottish schoolboys call a
sharp pocket-knife a 'libber'. He is generally able to authenticate
his alarming exhibits.

Truth, Beauty, and Bafflegab

The title of Jonathon Green's *Newspeak: A Dictionary of Jargon* contains a slight misnomer, in that Orwell's Newspeak entailed a reduction of vocabulary and hence of thought, whereas Green's version shows an increase in vocabulary pointing to an extension of thought, or knowledge, or supposition, whether admirable or otherwise. Green includes ironic and subversive expressions— something not found in the official language of Oceania—as well as the unexceptionable lingo of trades and professions.

Outside the admonitory slogans of Soviet Russia and China, the closest the book comes to Orwell is in its nastier euphemisms. *ABC warfare* isn't ructions in the primary class-room but Atomic, Biological, and Chemical weaponry. Nor is *absolute dud* the sort of comment a teacher is tempted to write on a report; it indicates the absence of one: a nuclear weapon that fails to explode on target. *Accidental delivery* isn't having someone else's groceries left on your doorstep, but the shelling of one's own troops. *Anticipatory retaliation* is double-think or *bafflegab* for surprise attack, and *BAMBI* stands for Ballistic Missile Boost Intercept, an orbiting satellite intended to destroy hostile ground installations. In Argentina *a chat with Susan* is shop slang for a session of torture by electric shock (no etymology given), whereas *happy talk* (US) is the style of newscasting in which all topics, however distressing, are given 'a jokey, light-hearted veneer', and much like *infotainment*, a mixture lower on information than on entertainment.

First Australians isn't a tactful way of referring to convicts: it signifies Aboriginals. *Bent spear* sounds anthropological or olde-worlde, but is US emergency code for an incident, not too serious, involving a nuclear device. *Heavy textiles* are mail-bags sewn by hand in HM prisons, not winter woollies, while *knitting* (Royal Navy) represents girls or girl-friends. In espionage circles *biographic leverage* describes the exploitation of personal indiscretions for blackmail purposes—*ladies*, it seems, initiate the seduction and *sisters* supply the sex: both categories belong to the *sanctifying* (i.e. blackmailing) team—while *family jewels* (borrowed from slang: 'male genitals') is CIA talk for an embarrassing secret that had best be kept secret. *Slimwear*, a fashion term, is here a fetishist mag genteelism for rubber garments.

Sex is a sickeningly rich field, with homosexuality a growth area. Many of the activities entered under this general head repel explication. *Dollar-an-inch-man* explains itself (*big Dick*, however, is a gambling expression for a throw of ten in dice), as perhaps do *plain-sewing*, *golden shower*, and *three-way girl*; the latter shouldn't be confused with *three-eye league*, a 'hypothetical club' consisting of politicians who have visited the homelands of the US's major minorities, Israel, Ireland, and Italy. *Coffee-queen* is a homosexual prostitute who obliges for food or drink, and among pimps *blow* is to 'lose a whore from your string of girls'— *whose* string?—while *bottom woman* is the tops: the most reliable or efficient component of your string. *Alimony drone* is neat for a divorced woman who declines to remarry solely to continue milking her ex-husband, but *boylesk* is rather contrived as burlesque/striptease featuring male performers, and needs to be distinguished from *butter-boy*, a young and ingenuous police constable in whose mouth, as the saying goes . . .

The author has a predilection for the Foreign Legion and its lingo, much of which comes from Arabic, like *bouzbir*: brothel, and *baraka*: luck; though *ravio*, anything obtained illegally, could be a corruption of the French *rabiot*, something extra to a soldier's rations, and *coup-de-bambon*, defined as 'a sudden physical or mental collapse with no apparent cause', may be a misprint for *coup de bambou*: sunstroke, and hence, with *avoir*, to go mad. *Abstauben*, we hear, is used by the Foreign Legion to denote anything acquired by irregular means; in ordinary use the German word means 'to wipe the dust off', and has taken on the same slang sense, I gather, with no hint of complicity on the Legion's part.

Green's definitions are occasionally less than adequate; *acoustical excitation* is glossed as '(milit.) sound'—a brass band, or bagpipes, or the Last Post? Obviously not the *Liebestod*. But he is not loath to betray his personal views on *affirmative action*, *caring professions*, and ('an insensitive flailing around of the subject's ego') *letting it all hang out*. Given sociology's aversion to judgemental or even plain language, *affectional preference minorities* is still a roundabout way of referring to homosexuals male or female. Probably *cabbage*: a tailor's perks, the bits of cloth left over, and *call a cab*: a jockey's action in waving a hand to keep his balance while taking a fence, are not very commonly heard. Similarly erudite or recherché are *res cogitans* (Descartes) and *res non verba* (things speak louder than words), *ABD* (US educational for All But Dissertation: the candidate has all the necessary credits for a Ph.D. but—a mere detail—hasn't yet written the thesis), and *unk-unks*. This last is an aerospace locution for phenomena tantalizingly defined as 'doubly unknown: in the first place they are not even known to exist, and if they were discovered, no one would have any idea what they were'.

It's good to know, though, that an *asymmetrical joking relationship* is the kind in which only one of the two partners has the right to practise joking towards the other (the latter, we suppose, is restricted to laughing or crying); that *bunny dip* describes how Hugh Hefner's staff serve food and drink backwards to prevent their breasts spilling out on the customer's table;* that activist groups fighting *ageism*, discrimination against the elderly, include the *Grey Panthers*; and that in America *the fabulous invalid* is the stage, which lives on despite persistent rumours of its demise. All the same, *Sadler's Wells make-up*—plaster from the walls, as pressed into service by impoverished companies— sounds a warning note.

Most heartening are the inventive and relatively wholesome coinages. Not *visagist(e)*, a pretentious word for (the pretentious) 'cosmetician', or *televisionary* (albeit 'humorous'), both of them in Volume IV of the *Supplement to the Oxford English Dictionary*. And not the rose-tinted linguistic pullulation on the drug scene: *angel dust*, *blue heaven*, *strawberry fields*, *white nurse*, *sweet Jesus* . . . (Quite different is *God's medicine*, morphine used medically, a designation attributed to Sir William Osler.) These examples illustrate a reference of Barzun's to the use, sometimes in conjunction with pseudo-technical language, of the

---

* But Michael Hulse, citing *Playboy* itself, has since pointed out that *bunny dip* is the forward bow, 'trained into Bunny girls', which enables the client to achieve the maximum view down the girl's front. It would seem that Green has bent over backwards to avoid the obvious.

metaphorical, 'which also blurs the contours of reality'. I am thinking, rather, of expressions, neither deceitfully euphemistic and obfuscatory nor inflated, which are legitimately eloquent. Such as *demented* for a badly designed computer programme; *pill palace*, hospital pharmacy; *black mist*, a literal translation of Japanese *kuro kiri*, for scandal and corruption inside the government and attempts made to mask them; *chew the scenery*, to over-act; *chop-socky*, oriental martial-arts movies, conflating chop-suey and sock; *carbolic soap*, soap opera set in a hospital; *fruit salad*, display of medal ribbons; *working for Jesus*, putting in extra time without asking for extra pay; and *citronella circuit* (US), small summer theatres in the sticks, from the insect repellant advisable in those places.

Brain candy is very light TV entertainment, but *caramel* belongs to a different department: it stands for lightweight reactor fuel which can be put only to peaceful purposes, and hence is the sweetest of euphemisms. *Co-op mix*, on the other hand, betokens home-made bombs in Northern Ireland, the materials for which are available in any supermarket. *Afghanistanism* used to be a pleasing idiom for the old device of turning public attention away from awkward domestic problems to some conveniently remote place, but it has suffered the fate risked by all neologisms; as Green notes, the USSR ruined the metaphor when they invaded the country in 1979. *Corgi and Bess*, we learn, is the commercial TV nickname for the Queen's Christmas broadcast, while *Kitty Hawk* is the coded whisper that goes round Heathrow when Her Majesty is about to appear—Kitty Hawk being the village in North Carolina where the Wright Brothers made their first aeroplane flight—and *Kitty Rainbow* signals the Duke of Edinburgh. The *Queen's pipe* turns contraband tobacco into ash, and the *Queen's sewer* swallows up contraband alcohol. The Royal Family certainly pull their weight.

Judd's dictum stems from an American sculptor who dealt with the embarrassing question 'But is it art?' by replying 'If someone calls it art, it's art.' Art, or what is called art, is continually popping up here, under such heads as *minimal art*, *idiot art*, *know nothing nihilism*, *drip painting*, *funk art*, *blow up* (or *gonflable*) *art*, *destructive art*, *art povera* (sounds grander than 'poor'), *l'art brut*, *expendable art*, *invisible painting* (more to it than meets the eye) . . . Not too surprisingly, *beauty* and *truth* now reside elsewhere, being properties of the bottom and the top quark respectively, with *charm* ascribed to the third of these three (hypothetical) fundamental particles from which other particles may be constructed. The word *quark* is on loan from *Finnegans Wake*.

As language at its finest, literature must surely be untainted by horrid jargon, we suppose. And in fact *stanza* in this context stands for either a segment of a television series or a week at a given cinema; *novelist*, in Soviet penology, is a prisoner who makes a confession, voluntarily or otherwise; the *Trollope ploy* (diplomatic) is the deliberate misinterpretation of some foreign situation enabling a country to respond in the fashion most advantageous to it: the expression is derived from the conscious tendency to take casual endearments too seriously ('Miss Trefoil must have thought that kissing and proposing were the same thing', *The American Senator*, 1877); *word-engineering* signifies the doctoring of information, telling the public only what is good for it (i.e. good for the agency that does the telling): cf. 'engineer of human souls'; and even *verbiage* is confined to schools, where it denotes any written material: 'no derogatory implication is involved'.

Admittedly we come across *Künstlerroman* (too narrowly defined as 'a novel that takes as its theme the making of a novelist': what about *Doktor Faustus*, *L'Œuvre*, *The Horse's Mouth*?), and *knockoffs*, instant hack publications, often non-fiction and 'tied into a major event, e.g. the Falklands War'. But the rot truly sets in with *engagé* (lit. crit.), *prequal* (which should perhaps read 'prequel', it being a substitute for a sequel: the thoughtless author has killed off his hero and is obliged to return to an earlier stage in the character's life), and *concrete poetry* with its swarming variants and associates, among them *evident poetry*, *poetry of surface*, *semiotic poetry*, *machine poetry*, *popcrete*, and *publit*. Ah, for the return of spring!—

> With beast and bird the forest rings,
> Each in his jargon cries or sings . . .

The sheer volume of official tergiversation, the escalation of rigmarole and its rapid turnover, point to the strain suffered by any government in a democracy—that is, in a society which, thanks to media too numerous and diverse to stifle, is aware or partially aware of what is going on and expects to have a say in it. In respect of obfuscation and equivocation, and in fields more private, *Newspeak* makes distressing reading. But it isn't totally unnerving. However shady, and squalid, and shaky, the world it evokes is at all events vigorous, ingenious, witty, and for better and for worse a fairly free one—a far cry from the bleak, bludgeoned world of *Nineteen Eighty-Four.*

The House of Joss

Arriving not so very long ago, as a relic of colonialism, in a newly independent and nominally socialist country, I was taken aback on hearing the university department's messenger called a *peon* (pronounced 'pewn'). In my book the term smacked of 'peasant' and 'pagan' and other ancient wrongs (in which my book was mistaken), or at the very least of 'pawn'; and true, the word comes by way of Portuguese from the Latin for 'foot'. It has been used in various places and at various times as 'serf', 'foot-soldier', 'orderly', 'bullfighter's assistant', 'footman'. However, no one in this new country considered the old word offensive, least of all the peon, and nor, before long, did I.

After all, as late as 1761 an honourable position in the East India Company was that of *Scavenger*, an official who inspected goods offered for sale and collected duty on them. That was what the word (of Germanic origin, cognate with 'show') originally signified, although back home the scavenger had been downgraded to cleaning the streets some two hundred years earlier.

We know words. Words are what we know. Or we think we know, for in practice they are continually surprising or discomfiting us. For one thing, as soon as we look into this language of ours, this cherished national heritage, it turns out to be largely other people's. Bosh, I hear you saying? That so indigenous, so British monosyllabic interjection, characteristic of our sharp eye for stuff and nonsense, comes from the Turkish *bo ş*, a word meaning 'empty, vain, useless, void of sense or utility'.

We may have guessed that, despite its deceptive 'low', *bungalow* was an Eastern import, from Hindi *banglā*, 'pertaining to Bengal', and that *bandanna* (Hindi), *cheroot* (Tamil, 'roll'), and *tariff* (via French, Italian, and Turkish from Arabic, 'the making known'), have a touch of the tar-brush about them. And similarly *banana* (from Guinea, though a pundit has suggested that the resemblance with Arabic *banāna*, 'a single finger or toe', can hardly be accidental), *sugar* (through Arabic from Sanskrit *sarkara*, 'grit or gravel'), and *candy* (from Sanskrit *khanda*,

216

'broken', or as we might say 'scotched', or possibly from the Dravidian for 'lump').

But did we know that *dinghy* ('legitimately incorporated in the vocabulary of the British navy, as the name of the smallest ship's boat') is Hindi from Sanskrit for 'trough', *shawl* comes from the Persian, itself possibly from the Sanskrit for 'variegated', and *punch* (potable) derives from Persian *panj* or Hindi *pānch*, 'five', i.e. consisting of five ingredients (though the *Concise Oxford Dictionary* says orig. unkn.)? Or that *chicanery*, immediately from the French for 'quibble', is traceable to Persian *chaugān*, the game of polo? (Our name *polo* is taken from a Kashmiri dialect word for 'ball'.) Henry Yule and A. C. Burnell propose that the modern sense of 'chicanery' is a reflection on the tactics resorted to in this up-market sport—taking every possible advantage of the terrain and so forth. In motor-racing parlance a *chicane* is a disadvantage, an artificial obstacle.

The first edition of *Hobson-Jobson*, monumentally subtitled 'A Glossary of Colloquial Anglo-Indian Words and Phrases, and of Kindred Terms, Etymological, Historical, Geographical and Discursive', appeared in 1886, and the latest reprint (1985) is of the second edition, edited and added to by William Crooke and published in 1903. In the original preface Colonel (later Sir) Henry Yule paid tribute to his collaborating correspondent, Arthur Burnell, of the Madras Civil Service, who died in 1882. Yule was then living in Palermo, presumably in retirement from overseas service; he died in 1889. In a foreword to the reprint Anthony Burgess observes that the work 'breathes the warmth of amateurism' while telling us more about the impact of Indian languages on English than any professional dictionary does. Random checks against up-to-date authorities suggest that, notwithstanding traces of rough-and-readiness, it is professional enough in its etymologies, as well as uniquely engaging in its annotations and graphic in its anecdotes. The expression 'Anglo-Indian', it should be noted, embraces practically anywhere and anything east of Alexandria.

Hobson-Jobson itself, 'a native festal excitement', is a garbling, a British soldiers' rendering of the cry, during the Muharram ceremonies, commemorating the deaths of the Shiite imams: 'Yā

Hasan! Yā Hosain!' Through the age-old contempt for foreign lingos, not always evident in practice, or perhaps as an attempt among the soldiery to domesticate the disease, *cholera morbus* emerges as *Corporal Forbes*. The French have shown themselves equally disrespectful: *mort-de-chien*, briefly anglicized in 1716 as 'Dog's Disease', is a corruption of Portuguese *mordexim*, itself deriving from Indian names for cholera, ultimately from a Marathi verb *modnen*, 'to collapse'. *Cheechee* is (or was) an odious term applied to people of mixed European and Indian race, alluding to their 'mincing accent' (*chī*, 'fie!', conveying genteel reproof), perhaps acquired in the Christian schools, and preserved as a defensive measure of identity *vis-à-vis* those of so-called pure blood. It is distinct in its history from the French *chi-chi*, adopted by us, albeit the expressions carry much the same sense—of affectation—and both are onomatopoeic. We gather that in the Dutch East Indies *lip-lap* was the equivalent of *cheechee*.

Buxee, 'a word of complex and curious history', signified 'military paymaster', though its original Sanskrit, *bhikshu*, denoted 'beggar' and hence religious mendicant. From early times *bakshi* and its variants were used by diverse peoples to signify variously a lama, scribe, doctor, teacher, minstrel. Confusion seems to have arisen with the Persian *bakhshīsh*, 'payment', from which, through the British presence in Egypt, *baksheesh*, 'tip, alms', entered our language. There is no mention here of the slang *buck-shee*, 'for free', which must have arrived on the scene too late for Yule and Burnell. The slang *dekko/deck*, in 'let's have a dekko', is a direct borrowing from Hindi *dekho*, imperative of the verb 'to look'. Eric Partridge gives an alternative derivation, or route, from Romany *dik*, 'to look'; and *Collins* lists a Northumbrian dialect imperative, *deck that!*, 'look at that', perhaps of Romany origin.

The entry on *pug*, an animal's footprint, from Hindi *pag/* Sanskrit *padaka*, 'a foot', provides a brief illustration of the 'Anglo-Indian' language at work, from a sporting magazine of 1831: '. . . sanguine we were sometimes on the report of a *burra* [great] *pug* from the *shikaree* [sportsman, whether native guide or trapper or European hunter].'

Not surprisingly, a *faux ami* raises its treacherous head on occasion. *Talisman* doesn't mean what it seems to say, but stands for 'mullah' and possibly (Yule and Burnell aren't quite sure) is a deformation of Arabic *talāmiza* or *talāmi*, 'disciples, students', whereas our 'talisman' comes from the Greek 'to complete a rite'. *Cowtail* is a distortion of *chowry*, from Sanskrit *chāmara*, the bushy tail of the Tibetan yak as used as a fly-swat or royal insignia or decoration attached to the horse-trappings of native warriors; thus it was absurd of a Mr Bogle to call yaks 'cow-tailed cows' in his Journal, when ' "horse-tailed cows" would have been more germane!' *Compound*, the enclosure in which a house or factory stands, in effect often a complex of buildings, has nothing to do with our Latinate word but is Malay *kampong*, a village or settlement. Yet a modern (1877) and 'most intelligent' but unnamed lady novelist is discovered in unseemly confusion: 'When the Rebellion broke out at other stations in India, I left our own compost.'

That *shampoo* (Hindustani *chāmpo*, 'kneading') was diverted in transit to signify the washing of hair may have had to do with the fact that massage was sometimes performed by barbers in the realms of Anglo-India. But *solar topee*, while indeed a sun-helmet, had no connection with the sun, since Urdu *solā* and Hindi *sholā* are the name of the plant from whose pith the topee (Hindi for 'hat') was made. A rather jolly accident in the *Hobson-Jobson* line is *upper roger*, for heir apparent or 'what we generally render in Siam as the "Second King" ': viz. the Sanskrit *yuva-rāja*, 'young king'. In like manner, *college-pheasant* is not a wise old bird or a swan reserved for the dons of St John's, but 'an absurd enough corruption' of *kālij*, the Himalayan name for a genus of birds intermediate between the pheasant and the jungle-fowl.

A not altogether false friend is *organ*, for an oriental form of mitrailleuse or machine-gun. It comes, Yule and Burnell say, from a Persian word deriving from the Greek *organon*, 'tool'— and this, others say, comes from an Indo-European word which gives us our 'work'. There is a lengthy entry on *typhoon*, rejecting the popular and plausible derivation from Chinese *tai fung*, 'big wind', on the grounds that there is no evidence that the expression is in Chinese use at all, and 'it would perhaps be as fair a suggestion to derive it from the English *tough 'un*'. Our two learned amateurs prefer to take it from the Greek *tuphon*, 'whirlwind', by way of the Arabic *tufan* (acquired through maritime intercourse or translations of Aristotle), and then (picked up from Arab pilots) the Portuguese *tufão*.

Umbrella, *padre*, and *pale ale* find a place here, not because they pose any difficulty, but simply because they were a common feature of everyday life, the last-named of them having been brewed specifically for consumption in India from the late eighteenth century onwards. *Suttee* gets an entry of eight columns, with illustrative quotations going back to 317 BC, although the word itself couldn't be found in any European work earlier than the seventeenth century. It is properly the Sanskrit *satī*, 'a good woman' or 'true wife', and the Sanskrit term actually used for the rite is horridly euphemistic: *sahagamana*, or 'keeping company'. Other generously informative entries are on *music* and *amok*. The one kind of Western music the mass of the Indians enjoyed was that of the bagpipe: 'they would much rather listen to this instrument a whole day than to an organ for ten minutes', according to Captain Munro's *Narrative* of Military Operations against the French, Dutch, and Hyder Ally Cawn (1789). A *muck/amok* is from the Malay 'to make a furious attack', possibly originating in the Sanskrit *amokshya*, 'that cannot be loosed' (i.e. bound by a vow). W. W. Skeat's theory that running amok was the national mode of suicide, of soliciting death, since no one had ever heard of Malays committing suicide in any other way is politely dismissed on the grounds that women and children, unlikely to hit back to fatal effect, have been frequent victims of such attacks.

Nine columns are devoted to *tea*, ultimately from Fukien dialect pronounced *tay*; Mandarin, *ch'a*. Pepys was introduced to tea, 'a China drink', in 1660, while a Dutch traveller first encountered it in 1681 and 'could not understand how sensible men could think it a treat to drink what tasted no better than hay-water'. *Caddy*, as in 'tea-caddy', is the Malay *kātī* or *catty*, a unit of weight, 1⅓ lb., in common use today.

Fun is had with *musk-rat*, a creature whose odour is 'so penetrative that it is commonly asserted to affect bottled beer by running over the bottles in a cellar'; *musk* is said to come, by way of Latin and Greek, through Persian, from Sanskrit *mushka*, the literal meaning of which is glossed here as 'in the old English phrase "a cod of musk" ', and in the *Concise Oxford*, less delicately, as 'scrotum (from shape of musk-deer's gland)'. *Caravan*, of course, is the Persian *kārwān*, a convoy of travellers; the watchful authors remark that the abbreviation 'van' seems to have acquired full rights in English whereas 'the altogether analogous "bus" is still looked on as slang'. While *chintz* (Sanskrit *chitra*, 'speckled') and *nankeen* (yellowish cotton cloth, from the city of Nanking) are listed, there is no reference to the wickedly appropriate material, 'the fabric that caresses the skin', from which the knickers of Joyce's Gerty MacDowell were made: nainsook, from Hindi *nain*, 'eye', and *sukh*, 'delight'.

Gong, once believed to be Chinese, is a Malay term, imitative of the sound produced. Yule and Burnell venture that the word *gum-gum*, which 'we had supposed to be an invention of the late Charles Dickens', is a genuine if rare Anglo-Indian locution, an approximation to the plural of *gong*. (In *Sketches by Boz*, 'The Steam Excursion', the article is associated with 'tom-tom' but its nature is never explained. 'I don't know what it may be in India,' a character says, 'but in England I think a gum-gum has very much the same meaning as a hum-bug.') Malay plurals are sometimes made by doubling the singular form: *pĕrĕmpuan*, 'woman', and *pĕrĕmpuan-pĕrĕmpuan*, 'women'; *mata* is 'eye'—as in Mata Hari, the Dutch dancer and beautiful spy, 'Eye of the Day', that's to say 'Sun'—and hence, by a slight change of process, *mata-mata* is a policeman (cf. 'private eye'), who needs at least two eyes.

It is intriguing to learn that among the various individuals credited with the invention of the *jennyrickshaw* or *jinricksha*, shortened to *rickshaw*, is an Englishman known as 'Public-spirited Smith'. The word is Japanese, *jin-riki-sha*, literally 'Man-Strength-Cart', and a humorous friend of the authors pointed out that the term was an exact equivalent of 'Pull-Man-Car'. More humour stems from the appellation *daimyō*, a feudal lord, this being the Japanese pronunciation of Chinese *tai ming*, 'great name'. A pertinent extract from Basil Hall Chamberlain's *Things Japanese* (1890), a fascinating compilation with which *Hobson-Jobson* has some affinity, notes that in medieval times warrior chiefs of lesser degree were known by the title *shōmyō*, 'small name', but this soon fell into disuse, perhaps because those who bore it didn't consider it grand enough.

Opium, we now discover, must be attributed to the noble Greeks (*opion*, 'poppy-juice'), and not to degenerate Arabs, whose *afyūn* was taken from the Greek, nor to depraved Chinamen, whose *a-fu-yung* came from the Arabic. A late-nineteenth-century lexicographer's attempt to trace the word (and possibly the blame) to Sanskrit *ahiphena*, 'snake venom', is gently put down as 'not probable'; and an extract dated 1726 states: 'It will hardly be believed that Java alone consumes monthly 350 packs of opium, each being of 136 catis [variant spelling of *catty*], though the East India Company make 145 catis out of it.' Sounds as if a *scavenger* had been at work there.

According to modern dictionaries the word *rice* comes to us from Old French, through Italian, through Latin, from Greek *oruza*, of oriental origin. With more space for speculation, Yule and Burnell dwell on the 'strong temptation' to derive the Greek term from Tamil *arisi*, 'rice deprived of husk'. Arabic *al-ruzz* may have been taken directly from the Dravidian, while the Greeks probably acquired their word during Alexander's expedition, on the Oxus or in the Punjab, possibly from the Sanskrit *vrīhi* in some such dialect form as *vrīsi*. Simpler, but nicely illustrative of the twists and turnabouts that happen in language, is the case of *joss*, as in *joss-stick*. To begin with, this was a borrowing from the European, *joss* being a pidgin reproduction in the Chinese ports of the Portuguese *deos* (Latin *deus*). (*Pidgin* or *pigeon*, represented here as a 'vile jargon', is reckoned to be the pidgin rendering of 'business'.) *Joss* was later taken back from the pidgin by Europeans under the misapprehension that it was a Chinese word referring to some native graven image. Accordingly *joss-house*, etymologically the house of God, came to denote an abhorred heathen temple. A well-judged act of linguistic revenge.

One of the epigraphs or mottoes decorating this rich and entertaining volume comes from a seventeenth-century document with the stirring title, *Restitution of Decayed Intelligence*: 'As well may we fetch words from the *Ethiopians*, or East or West *Indians*, and thrust them into our Language, and baptize all by the name of *English*, as those which we daily take from the *Latine* or Languages thereon depending . . .' Conceivably the writer is being sarcastic, a man of little faith, since he goes on to allege that when Englishmen discourse together, in what they call English, some of them can't grasp what the others are saying. As for our vocabulary, and where it comes from and how it was come by— in the words of the pious Anglo-Indian oath, it doesn't matter a dam. A *dām* is a small Indian coin, of copper, comparable on the metaphorical exchange to a brass farthing.

Death of a Thousand Typewriters

As *A Social History of English* will demonstrate, Slips of the Tongue have become so common in both Orality and Literacy that instead of Grammar and Good Taste we virtually depend on Nonverbal Communication Today. Well, it is always pleasing when we can show how the books we are discussing actually 'go together'.

'Deep emotions are often aroused by issues of language'; and no wonder when we have to cope with language like 'triglossic', 'verbomotor lifestyle', 'grapholect', 'noetic economy', 'para-language and kinesics', 'onset time in noncoactive episodes'. In *A Social History of English* Dick Leith has taken on more than can be safely digested within one set of covers: the development of English from the vernacular of 'certain Germanic tribes' through contacts with Celtic, Norman French, and Central French, a consideration of the distinction between dialect and patois, the importance of the 1611 Bible (distanced from everyday speech but lending dignity to the national language and presumably discouraging dialects) and of Johnson's *Dictionary*, the displacement of Latin in scientific writing . . . up to 'The Imposition of English in the British Isles' and (language following the flag) 'English Overseas'.

Leith is averse to authority, or whatever smells of it, and dislikes the notion that some forms of language are superior to others. 'Unfortunately, many people tend to treat dictionaries with reverence.' Many people never open one. 'Unfortunately, a great deal of public debate about words and their meanings is conducted in an atmosphere of prescriptivism.' Unfortunately for this supposedly democratic view, many people without the benefit (as they see it) of a decent education still *want* to know how to use words. And since prescriptivism is the only brake we have on the accelerating spread of chaos, let's find some other name for it, one less reminiscent of the National Health Service.

At this point the argument runs thus: If people had followed the rules, we wouldn't have the word *glamour*, created by 'so-called careless usage' blurring the differentiation between *r* and *l* in the word *grammar* (or in *gramarye*, magic spells having once been associated with learning). As it is, we now have two words, with separate meanings, 'for the price of one'; and so we shouldn't repine when by the same process usage blurs *disinterested* and *uninterested*: you lose on the swings, you gain on the roundabouts. Very true, as we have seen; but what our champions of *laissez-faire* ignore is the fact that today is *different* from the past in that language can be so swiftly blurred or perverted on a huge scale, most notably through the agency of television. (Radio is more careful because it is solely auditory.) It took a thousand years for *lewd* to change meaning from 'lay' ('unlearned'), by way of 'worthless', to 'lecherous'. It took about three weeks for *hopefully* to conquer the world in its new sense of 'it is hoped', and not much longer for the stress on *harass* to drop back from the first syllable to the second.

In their 1987 report the Oxford University Delegacy of Local Examinations bemoaned the strange things that happened in O and A levels when the spoken or heard word was transferred to the written paper; 'bone idol' was cited, and 'the barrier was an icesaw'. *The Times* once carried an advertisement seeking 'a French-speaking PA/secretary with floorless English', while the *Financial Times* reported complaints made about the 'bad grammer' and poor spelling common among younger employees. The people I grew up among made mistakes—'you was', 'the chimbley wants cleaning'—but they weren't the intelligentsia, they didn't prepare copy for the printer. A book called *The Temp*, published in 1985 by a fine old firm, bore a quaint claim in the blurb on its jacket: 'This first novel by an unknown writer illicited a passionate critical response.' Still, when you got to p. 12 you began to think that maybe the blurb-writer was on the level: 'Sometimes when I take my typewriter from its case I feel the same kind of guilt as when I used to pull down my underpants to masturbate.'

Not that the spoken word is always correct in the first place. In the London Underground, a place notorious for its linguistic mystery and mayhem, 'This escalator is defected' was scrawled in humble chalk, possibly by somebody in a hurry, but a warning that if you 'evade your fare' you could get a criminal record, 'something that would effect the rest of your life', was accorded the dignity of a printed poster. *Titillate* and *titivate* are etymologically discrete, but *Collins* allows the 'rare' use of the latter as another word for 'titillate'. Not rare at all; E. C. Tubb, a writer of science fiction, talks in the same book of 'lovers seeking new titivation' and 'deliberately managed slaughter for the titivation of a jaded crowd'. (It is touching to see another science-fiction writer, Gene Wolfe, going out of his way to underscore the pristine meaning of *decimate*: '. . . my own ten-times decimated people'.)

John Gross records an anchorman on American television speaking of a 'debiccle'—rhyming with 'medical' but nothing worse than a débâcle—in Washington; and I have heard an MP on British television declaring that something 'mitigated against' something else. The diarist of *The Times* reported that, instead of celebrating Harlow on its fortieth anniversary in 1987, London Weekend Television 'corruscated' the town. This involved both a misspelling (Latin *coruscare*, 'glitter') and, on the face of it, mistaken identity, and so—tempted by the ironic contiguity of a plea from the literary editor for more teaching of Latin and Greek in schools—I addressed a short letter to the editor, wondering whether the diarist had intended 'excoriated' or 'execrated' or 'castigated'. The letter wasn't printed, but later I received a polite note from the paper saying that the writer had indeed intended 'excoriated' but was too busy to check.

That was a solitary mishap, and some writers, we know, are too busy to write. And merely (if very) irritating are the bright little phrases that television eagerly pumps up into omnipresent, omnipurpose tags, such as 'the name of the game', 'having said which' (with no indication of who said it), and 'at the end of the day', albeit the latter has generated inadvertent comedy. 'It turned out to be quite a night at the end of the day,' said Jimmy Hill on *Match of the Day*. In a more serious category is the increasing misuse, also propagated by television, of *refute* to mean 'deny' instead of 'disprove'. 'I refute the suggestion categorically!' said someone, the other night, who was merely rejecting it. (But perhaps had a dim impression that he *was* disproving it.) Dr Johnson didn't think he was only rejecting Bishop Berkeley's theory—'I refute it *thus*'—when he kicked that large stone. Peter denied Christ thrice but didn't refute him once.

Niggling of this sort is sure to sound horribly priggish; and it's as well to remember the admonitory words of Saul Bellow's Herzog: the assumption that the deterioration or debasement of language is tantamount to dehumanization can itself lead to cultural Fascism. But I don't see that this lets scholars off the hook; by their cheerful, 'democratic' indifference, their purposeful slackness, they may be sowing new fields of professional endeavour for themselves, but they are laying rods in pickle for all of us. One of them has said, apropos of the fate of *disinterested*, that if a word is needed for something then it will be found. If we had a word, and it disappeared, does that mean we don't want the thing?

Dick Leith is strict, though, when it comes to sensitive spots. We mustn't use 'coon'—true, we can hardly bring ourselves to use it in saying we shouldn't use it. We mustn't use 'bent' or 'queer'— fair enough. But we are exhorted to use 'gay' on the grounds that it 'has become instrumental in the cause of homosexual equality'. If a word is needed for something it will be found; but this one wasn't found, it was maladroitly stolen. So 'authority', the authority of a minority, is OK here? I wonder how many of those homosexuals who perforce spent years in the closet are really happy with the expression.

With so much to cover, 'The Semantic Disparagement of Women' gets only two pages, but they are sensational. It has been estimated, we hear, that there are 'over 1000 words which in their history have denoted women and have also meant "whore" '. My *Roget* isn't up to scratch, it lists fewer than twenty; though Roget's original *Thesaurus* of 1852 gave twenty-nine, including 'wench' and 'hussy', as well as '*chère amie*' and 'Jezebel' and 'Messalina'. Since patronizing brothels and consorting with whores has generally been 'socially taboo', a covert language was needed, embracing 'even words like *nun* and *laundress*'. Presumably nuns have had too much dignity and laundresses too little clout to mount a counter-offensive. The conclusion, arrived at via the changing fortunes of the word *buxom*, originating as 'bowsome', 'submissive', and later influenced (maybe) by *bust*, is this: 'Men, it seems, have wanted women who are sexually submissive, and if possible comely and well-favoured too.' Well, they would, wouldn't they? (Another telly tag.) Perhaps somewhere here lies the reason why, according to

Otto Preminger, it was the word *virgin* that was objected to in the film *The Moon is Blue*.

Human society formed itself through oral communication, not written memos; only very late in its history did it become literate. Can it be that now, with television and its passion for chat shows and off-the-cuff pontificating, we are returning to orality, to the illiterate society foreshadowed by Melvyn Bragg? Is the race heading for its second childhood? If so, then it can count on the moral support of Walter J. Ong, who states that of all the thousands, tens of thousands, of languages spoken at one time or another 'only about 106 have ever been committed to writing to a degree sufficient to have produced literature', and that of the some 3000 languages spoken today, only some seventy-eight have a literature. 'The basic orality of language is permanent,' Ong states in this book he has written, *Orality and Literacy: The Technologizing of the Word*. 'Oral communication unites people in groups,' he observes, whereas 'writing and reading are solitary activities that throw the psyche back on itself': a truism which is less than wholly and purely true. More interestingly, in that the heroic and marvellous had the function of organizing knowledge which nowadays is organized elsewise, he associates with writing/printing the transition from the hero to the anti-hero, from Achilles to John Updike's Rabbit. We may not all take comfort from his assurance that this situation 'has nothing to do with a putative "loss of ideals" '. Homer couldn't write, but what a powerful memory the man had! Ong remarks of Homeric studies: 'Nowhere do the contrasts between orality and literacy or the blind spots of the unreflective chirographic or typographic mind show in a richer context.' Shouldn't he have said 'deaf spots'?

That speech came before writing, like fingers before forks, none of us disputes; nor—though, as Ong notes, it is difficult for fully literate people to imagine what a primary oral culture is or was like—that there has been great oral poetry. As for Plato, we wouldn't have known, let alone cared, that he rated speech above writing—the latter being presumptuous enough to pretend that what can be only in the mind has been established outside it—if somebody hadn't written him down. There is no mention here of the Etruscans, or of Richard Wilbur's touching address to their poets:

> Dream fluently, still brothers, who when young
> Took with your mothers' milk the mother tongue,
>
> In which pure matrix, joining world and mind,
> You strove to leave some line of verse behind
>
> Like a fresh track across a field of snow,
> Not reckoning that all could melt and go.

Or of Emerson's aphorism: 'The book written against fame and learning has the author's name on the title-page.'

Totally enigmatic, I find, is Ong's assertion that, without doubt, Chinese characters will be replaced by the Roman alphabet 'as soon as all the people in the Peoples' [*sic*] Republic of China master the same Chinese language ("dialect")', and consequently 'the loss to literature will be enormous, but not so enormous as a Chinese typewriter using over 40,000 characters'. What was that again? A joke? However, there are at least two fine remarks to carry away. One has it that 'It is bad pedagogy to insist that because there is nothing "wrong" with other dialects, it makes no difference whether or not speakers of another dialect learn the grapholect [established national written language], which has resources of a totally different order of magnitude.' This counsel should avert the death of a thousand typewriters. At least we shall all be able to converse by means of ball-point and paper, like speakers of different Chinese dialects who trace the ideograms in spilt beer on bar-tables. The second observation occurs in a description of the 'psychodynamics' of oral cultures: proverbial in style, 'redundant' or 'copious', 'empathetic and participatory', aggregative rather than analytic. Since all depends on memory, and you only know what you recall, he sums up: 'Think memorable thoughts.' That is a memorable thought, for writers a chastening one.

Ong seems to be in two minds, one oral and the other written. He is expressly concerned to 'undercut the chirographic and typographic bias', but he also concedes (if it is a concession) that 'writing is consciousness-raising'. It may be that what most sways him is the consideration that God *speaks*, he does not write, and

'Jesus, the Word of God, left nothing in writing, though he could read and write.' Ong follows with a gloss on 2 Corinthians 3: 6: 'The letter kills, the spirit [breath, on which rides the spoken word] gives life.' There is an altogether different book to be written around that passage.

Nonverbal Communication Today: Current Research, edited by Mary Ritchie Key, promises or threatens to take us several stages nearer the primeval. Actually the book is several degrees more modest; or possibly less comprehensible to the lewd laity. One contributor proposes as a 'new assumption' that 'long and exclusive emphasis on the verbal mode in education may have the effect of diminishing an individual's ability to make cognitive shifts in information-processing mode as required for specific tasks'. Since he is talking about the teaching of realistic drawing, and the proposal is hemmed about by qualifiers and particularizers, it may be considered fairly harmless, or meaningless.

Topics treated here include facial expression and intonation (both of which, as we have long suspected, assist speech by completing or clarifying meaning), finger-snapping, mother–child nonverbal interaction, animal communication, eye behaviour, and blushing. (It seems that women still tend to blush more than men, or did in 1977.) An article on 'Nonverbal Communication as Political Behaviour' sounds exciting, but ends in mystery. It seems that something was done to or by some twenty Swiss judges in the course of a field study in 1970, which drew from them smiles or scowls or head-movements or even caused them to get up and walk about behind the bench. Not one of them, we are told, actually slept. The conclusions drawn from these observations are either absent from the text or (quite likely) invisible to the untrained eye. Apart, that is, from this: 'Nonverbal communication itself was best predicted by emotional communication, economically conservative attitudes, and Romand language maternalism', in particular when the judges were relatively young and Roman Catholic. There must be conclusions to be drawn from this conclusion.

Despite the editor's effort to persuade us that the contributors are simply exploring the ever-popular question, 'What makes people tick?', these are specialist papers, copious in tables, graphs, and 'dendrograms', varying between the labouredly obvious and the reconditely tentative. My impression was that they were waiting for Walter J. Ong to come along and make them into a book.

In a similarly ecumenical spirit Anne Cutler, editor of *Slips of the Tongue and Language Production*, assures us that collecting speech errors is enjoyable and can justify such unscholarly pursuits as attending dinner parties and watching television interviews. But do not imagine it is a simple straightforward operation—if you listen for errors you may miss the content of what is said, if you attend to the content you may miss the errors. Also you have to watch out for deliberate witticisms, like 'my excess (Access) card'.

These papers analyse types of errors and classify them in linguistic categories. Since one concern is the implications that wrongness has for rightness, for 'the correct operation of the language production process'—when the argot isn't aspiring to be scientific it pretends to be industrial—emphasis is less on the psychological portent of such 'Freudian' slips as this: 'In the case of the female genitals, in spite of many *Versuchungen* [temptations]—I beg your pardon, *Versuche* [experiments] . . .', and more on 'pure' speech mishaps, like simple transpositions ('the Milo de Venus', 'I roasted a cook'), word-blends ('lection' for *lecture/lesson*), splices and spoonerisms, confusion between similar sounds or endings ('the coffee is copulating'), and word-division ('rubbish sheep'). A more complex error, in the 'substitution-blend' category, occurs when the speaker starts to say 'severely retarded', then thinks of 'profoundly retarded', and ends with 'When you're working with severely profound children . . .' This is glossed with the heavy-handedness generally in evidence when methodology is imposed on the humanities: 'We see that (part of) an adverb has substituted for an adjective. Note, however, that the adverb, *profoundly*, is composed morphologically of the adjective, *profound*, and the adverb-forming suffix, *-ly*,' and so on.

Then there is the 'crucial and largely unexplored' question, 'To what extent do children differ from adults in their storage and retrieval of lexical items?' An answer is attempted by comparing

adult and child malapropisms. One example taken has as its
'target word' *condiment(s)*:

1. Adult: We have a lovely Victorian *condom* set.
2. Child: Pass the *monuments*, please.
3. Child: Here you are, silly, you mean the *ornaments*.

It is pointed out that the adult preserves the initial consonant and
the stressed vowel while the children preserve the number of
syllables and the final consonant. Attention is also drawn to the
fact—which can no longer be a fact—that children are unlikely
to know the word *condom*, apparently one of the 'classical
malapropisms' collected from adults in 1978, ten long years ago.

Ignorance is acknowledged as a factor in the commission of
errors, notably in the field of medicine: 'frosted' and 'phosphate'
for *prostate*, 'muted' for *neutered*, 'polaroids' for *haemorrhoids*,
'fornications' for *fomentations*, 'tantalizers' for *tranquillizers*.
Comestibles run a close second, with 'corvettes' for *courgettes*,
'desecrated' coconut for *desiccated*, 'partisan' for *Parmesan*,
'armadillo' for *Amontillado*, 'Salome' for *salami*. But certain
errors can be put down to having a lot of things in one's head, as
when Heine referred to Faust's sweetheart as 'Käthchen' instead
of *Gretchen*. 'They are two of the most prevalent feminine
diminutives,' it is explained, 'and they are both names found in
Goethe, and even belong to persons in his *life*.' If you knew nothing about Goethe you probably wouldn't ever make that silly
mistake.

'To err is human . . .' is cited by Ong as an example of the
formulaic-mnemonic characteristic of oral cultures. In the present book we hear several times of the deletion-of-consonant error
in 'tendahl' for *Stendahl*; the context is such, or such by now is the
state of our minds, that we cannot be absolutely positive that
Stendahl is an error for *Stendhal*. The blurb on the back cover
adverts to 'the slips of the tongue in a large corpus of spantaneous
English conversation'. The corpus does cover quite a span, so it's
no wonder if the tongue slips on occasion.

Dennis E. Baron's *Grammar and Good Taste: Reforming the
American Language* is more of a book for the general reader: a
brisk and neatly documented history of the American concern ('or

mania') for correctness and the attendant suspicion ('or fear') of language regulation. The conclusion, exposed on p. 6, is foregone: 'The history of the failure of language reform in America should serve as a warning to those who would modify the language of its people.'

So, little suspense here, no use waiting for a thrilling denouement; but instead a lively sequence of vignettes from the early eighteenth century onwards, among them those figures who wanted to preserve the language of Hampden and Milton—and also the others, seemingly few, who wished to replace English with Greek or French or Hebrew. The last-mentioned proposal led the *Quarterly Review* of London to opine that the Americans considered themselves the new 'chosen people', while rather more wittily a member of the committee which drafted the Declaration of Independence recommended that they should keep the language as it was and make *the English* speak Greek. More than anything else, it must have been the taboo word 'English' that upset people, who accordingly sought for substitutes or circumlocutions—'American', 'the language of the United States'—although a comforting theory had it that before long English or more exactly American English would be the universal tongue and accordingly washed clean of original sin.

Encouraged by the Revolution, the great Noah Webster rejected British authority in linguistic matters in favour of national authority. 'A *national language* is a band of *national unity*' (1789). He was at least as much prescriptive as descriptive: usage is the law of speech, but 'only when custom is national, when the practice of a nation is uniform or general', and he was unsentimental about dialects, which in his view were disagreeable to strangers and could have 'an unhappy effect upon the social affections'. However, he failed in his attempt to redress the word 'bridegroom', an amalgam of *bride* and *guma* ('man') but corrupted by wrongful association with horses, and also in his efforts to reform spelling. The reforming of spelling is an area where the most intelligent of men soon begin to look like cranks. One of the reasons adduced by H. L. Mencken for the failure of these movements was that people lumped 'rationalized spelling' together with comic dialect writing and couldn't take it seriously. In a sense dissimilar from Ong's, the public was too literate.

Language

A procession of illustrious names bears witness to the zealous solicitude Americans have shown for their language. Benjamin Franklin ('Art is long, and their Time is short', so pupils had best concentrate on their native tongue); Thomas Jefferson (a believer in 'judicious neology'); Walt Whitman ('The Americans are going to be the most fluent and melodious voiced people in the world'); Ambrose Bierce (author of a guide to usage, *Write It Right*); Mark Twain (in the interests of spelling-reform he reported a script-ural revolt in ancient Egypt: it took forty-five minutes to render the Lord's Prayer in hieroglyphics and only four minutes to do it in the Roman alphabet); Henry James (addressing Bryn Mawr College in 1905: 'Against a care for tone, it would very much appear, the elements of life in this country, as at present conditioned, violently and increasingly militate') . . . It is to the balance struck by opposing forces—the drive for correctness and the desire for independence and individuality—that we owe the happy circumstance that, while American English certainly has its distinctiveness, Americans can understand British English pretty well and Britons can understand American English pretty well, despite the jokes both sides make—and other races manage to understand both.

Though Baron is not too well disposed towards 'high-handed purism', he is fair-minded, even to quoting as representative of a 'grass-roots attitude' a quite affecting passage from a recent undergraduate examination paper (Eastern Illinois University):

I think I support prescriptivisim . . . I believe there is one right and wrong for everyone. Perhaps what I think is right is not what you think is right but in the final analysis that isn't going to matter. What God thinks is right is what really matters and He doesn't have one right for you and one right for me.

Yes, these books do 'go together'. They share, in varying degrees and some of them artlessly, an excited predilection for primitivism and disdain for precedent, and a relish for what Pope called 'Mountains of Casuistry'. Also an unattractive turning against what has made their authors what they are. No doubt such procedures are amusing and risk-free—and they help in carving out one's niche or university chair in the edifice of Universal Darkness.

Broad Rumour

That by and large fame has had a bad press is partly because
saluting it looks much like soliciting it. 'What is honour?' A word,
an empty bubble. But now we have a history of it, a very full and
learned book, containing hundreds of thousands of words. In *The
Frenzy of Renown* Leo Braudy surmises that to document this
history thoroughly would be the work of at least a lifetime—a
modest estimate—'since everything preserved for us from the past
can in some sense be considered a message that perpetuates someone's fame.' Everything is a lot; and since it is impossible to be
exhaustive, was it necessary to be quite so exhausting? What
keeps Braudy's reader going, if at times stumbling, is not the
philosophy and psychology and sociology of fame—where repetitiousness is inevitable as century succeeds century—so much as
the diversity of witnesses brought to the stand. Anecdote is the
spur, story counts for more than history.

Everything, or a lot of it, is grist to Braudy's mill; and at times
we are ready to believe that he knows everything. Ovid has his
place, not only in fame but in the history of it: according to the
Metamorphoses Callisto competed with a goddess by lying with
Jupiter, was changed into a bear by jealous Juno, and then transformed into a constellation by Jupiter. (In modern parlance, she
became a star.) More generally, Braudy maintains, in this work
Ovid is pitting the human authority of the artist against the inhu-
man power of the gods. In another time and place the neglected
poet Enoch Soames is transported into the future, by courtesy of
the Devil, so that he can check on his posthumous fame. He finds
only one mention of himself, as an imaginary character in a story
by Max Beerbohm, who has thus added to his own reputation by
writing about someone who achieved nonentity.

Odysseus was helped towards fame by representing himself as a
nonentity, telling Polyphemus ('many fames') that his name was
'Nobody'. When the Cyclops cried out that 'Nobody' had blinded
him, nobody paid any attention. Safely back on his ship, but
loath to remain anonymous, Odysseus shouts: 'If anyone asks you

how you were shamed and blinded, say that Odysseus, son of Laertes, from Ithaca, did it!' This was imprudent, and Polyphemus promptly called on his father, Poseidon, to avenge him. But then, the ensuing misadventures suffered by the man from Ithaca plump out the *Odyssey* and make him world-famous. This can take time: a murderer complained to the police, in 1978, that only with his sixth killing had he begun to receive his rightful publicity. That infamy is fame is proved by the story of Herostratus, the shabby hero who burned down the Temple of Diana at Ephesus on the day of Alexander the Great's birth, in order to pre-empt some of the greatness in the offing. His name is found in reference books today whereas, in the spirit of a Brecht poem, the architects of the temple are lost to oblivion. Braudy might have reminded us, for the sake of extra piquancy, that when Herostratus was executed it was forbidden ever to mention his name on pain of death.

'Can a state survive its great men?' The question is first raised in connection with Pompey (named, at the age of twenty-five, the Great). In connection with the absurdity into which thirst for eminence can degenerate, Braudy mentions a later emperor who designated himself Magnus Maximus—a Spaniard, so my reference book states, who fought successfully against the Picts and Scots but was defeated by Theodosius I (himself subtitled 'the Great') and executed in 388. This moral is plain early in the story: like nails, one greatness drives out another.

Braudy's obsession with his subject—obsessions are not to be mocked, rather the reverse—leads him into fascinating byways, some of them once familiar and now largely forgotten. It can also lead him astray, though rarely. In respect of the desire felt by Hemingway's character, Colonel Cantwell, for a life of privacy 'where integrity and wholeness of being can finally flourish'—as the unknown yearn for fame so the famous yearn, often less whole-heartedly, for privacy—Braudy compares the Colonel with Shakespeare's Mark Antony, 'who tells Cleopatra that if she wants he will leave the world of public fame and live "as a private man in Athens" '. No, this was the plea conveyed to Octavius Caesar by Antony's ambassador, 'a Schoolmaster', after the defeat off Actium: could Antony please be allowed to live in Egypt or, at second best, as a private man in Athens? Nothing to do with integrity or wholeness of being or pleasing Cleopatra, but just a pathetic offer, under duress, to be a good boy in future. The cynical view of 'privacy' has been put vulgarly though effectively by Fred Allen: 'A celebrity is a person who works hard all his life to become known, then wears dark glasses to avoid being recognized.'

'Public esteem is the nurse of the arts and all men are fired to application by fame.' Cicero's assertion must often be true, but isn't always. The proposition has been repeated over and over, in varying forms, the finest and most celebrated being Milton's: fame is the 'last infirmity of noble mind', where 'last' presumably means the last weakness to be overcome or (echoing Tacitus) the last thing to be parted from, and also the least deplorable. Integrity and wholeness of being, adduced as the gift of privacy, can also be the fruit and indeed the intention of 'application'. We do sometimes work for love of the work. Not that this phenomenon is exactly disinterested, since we are enjoying what we do, but even this degree of disinterestedness, or of disinterested interest, gets insufficient publicity, so to speak, here. In a fairly humorous poem, 'When Earth's Last Picture is Painted', Kipling looked forward to the day when the last reviewer was dead and gone and the sole patron of the arts was God, and when

> no one shall work for money, and no one shall work for fame,
> But each for the joy of the working . . .

Regarding the Roman Republic, Braudy remarks that historians have spent many pages 'measuring the mix of political principle and personal ambition in the career of public figures', and adds, as a pragmatic rider, that in Latin *ambitio* means 'to walk around, canvassing for votes'. I don't see how that mix can be analysed and measured with much accuracy whatever the career may be.

Sterne is quoted to the effect that he wrote not to be *fed*, but to be *famous*. We have often heard that sentiment, just as we have often heard the contrary sentiment: 'Don't praise me, pay me.' Much of the time, I imagine, most of us would like both, to be world-famous and well paid. That thought too is a banality; the subject of fame is encompassed with commonplaces and half-truths, like the subject of money. Johnson is reported as declaring that no man but a blockhead ever wrote except for money, but we don't suppose he intended to utter a categorical and universal truth.

Milton's contention was that 'Fame is no plant that grows on mortal soil': it does not lie in 'broad rumour' but lives only in the 'pure eyes' of God. All the same, it is on mortal soil that one must promulgate one's message, for there is no need of teaching and improving in heaven. Braudy notes shrewdly that Satan tempts Eve with the novel notion of celebrity, and in the shape now enjoyed by film stars and television personalities.* Who is there to gaze on her in Eden, apart from some unappreciative animals and one sole man? She, who deserves to 'be seen a goddess among gods', adored and ministered to by a daily entourage of 'angels numberless'. But it is sadly inadequate to characterize Satan, as Milton (with or without knowing it) portrayed him, as 'an epic show-off' whose sin is 'not pride so much as an unquenchable desire for more and more appreciators, and a ravaging envy of anyone whom he thinks is celebrated in his stead'. (That parvenu man was due to be celebrated would try the patience of an angel!) *Paradise Regained* is more directly amenable to the argument at this stage: after resisting the temptation in the wilderness, and having listened to the acceptable acclamation of the angelic choir, Christ 'unobserved/Home to his mother's house private returned'.

The conventional invocation of the Muse, by Milton and others, Christian or pagan, displaces attention, moving it away from the writer and towards the message. Braudy talks of 'virtuous withdrawal' versus 'self-display', but the first expression sounds much like 'backing into the limelight', hardly to be distinguished from the 'ostentatious evasions of publicity' he imputes to J. D. Salinger and Thomas Pynchon. He cites Emily Dickinson's lines: 'To earn it by disdaining it / Is Fame's consummate fee', but goes on to style her 'the show-off of eternity' (outstripping even Satan?) because of 'the innumerable ways she devised to humble herself in the world even as she asserted herself to posterity and to heaven'. It is true that she had only four poems published in her

---

* Peter Conrad proposes a distinction between fame and celebrity: Orson Welles was already famous, but he achieved celebrity through his commercials for sherry and lager.

lifetime, whereas every word she penned would doubtless circulate in heaven. But it seems misdirected harshness to term 'ambivalent' the desire for immortality in one who scarcely had a mortal life.

> I'm Nobody! Who are you?
> Are you—Nobody—too?
> Then there's a pair of us!
> Don't tell! they'd banish us—you know!
>
> How dreary—to be—Somebody!
> How public—like a Frog—
> To tell your name—the livelong June—
> To an admiring Bog!

This poem of hers affects me as comic, light-hearted, and truthful, rather than a manifestation of the self-approval that stems from not seeking applause.

Braudy is strong on thinking, in general, somewhat low on feeling. My impression is that he underestimates the genuine distaste for fame, or distrust of it. It is the case that among those who profess contempt for fame some are simultaneously amassing it; it is only wise to declare that the grapes are sour once you have picked them, since false modesty is often taken for the real thing, and moreover you may actually manage to discourage potential rivals. All the same, after making heavy weather of the apparent contradiction in Keats, who scorned egotism and vanity in poets and yet said 'I think I shall be among the English poets after my death', Braudy gets it right by giving due weight to Keats's remarks about the poetical character which 'has no self'. To be modest or reticent does not involve you in abjectness; it may involve a lot of pride.

'In the new world of publicity'—the reference is to the late seventeenth century—'even the reclusive needed a public format if they wanted to have an effect.' Samuel Butler was more forthright:

> Honour is, like a Widow, won
> With brisk Attempt and putting on;
> With ent'ring manfully, and urging;
> Not slow approaches, like a Virgin.

Honour must be a tough old bird. Alongside those statements we should place what Coleridge wrote in *Biographia Literaria* concerning 'men of the greatest genius' as judged by contemporary accounts: 'In the inward assurance of permanent fame, they seem to have been either indifferent or resigned with regard to immediate reputation.' At all events, Braudy provides a sonorous summing-up of the urge to fame at its best, as 'a desire for recognition and appreciation that is interwoven with the nature of the human community, both socially valuable and personally enriching, beyond the rewards of comfort and status, in a worth inseparable from the good opinions of others'.

The Frenzy of Renown may be compared to a small pony hauling a huge pantechnicon, full to overflowing: the pony founders, the van falls apart, and a lot of curious and unexpected contents are scattered around. Not all the material is strictly germane, but the book constitutes an impressive anthology of human prowess, push, pathos, and perversity. Some of its themes, ranging far and wide, deserve to be itemized.

For instance, the interplay between the individual and his or her society or 'culture' (well, if you were the only person in the world you would be famous indeed, ripe for *The Guinness Book of Records*, except that there would be no one to take cognizance of you; cf. Eve in Eden), and 'the speed with which a president can change from an authority to a scapegoat'. The cost, and the irony, of fame: the baby son of Charles Lindbergh, the Lone Eagle, was kidnapped and murdered, along with Lindbergh's privacy. Julius Caesar's stage-managing of his image: Suetonius reports that, despite being stabbed twenty-three times, he arranged his toga decorously as he fell. Patronage, and the relation between political fame (Augustus) and literary (Horace): in the poet's words, 'Many brave men lived before Agamemnon, but all have gone down, unmourned and unknown, into the long night, for lack of their sacred poet.' The cult of saints and martyrs: St Simeon Stylites, the celebrated solitary on his pillar, 'had constant crowds of admirers'. The mixture in Dante of 'Christian humility and literary assertion'; Chaucer's *House of Fame* supplies an entertaining contrast, when the overweight Englishman, carried off by an eagle, wonders apprehensively whether 'Jove wol me stellifye'.

Portrait painting, printing, and then photography, all played their part in the swelling act of this strange eventful history: yet Joan of Arc became known to millions without the aid of any one of them. (There must be some early intimation here of the fearsome law of diminishing returns which takes a hectic and ever-increasing toll in our day.) And similarly the theatre and its impact, in particular Shakespeare's history plays with their 'exposure' of kingship and the private moments of monarchs; hence Elizabeth's nervous reflection (alleged, and not necessarily in response to Shakespeare's play): 'I am Richard II, know ye not that?'

Braudy quotes appositely from Boswell's *Journal*, 1764, a passage where Boswell asks Rousseau whether it is possible to live among men and still retain one's singularity, and Rousseau answers that yes, it is, he has done it. Boswell: 'But to remain on good terms with them?' Rousseau: 'Oh, if you want to be a wolf, you must howl.' Did Boswell subsequently enter into an affair with Rousseau's mistress purely in the hope that traces of genius or singularity and thus of fame would rub off on him? Then of course there is suicide, resorted to either because of failure to gain recognition or as a means of gaining it posthumously. Melancholia, tuberculosis, and (in moderate measure) madness have been deemed emblems of genius; and also, though a less agreeable cachet, syphilis. Byron serves as the exemplar of the hero-victim of the machinery of celebrity in the nineteenth century, 'the aristocrat who signals the effective end of aristocracy because he also wants to be famous'. (There may be a specifically American assumption there.) The most poignant gloss on 'Byronism' I know of, applicable as well to the phenomenon of 'dandies' and *poètes maudits*, lies in an anecdote purveyed by Matthew Arnold. When choosing a school for her son, Mary Shelley sought advice from a friend and was told the usual thing: 'Oh, send him somewhere where they will teach him to think for himself.' Mrs Shelley replied: 'Teach him to think for himself? Oh, my God, teach him rather to think like other people!'

Arriving at more recent times, Braudy introduces P. T. Barnum ('There's a sucker born every minute') and 'The Greatest Show on Earth'; Barnum dedicated his *Life*, written by himself, to 'The Universal Yankee Nation, of which I am Proud to Be

One', and made it known that the title of 'prince of humbugs' was first applied to him by himself. Mention is made of the typeface named after him—glory indeed!—with its brash, graceless alphabet and pointing fingers. In connection with the 'new' media, Braudy cites Hitler (1943): 'Imagine me going around with a pot-belly. It would mean political ruin.' And it appears that during the 1930s there was a famous (*sic*) brothel in Hollywood, called Mae's, where the girls all looked like, and acted like, famous actresses. The story casts a sad, chill light on Braudy's conclusion, that 'The more open a society we have, the more professedly equal we are before the law, the greater the urge to personal distinction. . . . In such a world the famous help answer the question: How do I live?' Come to think of it, though, Mae's did offer a fitting way of spending those fifteen minutes of fame we have all been promised in the near future.

In the relative privacy of the introduction Braudy allows himself to sound a rare (and welcome) personal note, in a brief recital of a 'marginal martyrdom'. He tells how his preliminary musings, specifically on how he himself wanted to be the best and yet noted for his humility, were painfully focused when in 1971 he read the manuscript of a book his first wife had written about the collapse of their marriage. Such a book could be socially valuable (a term in his exposition of the urge to fame at its best) as well as useful to the author's career in journalism (another term). But as he read on, he felt the book was self-absorbed and self-deceptive, though he couldn't decently resist its publication, nor could he ask her to change anything concerning himself. He began to realize, he says, that 'going public' meant being entrapped in the gaze of others, reduced by their definitions, and twisted into unforeseen shapes. 'Without severe cost, I had been privileged for a moment to stand outside the apparatus of modern fame and observe myself as a tiny element in its vast operation.'

On p. 594 Braudy speculates that his reference to Farrah Fawcett on p. 7 may now need footnoting. And, pardon my ignorance, but who is Richard Pryor, who announced in 1976 that he wanted people to be able to recognize him 'by just looking at a caricature of me that has no name on it', adding 'I know now that I can reach that level. I had doubts before but I don't have those doubts any more'? Joseph Epstein has unselfishly set out the five stages of a career thus: (1) Who is Joseph Epstein? (2) Get me Joseph Epstein. (3) We need someone like Joseph Epstein. (4) What we need is a young Joseph Epstein. (5) Who is Joseph Epstein? 'Who is what, finally?' asks a poem by C. H. Sisson called 'News': 'Finally nobody is anything.' Perhaps that's going it a bit. According to one of Canetti's aphorisms, what reconciles us to fame is that in the long run it is unpredictable.

'Do you by any chance know who a man called Russell Harty is?' asks the Englishman, in Jonathan Raban's *Foreign Land*, who has returned after long years abroad. He is astounded to discover that, whereas you have to wait ages for most things, a television set is delivered pronto, 'as if it was a medical emergency'. (And, should anything go wrong, the repair-man—unlike the doctor—comes running.) As early as p. 5, thinking of the ever-growing number of faces we see every day thanks to communications technology, Braudy comments that if these are famous then we may well ask, what is fame? His estimate has it that in the medieval world the average person saw one hundred other people in the course of a life-time, whereas now any city-dweller or anyone with a television set can see that many in an hour.

I well remember an occasion in the early 1950s, in Birmingham, when our two-year-old daughter, forcibly retrieved from watching a neighbour's television, pointed scornfully at our radio: 'No vision!', and stomped off to bed. You could be famous then for possessing a set. Later you could be famous for declining to possess one. Now you can be famous for appearing on a chat show; and even more so, of course, for having a show of your own.

Dame Edna Everage, that sweet old—sorry, mature—battle-axe, habitually mortifies her guests, yet there is no shortage of them, famous already, but willing to be made fools of for the sake of another appearance before the nation. Fame needs constant renewal. When I was a child, the people round our way were terrified at the idea of getting into the papers; but then, what would most likely have got them there was public drunkenness, fighting in the street, failure to pay the rent, or defaulting on hire-purchase. Nowadays you don't need actually to have been on television for someone on the bus to ask, 'Haven't I seen you on the telly?'

To be famous means to be in one way or another acceptable to—usable by—the media. The Medea, who can assist you to win the Golden Fleece and other prestigious prizes. Who gives, and who takes away soon afterwards. Time is like a fashionable host—said Shakespeare's Ulysses, discoursing on our present subject, ignorant though he was of televisionary hosts—who limply shakes the parting guest by the hand while eagerly greeting the newcomer. 'One touch of nature makes the whole world kin,/ That all with one consent praise new-born gawds.' Not infrequently one comes across the keyword of Braudy's title spelt 'reknown', as if it meant known just twice.

Putnam Smif, the young and ardent American in *Martin Chuzzlewit*, proclaims, 'I aspirate for fame. It is my yearning and my thirst'; but he has given the game away in declaring that 'Every alligator basking in the slime is in himself an Epic, self-contained.' So are we all, all self-contained epics, and if we are not to be alive and known in some other world, we want all the more to be remembered in this one. Alas, it would take more than a Homer to make a readable book of us, with appreciably more text than footnotes. Auden's verse is glumly to the point:

> Lucky the poets of old; for half their work was done for them:
> all would applaud when they named places or heroes or gods.
> Proper Names are *an-sich* poetic, but now there is hardly
> one that a poet will dare pen without adding a gloss.

Index

Abse, Dannie, 13
Adenauer, Konrad, 125
Agrippa, Cornelius, 102
AIDS—The Facts, 57
Albertus Magnus, 102
Alexander VI, Pope, 116
Alexander the Great, 222, 236
Allen, Fred, 237
Amis, Kingsley, 17
Andrew, Prince, 32, 33
Antony, Mark, 236–7
Aristotle, 220
Arnold, Matthew, 173–4, 180, 241
Auden, W.H., 244
Augustine, St, 115
Augustus, 236, 240
Austen, Jane, 5, 6, 53
Ayres, Pam, 13

Babel, Isaac, 149
Baker, Kenneth, 6–7, 16–17
Ballard, J.G., 39
Barnum, P.T., 241–2
Baron, Dennis E., 232–4
Barzun, Jacques, 40, 191–3, 212
Basil Brush Show, The, 72–6
Baudelaire, Charles, 159
Bauer, Carl, 90
Bauer, Felice, 89, 90
Bede, The Venerable, 116
Beerbohm, Max, 235
Beer-Hofmann, Richard, 150
Beethoven, Ludwig van, 6, 12
Bellow, Saul, 227
Benny Hill Show, The, 29
Berg, Alban, 150
Berkeley, George, 226
Bierce, Ambrose, 234
Big Bang in the Book World, 17–19
Birkett, Julian, 110
Birmingham, Bishop of, 55
Blake, William, 92, 166, 184
Bond, Edward, 70
Borges, Jorge Luis, 161
Boswell, James, 55, 191, 241
Bowie, David, 6
Bradbury, Malcolm, 13
Brady, Ian, 70, 71
Bragg, Melvyn, 15–16, 228
Braudy, Leo, 235–44
Brecht, Bertolt, 6, 95, 135, 236
Broch, Hermann, 145, 148, 149, 150, 151
Brond, 36
Brontë, Emily, 109
Brophy, Brigid, 199
Browning, Robert, 113, 207
Bruno, Giordano, 183
Burchfield, Robert, 205, 206
Burgess, Anthony, 165, 217

Burke, Edmund, 206
Burnell, A.C., 216–23
Butler, Samuel, 239
Byron, Lord, 10, 103, 106, 173, 241

Caesar, Julius, 240
Caesar, Octavius, *see* Augustus
Calder, John, 71
Canetti, Elias, 139, 140, 144–53, 243
Carlyle, Thomas, 174
Carmi, T., 152
Cartland, Barbara, 4–5, 15
Cary, Joyce, 214
Casanova, Giovanni Jacopo, 56
Cavafy, C.P., 94
Celts, The, 40
Chamberlain, Basil Hall, 221
Chaplin, Charlie, 164
Charles II, 75
Chateaubriand, François René, Vicomte de, 114
Chaucer, Geoffrey, 132, 202, 205, 240
Cheers, 28
Christie, Agatha, 208
Churchill, Sir Winston, 168
Cicero, Marcus Tullius, 237
Cleland, John, 38
Clement of Alexandria, 115
Cleopatra, 142, 236–7
Coleridge, Samuel Taylor, 9, 109, 110, 240
Collins, Jackie, 4–5, 15
Confucius, 130, 151
Conrad, Joseph, 166
Conrad, Peter, 8, 31, 238
Cook, Frederick A., 131, 132
Coronation Street, 20–32
Cosby Show, The, 28
Crisp, Quentin, 39
Critics' Forum, 64
Cromwell, Oliver, 197
Cromwell, Richard, 197
Crooke, William, 217
Crossroads, 33
Cutler, Anne, 231–2

Dallas, 26–8, 64, 69
Dante Alighieri, 62, 116, 154, 240
Davie, Donald, 186, 187
Davies, Robertson, 161–5
Davis, Angela, 170
Dead Head, 35
Dean, Brenda, 208
Debussy, Claude, 6
Delaney, Frank, 16, 40
DeLillo, Don, 85–7
Descartes, René, 212
Dickens, Charles, 5, 6, 7, 8, 9, 74, 87, 133, 221, 244
Dickinson, Emily, 238–9

Disney, Walt, 6, 53
Dixon, Reginald, 207
Donahue, Phil, 40
Donne, John, 87, 99
Draper, Hal, 172–82
Dryden, John, 100
Dunkley, Christopher, 28–9, 36–7, 46, 95
Dynasty 26, 27–8

EastEnders, 20–32, 45–6, 58, 77
Eastman, George, 192
Edinburgh, Duke of, 57–8, 213
Eliot, George, 87, 171, 174, 180, 181
Eliot, T.S., 114, 197, 198
Elizabeth I, 241
Elizabeth II, 31, 33, 44, 198–9, 213
Elizabeth the Queen Mother, Queen, 33
Elliot, Alistair, 180
Emerson, Ralph Waldo, 229
Emmerdale Farm, 67
Empson, William, 47
Engels, Friedrich, 179
Epstein, Joseph, 243
Ever Decreasing Circles, 29
Everett, Kenny, 46

Fawcett, Farrah, 242
Fawlty Towers, 29
Ferguson, Sarah, 32
Field, Frank, 133
First AIDS, 55–6
Flaubert, Gustave, 89, 90, 91, 92
Flexner, S.B., 197
Forman, Sir Denis, 68–70, 71, 202
Fowlds, Derek, 72, 73, 74, 75, 76
Franklin, Benjamin, 23–4
Franz Josef I, 142
Fresh Fields, 29
Freud, Sigmund, 64, 133, 157
Friedrich Wilhelm IV, 181
Funk, Charles Earle, 193–7, 199

Gaskell, Mrs Elizabeth Cleghorn, 207
Gaskill, William, 70
Genghis Khan, 36, 37, 69
George, St, 109
Gissing, George, 94–5, 96
Goering, Hermann, 164
Goethe, Johann Wolfgang von, 15, 98, 102, 103, 108, 109, 119, 135, 141, 142, 154, 163, 165, 170–1, 173, 174, 176, 177, 232
Goldbergs, The, 49
Good Life, The, 29
Grade, Michael, 63, 65
Graham, Billy, 6
Grahame, Kenneth, 73
Grass, Günter, 123–9, 135
Graves, Robert, 197
Green, Jonathon, 210–15
Greene, Graham, 3
Gregory the Great, St, 116
Grimm, Jacob and Wilhelm, 125, 127
Gropius, Walter, 150
Gross, John, 226
Gwyn, Nell, 75

Hampden, John, 233
Hanem, Kuchuk, 92
Hardy, Thomas, 100, 110
Harris, Rolf, 46
Harrison, Tony, 13
Harty, Russell, 243
Hašek, Jaroslav, 28, 170
Hayek, Friedrich August von, 198
Heath, Edward, 75
Hefner, Hugh, 212
Hegel, Georg Wilhelm Friedrich, 172
Heine, Heinrich, 44, 100, 131, 136, 172–82, 232
Heller, Erich, 130, 133, 139
Helmont, Jean Baptiste van, 192
Hemingway, Ernest, 236
Herostratus, 236
Heydrich, Reinhard, 169
Heym, Stefan, 117–22
Hill, Jimmy, 226
Hill Street Blues, 28
Hiller, Wendy, 8
Hitler, Adolf, 86, 142, 144, 242
Holroyd, Michael, 15–16
Homer, 154, 228, 235–6, 244
Horace, 240
Howerd, Frankie, 75
Hulse, Michael, 212
Humphries, Barry, 243
Hurt, John, 50
Huxley, Aldous, 53
Hyder Ali, 220

Ibsen, Henrik, 36

James, Henry, 7, 19, 89, 165, 234
James, William, 110
Jefferson, Thomas, 234
Jesus, 6, 16, 99, 100, 105, 116, 117, 120, 121, 122, 137, 165, 213, 226, 229–30, 238
Joan of Arc, 241
John, Elton, 6, 10
Johnson, Pamela Hansford, 70–1
Johnson, Samuel, 11, 55, 95, 136, 191, 205, 224, 226, 237–8
Jones, Mervyn, 4
Jonson, Ben, 16, 65, 109
Joyce, James, 53, 69, 150, 151, 214, 221
Judd, Don, 213

Kafka, Franz, 89, 90
Karloff, Boris, 106
Keats, John, 239
Keble, John, 203
Kershaw, H.V., 21, 23, 25, 26
Key, Mary Ritchie, 230–1
Kilroy-Silk, Robert, 41–2
King of the Ghetto, 35
Kingsley, Charles, 174
Kipling, Rudyard, 90, 237
Konrád, George, 170
Krafft-Ebing, Richard von, 70
Kraus, Karl, 53, 130–43, 145, 146, 148, 152
Kundera, Milan, 167

Lamb, Charles, 15
Last of the Summer Wine, 29

Index

Latini, Brunetto, 114
Lawrence, D.H., 51, 53
Leatherdale, Clive, 106, 107–8
Leavis, F.R., 132
Leavis, Q.D., 99
Lee, Christopher, 106, 108
Le Fanu, Sheridan, 107, 109, 110
Le Goff, Jacques, 114–16
Leith, Dick, 224–5, 227
Lem, Stanislaw, 60–1
Leys, Simon, 80
Lindbergh, Charles, 240
London, Bishop of, 99
Longfellow, Henry Wadsworth, 174, 202, 214
Longford, Lord, 75
Lovecraft, H.P., 166
Lowry, Malcolm, 10
Lu Xun, 80
Ludwig, Emil, 150
Lugosi, Bela, 106
Luke, David, 98
Luther, Martin, 115, 118, 120

Maddox, Brenda, 25
Magnus Maximus, 236
Mahler, Alma, 150
Mahler, Gustav, 150
Mallarmé, Stéphane, 6
Mann, Klaus, 91
Mann, Thomas, 12–13, 64, 88, 90–1, 101, 105, 122, 145, 146, 148, 151–2, 158, 164, 165, 214
Marlowe, Christopher, 16, 102, 119
Martin, Betty, 197
Martin, George, 72
Martin, St, 196
Marx, Groucho, 74
Marx, Karl, 157, 173
M*A*S*H, 28
Mata Hari, 221
Match of the Day, 226
McLuhan, Marshall, 13, 48, 142
Me and My Girl, 29
Mencken, H.L., 233
Miller, Jonathan, 7, 8, 9
Milne, A.A., 75
Milosz, Czeslaw, 145, 170, 183–7
Milton, John, 96, 101, 102, 103, 104, 105, 111, 117, 233, 237, 238
Mitford, Nancy, 192
Monro, Captain Innes, 220
Monroe, Marilyn, 194
Morris, Desmond, 197
Muir, Edwin, 53–4
Mullan, Bob, 26, 28, 39
Murnau, F.W., 106
Musil, Robert, 131, 133, 145, 146, 150, 151, 152

Nabarro, Sir George, 75
Nadherny, Sidonie, 135, 136, 137
Nagy, Imre, 170
Naked Video, 43
Nash, Robin, 72
Nestroy, Johann, 135

Nietzsche, Friedrich, 94
No Place Like Home, 29
Now—Something Else—Again, 56, 59

Offenbach, Jacques, 135
Ong, Walter J., 228–30, 231, 232, 233
Only Fools and Horses..., 29
Open All Hours, 29
Oprah Winfrey Show, The, 40
Origen, 115
Orwell, George, 168, 210, 215
Osler, Sir William, 212
Ovid, 235
Owen, Ivan, 73
Owen, Wilfred, 105

Paracelsus, Philippus Aureolus, 102
Parry, Idris, 130–1
Partridge, Eric, 29, 194, 196, 197, 206, 218
Patrick, St, 116
Paul, St, 230
Paz, Octavio, 110
Peary, Robert Edwin, 132
Pebble Mill at One, 44
Pepys, Samuel, 195, 197, 220
Perfect Strangers, 28
Peter, St, 226
Phoenix, Pat, 21
Plato, 115, 228
Plutarch, 102
Poe, Edgar Allan, 166
Polanski, Roman, 106
Polidori, John, 106
Pompey the Great, 236
Pope, Alexander, 43, 234
Porterhouse Blue, 60
Postman, Neil, 35
Potter, Beatrix, 72
Potter, Dennis, 27, 63, 64–6, 69
Powell, Anthony, 95
Preminger, Otto, 228
Presley, Elvis, 86
Prest, Thomas Peckett, 112
Prisoner, The, 49
Pritchett, V.S., 101
Procter & Gamble, 49
Professionals, The, 35
Pryor, Richard, 242
Pynchon, Thomas, 238

Quirk, Randolph, 197–200

Raban, Jonathan, 243
Reed, T.J., 181
Reynolds, Oliver, 10
Rhoda, 29
Richard II, 241
Richard III, 197
Riefenstahl, Leni, 167
Rilke, Rainer Maria, 90, 132
Rimbaud, Arthur, 96
Robinson, Anne, 8–9
Robinson, Kenneth, 43
Robinson, Robert, 21
Roch, St, 193
Roget, Mark, 11, 227

Index

Room, Adrian, 201-6, 207
Roosevelt, Franklin D., 196
Rosenberg, Julius and Ethel, 170
Ross, Betsy, 197
Rousseau, Jean-Jacques, 241
Rumpole of the Bailey, 29
Ruskin, John, 62
Russell, Jeffrey Burton, 98, 99, 100, 112
Russell, Ken, 6
Rymer, James Malcolm, 112

Saatchi & Saatchi, 49, 69
Sacco, Nicola, 170
Sackville-West, Victoria, 8
Sade, Marquis de, 62, 70, 87
Salinger, J.D., 238
Salten, Felix, 137
Sammons, Jeffrey L., 172
Scherchen, Hermann, 150, 152
Schiller, Friedrich von, 141
Schlegel, A.W., 100
Schnitzler, Arthur, 133
Schoenberg, Arnold, 133
Schumann, Robert, 131
Scott, Paul, 6-7
Scott, Sir Walter, 53
Shakespeare, William, 7-8, 15, 16, 45, 50,
    71, 74, 85, 87, 107, 114, 115, 131, 135,
    140, 153, 185, 194, 203, 204, 235, 236-7,
    241, 244
Shelley, Mary, 101-5, 106, 108, 110, 112,
    241
Shelley, Percy Bysshe, 6, 10, 78, 96, 102, 103,
    104, 105
Sidney, Sir Philip, 166
Siegl, Elsie, 132
Sienkiewicz, Henryk, 77, 80
Silverlight, John, 201, 202
Simeon Stylites, St, 240
Sinclair, Clive, 154
Singer, I.J., 155, 158, 159, 160
Singer, Isaac Bashevis, 154-60, 161
Sisson, C.H., 243
Skeat, W.W., 220
Skvorecky, Josef, 166-71, 207
Smith, Julia, 25
Soap, 27, 28
Sontag, Susan, 98
Sorry!, 29
Spenser, Edmund, 196
Spiegl, Fritz, 59, 199, 203, 206-9
Spitting Image, 43-4
Stalin, Joseph, 166, 171
Star Trek, 28
Starsky and Hutch, 36
Start the Week, 43
Steiner, George, 70, 113, 136
Stendhal, 232
Steptoe and Son, 29
Stern, J.P., 134
Sterne, Laurence, 237
Stocker, Margarita, 101
Stoker, Bram, 106, 107-11
Strindberg, August, 145
Suetonius, 240

Sweeney, The, 35
Swift, Jonathan, 36, 66, 135, 138, 142, 198
Szasz, Thomas, 133

Tacitus, Publius Cornelius, 237
Taggart, 37-8
Tagore, Rabindranath, 77
Taxi, 28
Taylor, D.J., 53
Taylor, Laurie, 26, 28, 39
Tell, William, 131
Terence, 170
Thackeray, William Makepeace, 8, 204
Thatcher, Margaret, 29, 32, 33, 43, 44
Theodosius I, 236
Timms, Edward, 133, 134-5, 137, 139
To the Manor Born, 29
Tolstoy, Leo, 154, 155
Tomlinson, Charles, 94
Torquemada, Tomás de, 36, 37
Toulouse-Lautrec, Henri de, 43
Trollope, Anthony, 5, 214
Trotsky, Leon, 120
Tsvetayeva, Marina, 15
Tubb, E.C., 226
Twain, Mark, 234

Ulbricht, Walter, 125
Updike, John, 52, 228

van Eyck, Hubertus, 164
Vanzetti, Bartolomeo, 170

Wagner, Richard, 211
Wassermann, Jakob, 150
Watson, Jack, 21
Waugh, Evelyn, 206
Webster, John, 57
Webster, Noah, 233
Weekley, Ernest, 206
Welles, Orson, 238
Wentworth, H., 197
Werfel, Franz, 150
White, Patrick, 198
Whitehouse, Mary, 24, 29, 75
Whitman, Walt, 187, 234
Wilbur, Richard, 229
Wilhelm II, Kaiser, 133
Wilson, A.N., 111
Wilson, Colin, 4
Wogan, Terry, 4-5, 40
Wolfe, Gene, 226
Wordsworth, William, 53, 60
Wotruba, Fritz, 150
Wright, Wilbur and Orville, 213

Yeats, W.B., 91, 93, 114
Yes, Minister, 29, 43
Yes, Prime Minister, 43
Yitshak, Avraham ben, 152-3
Yule, Henry, 216-23

Zagajewski, Adam, 12
Zohn, Harry, 130, 132, 134, 138, 141
Zola, Émile, 214